A Collection of
CLASSIC
SOUTHERN
HUMOR

Fiction and Occasional Fact
by Some of the South's
Best Storytellers.

Edited by George William Koon

PEACHTREE   PUBLISHERS,   LIMITED

Published by
PEACHTREE PUBLISHERS, LTD.
494 Armour Circle, N.E., Atlanta, Georgia 30324

Copyright © 1984 Peachtree Publishers, Ltd.

Manufactured in the United States

Jacket design by Cynthia McDaniel

First edition
3rd printing
Library of Congress Catalog Number 84-60018

ISBN: 0-931948-55-X Hardcover
ISBN: 0-931948-59-2 Trade Paper

For Barbara Anne Donovan

Contents

Preface

William Faulkner said much about Southern writing when he called Henry James "the nicest old lady I ever met." He indicated, of course, the sense of humor that the region has always had. And he indicated his disregard for the kind of psychological drama that identifies the target of his joke. If James liked to have a character such as Fleda Vetch go into serious depression over wallpaper, as he did in *The Spoils of Poynton,* Faulkner was likely to come up with a well armed Sutpen or Sartoris for some blood and guts violence.

The South has always done it that way. We tend to express our conflicts with dramatic external gestures rather than let them rest on the psychological level. Our literary heritage accepts easily that Oedipus would actually gouge out his eyes when he discovers just how useless they have been. And the terrible violence at the end of *Hamlet* seems perfect as it brings to the surface the psychological conflicts that have gone before it.

An agrarian economy probably explains this literal approach best. Life close to the land just does not call for much abstraction or much despair over wallpaper. The Greeks showed us that as they gave their gods human form and brought them to earth. Things are equally definite for Southerners. Our guilt is not something in the back of the mind; it stands before us in the black man. Our religion often comes straight off the pages of the Bible and can call for baptisms in the river as well as for taking up serpents. And our conflicts with each other take physical form often enough to give us a grand rate of violent crime. We owe that curious and ironic mix of intense religion and real violence to the same source—our inclination to the literal and dramatic.

Perhaps the familiar tale of the Mississippi father, who had sent his son off to an eastern college, makes the point. The father heard the boy, home from college, swear "Jesus Christ" and was quick to point out that Southerners say "goddamn." The former curse is ambiguous enough even to be taken as a prayer. The latter gets the job done with some drama and without any doubt.

Our comedy comes forward in the same way. Humor thrives on incongruity—a pie in the face when we have on our best outfits, a Charlie Chaplin carving up a boiled boot as if it were a Thanksgiving turkey. Thus the South's particular advantage, for its incongruities emerge in literal and dramatic form. We are not talking so much about wit and word play but about our good old boys and girls who are forever having head-on conflicts with each other and with modernity. Roy Blount illustrates the point as he follows the Carters—Velveeta Carter, Martha Carter Kelvinator, and Jimmy among them—from Plains, Georgia, to the White House. The outrageous inconsistencies were just too much for a Southern writer to ignore, and they made Blount's fine book, *Crackers*.

Marion Montgomery was not content to philosophize about the effect of the machine age on the South's garden. He preferred to bring a car into the domestic life of a particular farmer who would rather stick with the mules he knew, stubborn as they were, than deal with Henry Ford's assembly-line product. Florence King could have told us what we know already about social climbing. But like Faulkner, she found some real Snopeses, in this case the debutantes of small town society pages, to carry the case. Eudora Welty knew about sibling rivalry, as the psychologist would have it, and she worked it out in the marvelous terms of a sisterly squabble that leaves one character living in a rural post office.

Subtlety may not always be our long suit, but good broad comedy is. And the collection to follow is designed to make that point. The pieces range widely—from some of our best known fiction writers and their followers through some of the many essayists who have brought Southern ways to what is loosely called the new journalism. These stories and essays, I believe, add up to the point that Southern humor is thriving, that we still have a variety of good writers who see things in definite terms and who are exuberant about telling their tales.

I want to make one additional point. The South's comic sensibility almost always indicates a general acceptance of the human situation. Our foibles are conspicuous enough; but the approach of our best writers is to let that be what it may, perhaps even to enjoy some of it. Almost never do they pass large moral judgments. Flannery O'Connor may have had the sternest vision; yet her characters are notably human, and moral superiority just does not exist, even when, as in "Revelation," she brings her Wellesley girl face to face with her woman from the hog farm. William Price Fox's Doug Broome is the ultimate con artist, a fast food man who knows that there is no such thing as a small Coke, and yet he turns out to be notably humane as he takes care of the haphazard folks who drift through his establishment. Lewis Grizzard's preacher, Brother Roy Dodd, who heals only internal organs and no broken bones, calls for our laughter and our sympathy in his wackiness. And Larry King's whores, just one more fact of life, do have hearts of gold.

Thus the hope that the good times here come with some reassurances. All of these writers, with the exceptions of Flannery O'Connor and John Kennedy Toole, whose deaths were so untimely, are still alive and productive. The additional comfort lies in their extraordinary ability to both understand and accept human nature. Perhaps the cultivation of this particular ability led them to comedy in the first place since the laughs are the best mark of a forbearance of humanity, since they make happy the business of seeing ourselves so clearly.

George William Koon
Clemson University

Eudora Welty

Why I Live at the P.O.

I WAS GETTING ALONG fine with Mama, Papa-Daddy and Uncle Rondo until my sister Stella-Rondo just separated from her husband and came back home again. Mr. Whitaker! Of course I went with Mr. Whitaker first, when he first appeared here in China Grove, taking "Pose Yourself" photos, and Stella-Rondo broke us up. Told him I was one-sided. Bigger on one side than the other, which is a deliberate, calculated falsehood: I'm the same. Stella-Rondo is exactly twelve months to the day younger than I am and for that reason she's spoiled.

She's always had anything in the world she wanted and then she'd throw it away. Papa-Daddy gave her this gorgeous Add-a-Pearl necklace when she was eight years old and she threw it away playing baseball when she was nine, with only two pearls.

So as soon as she got married and moved away from home the first thing she did was separate! From Mr. Whitaker! This photographer with the popeyes she said she trusted. Came home from one of those towns up in Illinois and to our complete surprise brought this child of two.

Mama said she like to make her drop dead for a second. "Here you had this marvelous blonde child and never so much as wrote your mother a word about it," says Mama. "I'm thoroughly ashamed of you." But of course she wasn't.

Stella-Rondo just calmly takes off this *hat*, I wish you could see it. She says, "Why, Mama, Shirley-T.'s adopted, I can prove it."

"How?" says Mama, but all I says was, "H'm!" There I was over the hot stove, trying to stretch two chickens over five people and a

1

completely unexpected child into the bargain, without one moment's notice.

"What do you mean—'H'm!'?" says Stella-Rondo, and Mama says, "I heard that, Sister."

I said that oh, I didn't mean a thing, only that whoever Shirley-T. was, she was the spit-image of Papa-Daddy if he'd cut off his beard, which of course he'd never do in the world. Papa-Daddy's Mama's papa and sulks.

Stella-Rondo got furious! She said, "Sister, I don't need to tell you you got a lot of nerve and always did have and I'll thank you to make no future reference to my adopted child whatsoever."

"Very well," I said. "Very well, very well. Of course I noticed at once she looks like Mr. Whitaker's side too. That frown. She looks like a cross between Mr. Whitaker and Papa-Daddy."

"Well, all I can say is she isn't."

"She looks exactly like Shirley Temple to me," says Mama, but Shirley-T. just ran away from her.

So the first thing Stella-Rondo did at the table was turn Papa-Daddy against me.

"Papa-Daddy," she says. He was trying to cut up his meat. "Papa-Daddy!" I was taken completely by surprise. Papa-Daddy is about a million years old and's got this long-long beard. "Papa-Daddy, Sister says she fails to understand why you don't cut off your beard."

So Papa-Daddy l-a-y-s down his knife and fork! He's real rich. Mama says he is, he says he isn't. So he says, "Have I heard correctly? You don't understand why I don't cut off my beard?"

"Why," I says, "Papa-Daddy, of course I understand, I did not say any such of a thing, the idea!"

He says, "Hussy!"

I says, "Papa-Daddy, you know I wouldn't any more want you to cut off your beard than the man in the moon. It was the farthest thing from my mind! Stella-Rondo sat there and made that up while she was eating breast of chicken."

But he says, "So the postmistress fails to understand why I don't cut off my beard. Which job I got you through my influence with the government. 'Bird's nest'—is that what you call it?"

2

Not that it isn't the next to smallest P.O. in the entire state of Mississippi.

I says, "Oh, Papa-Daddy," I says, "I didn't say any such of a thing, I never dreamed it was a bird's nest, I have always been grateful though this is the next to smallest P.O. in the state of Mississippi, and I do not enjoy being referred to as a hussy by my own grandfather."

But Stella-Rondo says, "Yes, you did say it too. Anybody in the world could of heard you, that had ears."

"Stop right there," says Mama, looking at *me.*

So I pulled my napkin straight back through the napkin ring and left the table.

As soon as I was out of the room Mama says, "Call her back, or she'll starve to death," but Papa-Daddy says, "This is the beard I started growing on the Coast when I was fifteen years old." He would of gone on till nightfall if Shirley-T. hadn't lost the Milky Way she ate in Cairo.

So Papa-Daddy says, "I am going out and lie in the hammock, and you can all sit here and remember my words: I'll never cut off my beard as long as I live, even one inch, and I don't appreciate it in you at all." Passed right by me in the hall and went straight out and got in the hammock.

It would be a holiday. It wasn't five minutes before Uncle Rondo suddenly appeared in the hall in one of Stella-Rondo's flesh-colored kimonos, all cut on the bias, like something Mr. Whitaker probably thought was gorgeous.

"Uncle Rondo!" I says. "I didn't know who that was! Where are you going?"

"Sister," he says, "get out of my way, I'm poisoned."

"If you're poisoned stay away from Papa-Daddy," I says. "Keep out of the hammock. Papa-Daddy will certainly beat you on the head if you come within forty miles of him. He thinks I deliberately said he ought to cut off his beard after he got me the P.O., and I've told him and told him and told him, and he acts like he just don't hear me. Papa-Daddy must of gone stone deaf."

"He picked a fine day to do it then," says Uncle Rondo, and before you could say "Jack Robinson" flew out in the yard.

3

What he'd really done, he'd drunk another bottle of that prescription. He does it every single Fourth of July as sure as shooting, and it's horribly expensive. Then he falls over in the hammock and snores. So he insisted on zigzagging right on out to the hammock, looking like a half-wit.

Papa-Daddy woke up with this horrible yell and right there without moving an inch he tried to turn Uncle Rondo against me. I heard every word he said. Oh, he told Uncle Rondo I didn't learn to read till I was eight years old and he didn't see how in the world I ever got the mail put up at the P.O., much less read it all, and he said if Uncle Rondo could only fathom the lengths he had gone to get me that job! And he said on the other hand he thought Stella-Rondo had a brilliant mind and deserved credit for getting out of town. All the time he was just lying there swinging as pretty as you please and looping out his beard, and poor Uncle Rondo was *pleading* with him to slow down the hammock, it was making him as dizzy as a witch to watch it. But that's what Papa-Daddy likes about a hammock. So Uncle Rondo was too dizzy to get turned against me for the time being. He's Mama's only brother and is a good case of a one-track mind. Ask anybody. A certified pharmacist.

Just then I heard Stella-Rondo raising the upstairs window. While she was married she got this peculiar idea that it's cooler with the windows shut and locked. So she has to raise the window before she can make a soul hear her outdoors.

So she raises the window and says, *"Oh!"* You would have thought she was mortally wounded.

Uncle Rondo and Papa-Daddy didn't even look up, but kept right on with what they were doing. I had to laugh.

I flew up the stairs and threw the door open! I says, "What in the wide world's the matter, Stella-Rondo? You mortally wounded?"

"No," she says, "I am not mortally wounded but I wish you would do me the favor of looking out that window there and telling me what you see."

So I shade my eyes and look out the window.

"I see the front yard," I says.

"Don't you see any human beings?" she says.

"I see Uncle Rondo trying to run Papa-Daddy out of the hammock,"

I says. "Nothing more. Naturally, it's so suffocating-hot in the house, with all the windows shut and locked, everybody who cares to stay in their right mind will have to go out and get in the hammock before the Fourth of July is over."

"Don't you notice anything different about Uncle Rondo?" asks Stella-Rondo.

"Why, no, except he's got on some terrible-looking flesh-colored contraption I wouldn't be found dead in, is all I can see," I says.

"Never mind, you won't be found dead in it, because it happens to be part of my trousseau, and Mr. Whitaker took several dozen photographs of me in it," says Stella-Rondo. "What on earth could Uncle Rondo *mean* by wearing part of my trousseau out in the broad open daylight without saying so much as 'Kiss my foot,' *knowing* I only got home this morning after my separation and hung my negligee up on the bathroom door, just as nervous as I could be?"

"I'm sure I don't know, and what do you expect me to do about it?" I says. "Jump out the window?"

"No, I expect nothing of the kind. I simply declare that Uncle Rondo looks like a fool in it, that's all," she says. "It makes me sick to my stomach."

"Well, he looks as good as he can," I says. "As good as anybody in reason could." I stood up for Uncle Rondo, please remember. And I said to Stella-Rondo, "I think I would do well not to criticize so freely if I were you and came home with a two-year-old child I had never said a word about, and no explanation whatever about my separation."

"I asked you the instant I entered this house not to refer one more time to my adopted child, and you gave me your word of honor you would not," was all Stella-Rondo would say, and started pulling out every one of her eyebrows with some cheap Kress tweezers.

So I merely slammed the door behind me and went down and made some green-tomato pickle. Somebody had to do it. Of course Mama had turned both the Negroes loose; she always said no earthly power could hold one anyway on the Fourth of July, so she wouldn't even try. It turned out that Jaypan fell in the lake and came within a very narrow limit of drowning.

So Mama trots in. Lifts up the lid and says, "H'm! Not very good

5

for your Uncle Rondo in his precarious condition, I must say. Or poor little adopted Shirley-T. Shame on you!"

That made me tired. I says, "Well, Stella-Rondo had better thank her lucky stars it was her instead of me came trotting in with that very peculiar-looking child. Now if it had been me that trotted in from Illinois and brought a peculiar-looking child of two, I shudder to think of the reception I'd of got, much less controlled the diet of an entire family."

"But you must remember, Sister, that you were never married to Mr. Whitaker in the first place and didn't go up to Illinois to live," says Mama, shaking a spoon in my face. "If you had I would of been just as overjoyed to see you and your little adopted girl as I was to see Stella-Rondo, when you wound up with your separation and came on back home."

"You would not," I says.

"Don't contradict me, I would," says Mama.

But I said she couldn't convince me though she talked till she was blue in the face. Then I said, "Besides, you know as well as I do that that child is not adopted."

"She most certainly is adopted," says Mama, stiff as a poker.

I says, "Why, Mama, Stella-Rondo had her just as sure as anything in this world, and just too stuck up to admit it."

"Why, Sister," said Mama. "Here I thought we were going to have a pleasant Fourth of July, and you start right out not believing a word your own baby sister tells you!"

"Just like Cousin Annie Flo. Went to her grave denying the facts of life," I remind Mama.

"I told you if you ever mentioned Annie Flo's name I'd slap your face," says Mama, and slaps my face.

"All right, you wait and see," I says.

"I," says Mama "*I* prefer to take my children's word for anything when it's humanly possible." You ought to see Mama, she weighs two hundred pounds and has real tiny feet.

Just then something perfectly horrible occurred to me.

"Mama," I says, "can that child talk?" I simply had to whisper! "Mama, I wonder if that child can be—you know—in any way? Do you realize," I says, "that she hasn't spoken one single, solitary word

6

to a human being up to this minute? This is the way she looks," I says, and I looked like this.

Well, Mama and I just stood there and stared at each other. It was horrible!

"I remember well that Joe Whitaker frequently drank like a fish," says Mama. "I believed to my soul he drank *chemicals.*" And without another word she marches to the foot of the stairs and calls Stella-Rondo.

"Stella-Rondo? O-o-o-o-o! Stella-Rondo!"

"What?" says Stella-Rondo from upstairs. Not even the grace to get up off the bed.

"Can that child of yours talk?" asks Mama.

Stella-Rondo says, "Can she what?"

"Talk! Talk!" says Mama. "Burdyburdyburdyburdy!"

So Stella-Rondo yells back, "Who says she can't talk?"

"Sister says so," says Mama.

"You didn't have to tell me, I know whose word of honor don't mean a thing in this house," says Stella-Rondo.

And in a minute the loudest Yankee voice I ever heard in my life yells out, "OE'm Pop-OE' the Sailor-r-r-r Ma-a-an!" and then somebody jumps up and down in the upstairs hall. In another second the house would of fallen down.

"Not only talks, she can tap-dance!" calls Stella-Rondo. "Which is more than some people I won't name can do."

"Why, the little precious darling thing!" Mama says, so surprised. "Just as smart as she can be!" Starts talking baby talk right there. Then she turns on me. "Sister, you ought to be thoroughly ashamed! Run upstairs this instant and apologize to Stella-Rondo and Shirley-T."

"Apologize for what?" I says. "I merely wondered if the child was normal, that's all. Now that she's proved she is, why, I have nothing further to say."

But Mama just turned on her heel and flew out, furious. She ran right upstairs and hugged the baby. She believed it was adopted. Stella-Rondo hadn't done a thing but turn her against me from upstairs while I stood there helpless over the hot stove. So that made Mama, Papa-Daddy and the baby all on Stella-Rondo's side.

Next, Uncle Rondo.

I must say that Uncle Rondo has been marvelous to me at various times in the past and I was completely unprepared to be made to jump out of my skin, the way it turned out. Once Stella-Rondo did something perfectly horrible to him—broke a chain letter from Flanders Field—and he took the radio back he had given her and gave it to me. Stella-Rondo was furious! For six months we all had to call her Stella instead of Stella-Rondo, or she wouldn't answer. I always thought Uncle Rondo had all the brains of the entire family. Another time he sent me to Mammoth Cave, with all expenses paid.

But this would be the day he was drinking that prescription, the Fourth of July.

So at supper Stella-Rondo speaks up and says she thinks Uncle Rondo ought to try to eat a little something. So finally Uncle Rondo said he would try a little cold biscuits and ketchup, but that was all. So *she* brought it to him.

"Do you think it wise to disport with ketchup in Stella-Rondo's flesh-colored kimono?" I says. Trying to be considerate! If Stella-Rondo couldn't watch out for her trousseau, somebody had to.

"Any objections?" asks Uncle Rondo, just about to pour out all the ketchup.

"Don't mind what she says, Uncle Rondo," says Stella-Rondo. "Sister has been devoting this solid afternoon to sneering out my bedroom window at the way you look."

"What's that?" says Uncle Rondo. Uncle Rondo has got the most terrible temper in the world. Anything is liable to make him tear the house down if it comes at the wrong time.

So Stella-Rondo says, "Sister says, 'Uncle Rondo certainly does look like a fool in that pink kimono!'"

Do you remember who it was really said that?

Uncle Rondo spills out all the ketchup and jumps out of his chair and tears off the kimono and throws it down on the dirty floor and puts his foot on it. It had to be sent all the way to Jackson to the cleaners and re-pleated.

"So that's your opinion of your Uncle Rondo, is it?" he says. "I look like a fool, do I? Well, that's the last straw. A whole day in this house with nothing to do, and then to hear you come out with a remark like that behind my back!"

"I didn't say any such of a thing, Uncle Rondo," I says, "and I'm not saying who did, either. Why, I think you look all right. Just try to take care of yourself and not talk and eat at the same time," I says. "I think you better go lie down."

"Lie down my foot," says Uncle Rondo. I ought to of known by that he was fixing to do something perfectly horrible.

So he didn't do anything that night in the precarious state he was in—just played Casino with Mama and Stella-Rondo and Shirley-T. and gave Shirley-T. a nickel with a head on both sides. It tickled her nearly to death, and she called him "Papa." But at 6:30 A.M. the next morning, he threw a whole five-cent package of some unsold one-inch firecrackers from the store as hard as he could into my bedroom and they every one went off. Not one bad one in the string. Anybody else, there'd be one that wouldn't go off.

Well, I'm just terribly susceptible to noise of any kind, the doctor has always told me I was the most sensitive person he had ever seen in his whole life, and I was simply prostrated. I couldn't eat! People tell me they heard it as far as the cemetery, and old Aunt Jep Patterson, that had been holding her own so good, thought it was Judgment Day and she was going to meet her whole family. It's usually so quiet here.

And I'll tell you it didn't take me any longer than a minute to make up my mind what to do. There I was with the whole entire house on Stella-Rondo's side and turned against me. If I have anything at all I have pride.

So I just decided I'd go straight down to the P.O. There's plenty of room there in the back, I says to myself.

Well! I made no bones about letting the family catch on to what I was up to. I didn't try to conceal it.

The first thing they knew, I marched in where they were all playing Old Maid and pulled the electric oscillating fan out by the plug, and everything got real hot. Next I snatched the pillow I'd done the needle-point on right off the davenport from behind Papa-Daddy. He went "Ugh!" I beat Stella-Rondo up the stairs and finally found my charm bracelet in her bureau drawer under a picture of Nelson Eddy.

"So that's the way the land lies," says Uncle Rondo. There he was, piecing on the ham. "Well, Sister, I'll be glad to donate my army cot if you got any place to set it up, providing you'll leave right this minute and let me get some peace." Uncle Rondo was in France.

"Thank you kindly for the cot and 'peace' is hardly the word I would select if I had to resort to firecrackers at 6:30 A.M. in a young girl's bedroom," I says back to him. "And as to where I intend to go, you seem to forget my position as postmistress of China Grove, Mississippi," I says. "I've always got the P.O."

Well, that made them all sit up and take notice.

I went out front and started digging up some four-o'clocks to plant around the P.O.

"Ah-ah-ah!" says Mama, raising the window. "Those happen to be my four-o'clocks. Everything planted in that star is mine. I've never known you to make anything grow in your life."

"Very well," I says. "But I take the fern. Even you, Mama, can't stand there and deny that I'm the one watered that fern. And I happen to know where I can send in a box top and get a packet of one thousand mixed seeds, no two the same kind, free."

"Oh, where?" Mama wants to know.

But I says, "Too late. You 'tend to your house, and I'll 'tend to mine. You hear things like that all the time if you know how to listen to the radio. Perfectly marvelous offers. Get anything you want free."

So I hope to tell you I marched in and got that radio, and they could of all bit a nail in two, especially Stella-Rondo, that it used to belong to, and she well knew she couldn't get it back, I'd sue for it like a shot. And I very politely took the sewing-machine motor I helped pay the most on to give Mama for Christmas back in 1929, and a good big calendar, with the first-aid remedies on it. The thermometer and the Hawaiian ukulele certainly were rightfully mine, and I stood on the step-ladder and got all my watermelon-rind preserves and every fruit and vegetable I'd put up, every jar. Then I began to pull the tacks out of the bluebird wall vases on the archway to the dining room.

"Who told you you could have those, Miss Priss?" says Mama, fanning as hard as she could.

"I bought 'em and I'll keep track of 'em," I says. "I'll tack 'em up one on each side the post-office window, and you can see 'em when you come to ask me for your mail, if you're so dead to see 'em."

"Not I! I'll never darken the door to that post office again if I live to be a hundred," Mama says. "Ungrateful child! After all the money we spent on you at the Normal."

"Me either," says Stella-Rondo. "You can just let my mail lie there and *rot,* for all I care. I'll never come and relieve you of a single, solitary piece."

"I should worry," I says. "And who you think's going to sit down and write you all those big fat letters and postcards, by the way? Mr. Whitaker? Just because he was the only man ever dropped down in China Grove and you got him—unfairly—is he going to sit down and write you a lengthy correspondence after you come home giving no rhyme nor reason whatsoever for your separation and no explanation for the presence of that child? I may not have your brilliant mind, but I fail to see it."

So Mama says, "Sister, I've told you a thousand times that Stella-Rondo simply got homesick, and this child is far too big to be hers," and she says, "Now, why don't you all just sit down and play Casino?"

Then Shirley-T. sticks out her tongue at me in this perfectly horrible way. She has no more manners than the man in the moon. I told her she was going to cross her eyes like that some day and they'd stick.

"It's too late to stop me now," I says. "You should have tried that yesterday. I'm going to the P.O. and the only way you can possibly see me is to visit me there."

So Papa-Daddy says, "You'll never catch me setting foot in that post office, even if I should take a notion into my head to write a letter some place." He says, "I won't have you reachin' out of that little old window with a pair of shears and cuttin' off any beard of mine. I'm too smart for you!"

"We all are," says Stella-Rondo.

But I said, "If you're so smart, where's Mr. Whitaker?"

So then Uncle Rondo says, "I'll thank you from now on to stop reading all the orders I get on postcards and telling everybody in

11

China Grove what you think is the matter with them," but I says, "I draw my own conclusions and will continue in the future to draw them." I says, "If people want to write their inmost secrets on penny postcards, there's nothing in the wide world you can do about it, Uncle Rondo."

"And if you think we'll ever *write* another postcard you're sadly mistaken," says Mama.

"Cutting off your nose to spite your face then," I says. "But if you're all determined to have no more to do with the U.S. mail, think of this: What will Stella-Rondo do now, if she wants to tell Mr. Whitaker to come after her?"

"Wah!" says Stella-Rondo. I knew she'd cry. She had a conniption fit right there in the kitchen.

"It will be interesting to see how long she holds out," I says. "And now—I am leaving."

"Good-bye," says Uncle Rondo.

"Oh, I declare," says Mama, "to think that a family of mine should quarrel on the Fourth of July, or the day after, over Stella-Rondo leaving old Mr. Whitaker and having the sweetest little adopted child! It looks like we'd all be glad!"

"Wah!" says Stella-Rondo, and has a fresh conniption fit.

"*He* left *her*—you mark my words," I says. "That's Mr. Whitaker. I know Mr. Whitaker. After all, I knew him first. I said from the beginning he'd up and leave her. I foretold every single thing that's happened."

"Where did he go?" asks Mama.

"Probably to the North Pole, if he knows what's good for him," I says.

But Stella-Rondo just bawled and wouldn't say another word. She flew to her room and slammed the door.

"Now look what you've gone and done, Sister," says Mama. "You go apologize."

"I haven't got time, I'm leaving," I says.

"Well, what are you waiting around for?" asks Uncle Rondo.

So I just picked up the kitchen clock and marched off, without saying "Kiss my foot" or anything, and never did tell Stella-Rondo good-bye.

There was a girl going along on a little wagon right in front.

"Girl," I says, "come help me haul these things down the hill, I'm going to live in the post office."

Took her nine trips in her express wagon. Uncle Rondo came out on the porch and threw her a nickel.

And that's the last I've laid eyes on any of my family or my family laid eyes on me for five solid days and nights. Stella-Rondo may be telling the most horrible tales in the world about Mr. Whitaker, but I haven't heard them. As I tell everybody, I draw my own conclusions.

But oh, I like it here. It's ideal, as I've been saying. You see, I've got everything cater-cornered, the way I like it. Hear the radio? All the war news. Radio, sewing machine, book ends, ironing board and that great big piano lamp—peace, that's what I like. Butter-bean vines planted all along the front where the strings are.

Of course, there's not much mail. My family are naturally the main people in China Grove, and if they prefer to vanish from the face of the earth, for all the mail they get or the mail they write, why, I'm not going to open my mouth. Some of the folks here in town are taking up for me and some turned against me. I know which is which. There are always people who will quit buying stamps just to get on the right side of Papa-Daddy.

But here I am, and here I'll stay. I want the world to know I'm happy.

And if Stella-Rondo should come to me this minute, on bended knees, and *attempt* to explain the incidents of her life with Mr. Whitaker, I'd simply put my fingers in both my ears and refuse to listen.

Lee Smith

Cakewalk

THEY CALL FLORRIE the "cake lady" now and don't think Stella doesn't know it, even though of course no one has dared to say it to her face. Stella's face is smooth, strong, and handsome still—you'd have to say she's a handsome woman, instead of a pretty one—but her face is proud and stand-offish, too, sealed up tight with Estée Lauder makeup, ear to ear. Stella has run the cosmetics department at Belk's for twenty years and looks like it. Florrie, on the other hand, doesn't care what she looks like or what anybody thinks about it, either, and never has. Florrie wears running shoes, at her age, and wooly white athletic socks that fall in crinkles down around her ankles, and whatever else her eye lights on when she wakes up. At least that's what she looks like. Sometimes she'll have on one of those old flowered dresses that button all the way up the front, or sometimes she'll have on turquoise toreador pants or a felt skirt with a poodle on it—stuff she must have kept around for years and years, since she never throws anything at all away, stuff Stella wouldn't be caught dead in, as Stella frequently remarks to her husband, Claude, but whatever Florrie puts on, you can be sure she'll have white smudges all over it, at the skirt or on the sleeve, like she's been out in her own private snowfall. That's flour. She's always making those cakes. And then you can see her going through town carrying them so careful, her tired plump little face all crackled up and smiling, those Adidas just skimming the ground. She never wears a coat.

Oh Stella knows what they say! Just like Florrie is some poor soul on the order of Red Marcus' son who used to ride his blue bike around and around the Baptist Church until he either had a fit or somebody stopped him, or Martin Quesenberry's wife, Eloise, who is hooked on arthritis dope and has not come out of her nice Colonial frame house for eleven years, Stella knows the type and you do, too: a town character. It breaks Stella's heart. Because they were not raised to be town characters, the Ludington girls, they were brought up in considerable refinement thanks entirely to their sweet mother, Miss Bett, and not a day went by that she did not impress upon them in some subtle or some not-so-subtle way their obligations in this town as the crème de la crème, which is what she called them, which is what they were. Miss Bett learned this expression, and others, when she resided for one solid year on a tree-lined street in Europe in her youth. "Resided"—that's what she said.

Florrie and Stella resided in the big gray house on the corner of Lambert and Pine, the house with the gazebo, the handcarved banisters and heart pine floors, the same house that Florrie has made a shambles of and lives in, to this day, in the most perverse manner Stella can think of. But in those days it was the loveliest house in town and the Ludington family had always lived there, "aloft," as Stella told Claude, "on the top rung of the social crust."

So Stella was born with a natural gift for elegance, and this is why she loves Belk's. She goes in to work twenty minutes early every day with her own key on a special key ring by itself, a shiny brass key ring that spells out STELLA. After she lets herself in, she goes straight to the cosmetics department where everything is elegant, gleaming glass counters cleaned the night before by the hired help, all the shiny little bottles and tubes and perfume displays arranged just so, and she pours the tea from her thermos into a china cup and puts the thermos out of sight under the counter and settles herself on her high pink tufted stool and slowly sips her tea; she uses a saucer, too. The cosmetics department rises like an island on a rose pink carpet in the center of the store, close to the accessories but not too close, a long way from the bedspreads. After Stella has been there for about ten minutes or so, everybody else comes trickling in, too, and she speaks to them pleasantly one by one and pities their makeup and the way they look so thrown together, some of them, with their slips showing and sleep at the edges of their eyes. Then, five minutes before Mr. Thomas slides open the huge glass door to the rest of the mall, just when she has reached the hand-painted violet at the bottom of the china cup, then comes the moment she has been waiting for, the reason she gets up one whole hour before she has to and does her makeup by artificial light, which is not the way to do it, anybody can tell you that, and leaves the house in the pitch black frosty morning with Claude still sleeping humped up in the bed: this is it, the moment when Mr. Thomas flicks that master switch and her chandelier comes on. Of course, the cosmetics department is the only section in the store that has a chandelier, and it's a real beauty, hundreds and hundreds and maybe thousands of glass teardrops glowing like a million little stars, and all those shiny tubes and bottles winking back the light. The chandelier is as big as a Volkswagen, hanging right down over Stella, dead center at the soul of Belk's. It's just beautiful; Stella sighs when it comes on.

She checks her merchandise, then, and maybe she'll add something new or drape a bright silk scarf around a mirror. Stella carries Erno Laszlo, Estée Lauder, Revlon, Clinique—all the most exclusive lines, and she sells to the very best people in town. Nobody else can afford these cosmetics, and Stella keeps it that way. The ladies she helps are the crème de la crème, so she never rushes them, and they will linger for hours sometimes in the sweet-smelling pink air of the cosmetics department, trying teal eyeliner or fuchsia blush, in the soft glow of the chandelier. Stella is calm, aloof, and refined, and it's a pleasure, in this day and age, to deal with someone like that. She doesn't seem to care if anybody buys anything or not, so the ladies buy and buy, just to *show* her. Stella makes a mint, her salary plus commissions, and whatever you read about in *Vogue*, she's already got it, she ordered it last month. If Pearls-in-Your-Bath are in, for instance, Stella has some pearls thrown out on black velvet in a tasteful little way to catch your eye, and the product set up in a pyramid at the side. Stella says she keeps one foot on the pulse of the future, and it's true. Stella has always stayed up with the times.

Florrie doesn't, though. If she made any real money from all those cakes, that would be different. But the way Stella figures it, Florrie just barely covers expenses. She won't use a mix, for one thing. And the way she gets herself up looking so awful, and the people she deals with—why, Florrie will make a cake for anybody, any class of person, and that's the plain truth, awful as it is. Stella shudders, thinking of it on this mid-October day, this cool nippy day with a jerky wind that whistles and whistles around the corner of Belk's although not one teardrop of the chandelier above Stella's cosmetics counter ever moves. Stella shudders, because today is the day she has circled in her mind to go over there (since she gets off early on Thursdays anyway) and try to talk some sense into Florrie for the umpteenth time.

She's got it all worked out in her head: if Florrie will quit making those embarrassing cakes and running around town like a mental person, Stella is prepared to be generous and let bygones be bygones, to let Florrie move in with her and Claude where she can do the cooking, since she likes to cook so much, and then they can sell Mama's house for a pretty penny. And all of this might be good for Claude, too, who has acted so funny since he retired from the electric company two years ago. Claude just bats around the house these days with his pajama top on over his slacks, leaving coffee cups any old place, which makes rings on all the furniture, smoking his pipe and smelling up the house, or taking that boat of his up to Kerr Lake and driving it around in the water all day by himself. It would be one thing if he were fishing, but he's not. He's just driving around in the water and looking back at the wake. Stella has colitis—that's why she's switched to tea instead of coffee—and the very thought of Claude out in that boat goes straight to her bowels. Well. At least she can go over and talk some sense into Florrie, something she's been trying to do ever since she can remember.

She can't remember a time when Florrie didn't need it, either, but she *can* remember, or thinks she can, when Florrie started making those cakes. In fact Stella can recall precisely, because she's got such a good head for business, several cakes in particular, and she narrows her frosty green eyelids and totally ignores the tacky woman on the other side of the counter asking if they carry Cover Girl, which of course they do *not,* and recalls these cakes one by one.

To understand the circumstances of Florrie's first cake, which she made practically over her mama's dead body when she was in the eighth grade—it was the dessert for a Methodist Youth Fellowship Progressive Dinner—you have to understand the way they used to live then, in that fine old house on the corner of Lambert and Pine. The house was number one on the House Tour every year, and you couldn't find a speck of dust in it, either, or one thing out of place. That Miss Bett kept her house this way was a triumph of mind over matter, because she was not a well woman, ever, and it wore her out to keep things so straight. But she did it anyway, and held her head up high in the face of her husband's failings, and even the towels were ironed. So you can see why the idea of fifteen teenagers tromping in for dessert would have run her right up the wall.

"But Mama," Florrie said, "they're *coming*. It's all settled. We're going to have the first course at Rhonda's house, and the main course at Sue and Joey's, and then I invited them here for dessert. After that we'll go back to the church for the meeting."

"I never heard of such a thing," Miss Bett said. Miss Bett was a tall frail woman with jet black hair in a bun on the top of her head, and big dark eyes that could flash fire, as they did right then at Florrie. Miss Bett held famous dinner parties every year or so, which involved several weeks of preparations, all the silver polished and the china out, dinner parties that were so lovely that she had to go to bed for a day or two afterward to recover. "A Progressive Dinner!" she snorted. "The very idea!"

"Well, they're coming," Florrie said sweetly. That was her way— she never argued with her mother, or cried, just acted so sweet and did whatever she wanted to do. Stella wasn't fooled by this and neither was Miss Bett, but Florrie had everybody else in town eating out of the palm of her hand, including, of course, her daddy.

"Come on, Bett," Oliver Ludington said, standing in the kitchen doorway. "Don't embarrass her."

"I would talk about embarrassment if I were you," Miss Bett said. She stared at him until he said something under his breath and started to turn away, and then she looked back at her two daughters just in time to see Florrie give him a wink. That wink was the last straw.

"All right." She bit off the words. "Since Florrie has invited fifteen perfect strangers into our home, we will entertain them properly.

Stella," she directed, "go out and cut some glads and some of those snapdragons next to the lily pond."

Florrie giggled. "We don't have to have *flowers*," she said.

"*Stella!*" said Miss Bett, and Stella went out, furious because she was three years older and had never joined the MYF in the first place, even though she was more religious than Florrie, and now she had to cut the flowers.

Miss Bett began removing vases from the sideboard, considering them one by one.

"I'll just make a cake," Florrie suggested. She knew it would take her mother hours to arrange the flowers.

"You've never made a cake in your life," said Miss Bett. "You don't know the first thing about it."

"I won't make a mess," Florrie said.

"Florrie—" their mother began.

But Oliver Ludington, from the parlor, said, "That's all right, honey, Bessie can clean it up."

"Bessie doesn't come until *Monday*," Miss Bett reminded everybody, and of course it was only Sunday afternoon.

"I think I'll make a yellow cake with white icing," Florrie said. She had taken all the cookbooks out of their drawer and piled them on the table in a heap, and now she was flipping through them in her disorganized way. "Where's that big flat cake pan?"

A sound that could have been a laugh, or maybe a cough, came from the parlor as Miss Bett found the pan and slammed it out on the table for Florrie.

"Stella, don't put the flowers right down on the counter like that, honey, put them on *newspaper,* they could have anything on them, and then please take sixteen salad forks out of the silver chest and polish them."

"*Mama*," Stella said, but after one look at Miss Bett, she did it.

By the time the members of the MYF arrived three hours later, the dining room looked just like a picture, silver forks and pink linen on the table and flowers in a cut-glass vase from Europe in the center. Stella was fit to be tied and refused to have dessert with the group, even though Florrie begged her, and Miss Bett had taken to her bed with a sick headache after one look at Florrie's cake. The cake would have been fine if Florrie had not gotten into the food coloring, which was never used in that house except at Christmas when Miss Bett made cookies for the help. But Florrie had found it, and she had tinted some of the white icing yellow and had made a great big wobbly cross in the center of the cake. Then she tinted the rest of the icing dark blue and wrote MYF on the cross, and put a little blue border all around its sides.

"Oh!" Miss Bett shrieked, and her hand fluttered up to her high pale forehead, and she turned without a word and climbed the steps, clutching the handsome banister all the way.

Florrie had cleaned up the kitchen the best she could, not really knowing how to do it, but she couldn't get the blue food coloring off her fingers so they stayed that way for the Progressive Dinner, even though she looked very nice otherwise, with her curly blond hair pinned back out of her eyes by silver barrettes, and wearing her pleated skirt. Oliver Ludington went upstairs and took a bath, singing "Bicycle Built for Two" as loud as he could, and then he appeared at the door in a sparkling white shirt, a red bow tie, and his best seersucker suit, just in time to welcome the whole Progressive Dinner to his house. "Come right in!" He bowed. "Glad to have you," he said, and Florrie smiled her full happy smile at him, showing her dimples, and giggled "Oh Daddy!" as she came through the hall trailed by the whole MYF in which all the boys had a crush on her, even then, and even then she knew how to flirt back, and laugh, and shake her blond curls, but that's *all* she did in those days—it was later, in high school, that boys became a problem.

Oliver Ludington died when Florrie was sixteen and Stella was off at college. He died of cirrhosis of the liver, as everyone knew he would, and it was a funny thing how many people showed up for his funeral, filling up the whole Methodist Church and then spilling out to fill up all that space between the church and the street. It was awful how Florrie took on. Miss Bett and Stella cried too, into their handkerchiefs, but to tell the truth everybody expected Miss Bett to be *relieved*, after it was all over, since Oliver Ludington drank so and since she had never been happy with the way he had refused to practice law and taught at the high school instead. But Miss Bett was not relieved, or at least she didn't seem to be. After Oliver died, all that fine dark fire went right out of her, and she crept around like a pastel ghost of herself for the rest of her life. It was like she had used herself completely up in her long constant struggle with Oliver, and lacking anybody to fight with or try to raise up by their bootstraps, she paled and died back like one of the flowers in her own garden, going to seed. She let the house go, too, even though Bessie still came in. The house seemed to sag at all its corners, the gazebo started to peel, worn places in the upholstery were left unrepaired, and a loose shutter flapped in the wind. She didn't even try to control Florrie, who went out with any boy who asked her, and when Stella tried to talk some sense into her, she didn't seem to hear.

"Mama," said Stella, just home from business school where she had a straight A average, "you have got to do something about Florrie. She's getting a *reputation.*" Stella paused significantly, but her mother's dark eyes were looking beyond her face. "I might as well come right out and say it, Mother, I think she's fast. And Daddy used to think she was so smart, but look at her grades now! They're terrible, and she'll never make it to college at the rate she's going. Besides, I don't like the crowd she hangs around with, for instance that Barbara Whitley. Those people are common."

Miss Bett's fingers trembled on her lap, like she was brushing some insect, or some speck, off the flowered voile. "You haven't asked me how my stomach is," she said to Stella.

Stella sat straight up in her chair. "Well, how *is* it?" she said.

"I have my good days and I have my bad days," Miss Bett told her. "I just eat like a bird. Sometimes I have a little rice or a breast of chicken"—but just then Florrie came in from the kitchen with her lipstick on crooked, bringing her mama some tea, and Miss Bett sighed like she was dying and then drank it up in one gulp.

"Come on and go to the sidewalk carnival," Florrie said to Stella. "It's for the Fire Department, and they've got a band."

"I think somebody should stay here with Mama," Stella said.

21

"I think I could stand another cup of tea with a little more lemon in it," Miss Bett said, and then Stella decided to go after all, and she changed her dress while Florrie fixed Miss Bett's tea.

Florrie had made a cake for the carnival, a white sheet cake with yellow icing and a fire engine outlined on it in red, the engine's wheels made out of chocolate nonpareils. The sisters walked downtown along the new sidewalk and Stella thought how the town was growing since the aluminum company had come, and how many new faces she saw. Everybody spoke to Florrie, though, and stopped to admire her cake, and Florrie introduced them all, complete strangers, to Stella. "She's away at school," Florrie would say.

"I wish you wouldn't do that," Stella told her finally, because she could tell after twenty minutes or so that there was no one she wanted to meet.

The square had been roped off for the carnival, and Florrie took her cake carefully up to the table in the center of it, a long table draped with red, white, and blue, and put it right down in the middle. Everybody went "ooh, ah," and Stella turned away and went to sit on the steps of the North Carolina National Bank where to her surprise she fell into a conversation with Claude Lambeth, a boy she hadn't seen since high school, a tall serious-looking boy who was studying electrical engineering at State. Now Stella was a beauty at that time. She had Miss Bett's looks and her own way of walking so straight and inclining her head. Stella and Claude Lambeth sat on the high steps of the bank, back from the action, and watched the crowd mill around and watched the kids dancing in front of the fountain to the band. They had a lot in common, Stella learned, as they talked and talked and watched the dancing. Florrie was like a little whirlwind out there. First she went with one and then another, and even Stella had to admit she was pretty, or would have been if her hair didn't fly out so much on the turns and she didn't look quite so messy in general.

"That's your sister, isn't it?" Claude Lambeth said to Stella, and Stella said yes it was. Claude Lambeth just shook his head, and then later, at the cakewalk, he shook it again when the music stopped and five or six boys jumped on the painted red dot for Florrie's cake and the right to walk her home. The boy who ended up on the bottom was Harliss Reeves, who was generally up to no good, and when the whole cakewalk was over, Claude Lambeth told Harliss Reeves thanks anyway, he had promised their mother that he would drive Florrie and Stella home in his car. And he did, leaving Harliss on the sidewalk with his cake in both hands and his mouth wide open, Florrie mouthing apologies at him through the closed glass window of Claude Lambeth's car. "What'd you do *that* for?" she screamed at Claude, jerking her arm away from Stella, but Stella was taken with Claude and approved his action with all her heart.

Which was broken when Claude Lambeth failed to write to her and dated her little sister instead, all that spring and summer while Stella graduated and then worked so hard in her first job as a teller trainee in Charlotte. Stella was so mad she wouldn't come home at all, not even to try to talk some sense into Florrie when her mama wrote that Florrie refused to go to college and was selling toys in the five-and-dime, but then her mama wrote that Florrie and that nice Claude Lambeth were unfortunately no longer seeing each other, and Stella knew he had seen the light. She came home for a visit and married him on the spot, and Florrie made them a three-tiered Lady Baltimore wedding cake.

"You ought to charge," Stella told her, eyeing the cake at her wedding reception. "You'll never get anywhere at the five-and-dime," she said, and Florrie stopped playing with all their squealing little girl cousins long enough to say maybe she would.

Florrie never had a wedding cake of her own, poor thing, or a wedding reception either—she ran off in a snowstorm two years later with Earl Mingo, a drifter from northern Florida, and married him in a J.P.'s office in the middle of the night in Spartanburg, South Carolina, under a bare hanging light bulb. Now Earl Mingo was good looking, you would have to say that—but who knows what else she saw in him? Because Florrie could have had her pick in this town, and she didn't, she ran off with Earl Mingo instead, a man with Indian blood in him who had never made a decent living for himself or anybody else. He painted houses, or so he said, but if it was too cold, or too hot, or he didn't like the color of paint you had picked out, forget it. Earl Mingo kept guns and he went hunting a lot, out in the river woods or up on the mountain, and sometimes when you were trying to hire him he'd stare right past you, to where the road went off in the trees. Everybody knew who he was. He had men friends, hunting buddies, but they never asked him over for dinner, and neither did anyone else.

Stella didn't speak to Florrie for months after she did it, and Miss Bett had to be hospitalized it was such a shock. After her mother got out of the hospital, Stella used to drive over there to pick up Miss Bett and take her to church—of course Florrie and Earl didn't attend—and then she would drop her off again, but finally when Miss Bett told Stella that Florrie was pregnant, she decided to walk back in that house, meet Earl Mingo face to face, and make peace. Because Stella had had a baby herself by then, little Dawn Elizabeth, and this had softened her heart.

So finally, on this particular Sunday after church, Stella parked the car and walked her mother right up to the door in the pale March sunlight, her hand under Miss Bett's arm, and she couldn't help but notice how nobody had ever fixed that shutter, and how dirty the carpet was in the front hall. While her mother went upstairs to lie down, Stella stood at the last step, holding on to the banister, and hollered for Florrie.

Nobody answered.

But Stella smelled coffee and so she pressed her black patent leather purse up tight against her bosom and put her lips in one thin line and headed back toward the kitchen without another word. Forgive and forget, she thought. The swinging kitchen door was closed. When Stella pushed it open, the first thing she noticed was the *color,* of course, which her mother had never said the first word about and which was a big surprise as you can imagine, her mama's nice white kitchen painted bright blue like the sky. Now if it had been a kitchen color that would be one thing, such as pale blue or beige or yellow, but whoever heard of a sky blue kitchen? Even the cabinets were blue. Stella was too surprised to say a word, so she kept her mouth shut and blinked, and then she saw what she would have seen right away if that color hadn't been such a shock: Earl Mingo seated big

as life at the kitchen table with Florrie on his lap, both their faces
hidden by Florrie's tumbling yellow hair. Florrie was laughing and
Earl Mingo was saying something too low for Stella to hear. Earl
Mingo didn't even have a shirt on, and the kitchen table was cluttered
with dishes that no one had bothered to wash.

When Stella said "Good morning!" though, Florrie jumped up giggling and pulled the tie of her pink chenille robe around her and
tied it as fast as she could, but not before Stella could see she was
naked as a jaybird underneath. This was in the *afternoon,* close to
one o'clock.

"Stella, this is Earl," Florrie said exactly as if people ran around
in nothing but pink chenille robes all day long.

"I'm pleased to meet you." Earl stood up in his bare chest and
stuck out his hand to Stella, who seized it in her confusion and pumped
it up and down too long. Later, she hoped Earl Mingo didn't think
she meant anything by that because she could see in one glance that
he was the kind of man who thinks a woman is only good for one
thing, and Stella was not that kind of woman by a long shot.

Earl Mingo stood over six feet tall, with black hair, too long, brushed
straight back from his high dark forehead and black eyes that looked
right through you. He had a big nose, straight thick eyebrows, a
hard chin and a thin crooked mouth that turned up at the corners,
sometimes, in the wildest grin. When Earl Mingo grinned, he showed
the prettiest, whitest teeth you can imagine on a man. He grinned
at Stella like he was just delighted to meet her after all. "Have a
cup of coffee," he said.

"Why don't you take off your hat and sit down," Florrie said, which
is what she and Earl proceeded to do themselves, only this time Florrie
sat in a separate chair. "That's a pretty hat," Florrie said. "I like
that little veil."

"I'd just love to stay but I can't." Stella was lying through her
teeth. "Claude is watching Dawn Elizabeth and I have to get right
back. I just wanted to run in and say I'm real happy about the baby,
Florrie, and I never have said congratulations either, so congratulations." Stella's eyes filled up with tears then—she had been having
those crying spells ever since Dawn Elizabeth was born—and Florrie

jumped right up and hugged her on the spot. Stella remembered holding her little sister by the hand when she started first grade, walking Florrie to school.

"Well, I've got to go," Stella said finally, and then for no reason at all she said, backing out that bright blue kitchen door, "You all be careful, now," and Earl Mingo threw back his head and laughed.

There comes a time in a woman's life when the children take over, and what you do is what you have to, and it seems like the days go by so slow then while you're home with them, and nothing ever really gets done around the house before you have to go off and do something else that doesn't ever get done either, and it can take you all day long to hem a skirt. Every day lasts a long, long time. But then before you know it, it's all over, those days gone like a fog on the mountain, and the kids are all in school and there you are with this awful light empty feeling in your stomach like the beginning of cramps, when you sit in the chair where you used to nurse the baby and listen to the radio news.

Not that Stella ever nursed Dawn Elizabeth or Robert either one, but Florrie had two babies in a row and nursed them all over town. Anyway, with Robert in school at last, Stella had her hair frosted, bought some new shoes, took a part-time job in the accounting department at Belk's, and started working her way up into her present job in the cosmetics department. It was like she just woke up from a long, long sleep. She had done her duty and stayed home with those babies, and then she went back to the real world where she belonged. Not that Stella ever neglected those kids while she worked: she had them organized like the army, the whole family. Everybody had a chore, and she and Claude gave them every advantage in the world— piano lessons, dancing lessons, braces, you name it. Claude advanced steadily in his job at the electric company, a promotion every six years, and they built a nice brick ranch-style house with wall-to-wall carpeting and a flagstone patio. Claude was elected president of the Kiwanis Club, and Stella went on buying trips to New York City, where she stayed in hotels by herself.

And Florrie? Florrie never could seem to understand that those baby days were over. She had Earlene—six months after she got married—and then she had Earl Junior and then she had Paul who was born too soon and died, and anybody else would have left it at that. But nine years later, along came Bobby Joe, and then Floyd, and Florrie seemed tickled pink. She raised her children in the scatter-brained way she did everything else, and they ran loose like wild Indians and stayed up as late as they pleased on a school night, and spent all their money on gum. Then when they got to be older, they used to have all the other kids in town over there in that big house, too, dancing to the radio in the parlor and who knows what all, smoking cigarettes out in the yard. Florrie was always right there in the middle of it, making a cake as often as not.

Because her business had grown and grown—she never gave it up even when she had two of them in diapers at one time. And she never switched to cake mixes either, although she would have saved herself hours if she had. Florrie still made plenty of birthday cakes with roses on them, and happy anniversary cakes with bells, and seasonal cakes such as a green tree cake for Christmas with candy ornaments on it, or a chocolate Yule log, or an orange pumpkin cake for Halloween, and she had four different sizes of heart molds she used for Valentine's Day. But the town was growing and changing all the time, and you could tell it by Florrie's cakes. After the new country club opened up, she made a cake for Dolph Tillotson's birthday that was just like a nine-hole golf course, a huge green sheet cake with hills and valleys and little dime store mirrors for the water hazards, flags on all the greens, and a tiny sugar golf ball near the cup on the seventh hole. When the country club team won the state swim meet, they ordered an Olympic pool cake with a chocolate board and twelve different lap lanes. Once she worked for two solid days on a retirement cake for the head of the secretarial pool out at the aluminum plant. This cake involved a lot of oblong layers assembled just so to form a giant typewriter with Necco wafers as keys. The sheet of paper in the blue typewriter was smooth white icing, and on it Florrie had put "We'll Miss You, Miss Hugh" in black letters that looked like typing. When the new Chevrolet agency opened, she filled an order for a chocolate convertible; and after the community college started up, she made cakes and cakes for the students, featuring anything they told her to write, such as "Give 'Em Hell, Michelle" on a spice cake for a roommate's birthday.

The cake business and the children kept Florrie happy then, or seemed to, a good thing since Earl Mingo did not amount to a hill of beans, which surprised nobody. He painted houses for a while, and then he put in insulation, and then he went away working on a pipeline. In between jobs he would go off hunting by himself, or so he said, and stay gone for as long as a month. Then he'd show up again, broke and grinning, and Florrie would be so happy to see him and all the children would be too, and things would go on like that for a while before Earl Mingo went off again.

It was a marriage that caused a lot of talk in the beginning, talk that started up again every time Earl Mingo went away and then died back every time he came home, but since he kept on doing it, the talk slacked off and finally stopped altogether and everybody just accepted the way it was with them, the way he came and went. Since it didn't seem to bother Florrie, it stopped bothering everybody else too—except Stella, who felt that Florrie had stepped off the upper crust straight into scum. Into *lowlife,* which is where in her opinion Florrie had been heading all along.

For years Miss Bett had her own rooms upstairs, with her pressed flowers and her pictures from Europe in silver frames, her little brocade settee and her Oriental rug and her gold-tasseled bed. So many of the other fine things in the rest of the house had been broken by Florrie's children. Which wasn't their *fault,* exactly, since nobody ever taught them any better or ever told them "no" in all their lives.

"It's just a madhouse over here!" Stella said, not for the first time, one day after work when she was sitting with her mama in what used to be called the east parlor, looking out on the front yard where Earl Junior and a whole gang of boys were playing football in spite of the boxwood hedges on either side of the walk. Stella and Miss Bett watched through the wavy French doors as Earl Junior and his friends caught the ball, and ran, and fell down in a pile and then got up. They watched as Earl Junior and his friends waved their arms frantically and shouted at one another, the breath of their words hanging white in the cold fall air. Sometimes they had a fight, but nobody stepped in to stop it, and after a while they would get tired of fighting it seemed, and roll over on their backs and start laughing. Stella was glad that her own son, Robert, was not out in that pile of boys. In the west parlor, Earlene was playing the piano—practically the only stick of furniture in that room that was left in one piece— practicing for a talent show at school. Her fingers ran over the same thing again and again, a tinkly little melody that got on Stella's nerves. Floyd and Bobby Joe were wrestling in the hall. Every now and then they rolled past the east parlor door, for all the world like two little monkeys. Back in the kitchen the TV set was on, Florrie watching her stories and smoking cigarettes, no doubt, while she cooked. Earl Mingo was gone.

Cold sunlight came in through those high French doors and fell across the worn blue carpet, pale fine golden sunlight that reminded Stella suddenly of their childhood in such a way that it caused her to suck in her breath so hard it hurt her chest, and blurt out something she didn't even know she'd been thinking about until she said it out loud.

"Mama," she said, "you don't have to stay here, you know. You could come to live with Claude and me, we'd be glad to have you."

Miss Bett looked so pitiful and small, her eyes like puddles in her little white face. She's *shrunk!* Stella noticed. She's shrinking up like a little old blow-up doll, and no one has noticed but me. *"Mama,"* Stella said. "We could build you a little apartment over the garage."

"I had a bad day yesterday," Miss Bett said, looking past Stella out the French doors where Earl Junior was catching a pass. "Everything went through me like a sieve."

"Wouldn't you like to have your own apartment, Mama?" Stella went on. "Wouldn't you like to have some peace?"

"I'd like a little peace." Miss Bett said this like she was in a dream.

"Well then!" Stella stood up. "I'll just talk to Florrie about it, and we'll—"

"No!" Miss Bett got all excited suddenly and twisted her hands around and around in her lap. She said it with such force that Stella stopped, halfway out the door.

"We'd love to have you," Stella said.

"I—" Miss Bett said. "I—" She moved her little blue hand in a circle through the sunlight, then let it drop back in her lap. She

29

looked straight at Stella. "I'll try to stand it a little longer," she said.

"We'll buy you a new TV."

Miss Bett lifted her head the way she used to, and touched a white wisp of her hair.

"I'll just have to bear it," she said.

But Stella sailed right past her into the kitchen where, sure enough, Florrie was sitting at the kitchen table reading a magazine and smoking a cigarette. The table was half covered up with newspapers and Popsicle sticks and glue.

"What's all that?" Stella pointed at the mess.

"Earl Junior is making this little old theater, like Shakespeare had, for school. It's the cutest thing," Florrie said.

"Listen." Stella sat down and started right in. "Listen here, I'm worried about Mother."

"Mother?" Florrie said it like she was surprised.

"I think she needs a change." Stella was going to be tactful, but then she just burst into tears. "Poor little thing. She's *shrinking*, Florrie. I swear she's just shrinking away."

Florrie put her cigarette out and giggled. "She's not shrinking, Stella," she said.

"But what do you think about her *health*, Florrie? Now really—I wouldn't be surprised if it turned out to be all mental myself, if you want to know. I hope you won't take this wrong, but I just don't think it's good for her to live under such a strain. I don't think there's a thing wrong with her stomach, if you want to know what I think. I think if she could get a little peace and quiet, and if she had some *hobbies* or something—"

Florrie threw back her head and laughed. "I can just see Mama with a hobby!" she said. "Lord! Mama's already got a hobby, if you ask me."

"No, *really*, Florrie," Stella said. "Wouldn't it be a whole lot easier for you and Earl if she came and lived over our garage?" Floyd came in the kitchen crying then, and Florrie got him a Coke, and Stella went on. "Just think about it. Think about how much easier your life would be. What do you think about her health, anyway? I've been meaning to ask you."

Florrie looked at Stella. "Well, she has her good days and she has her bad days," Florrie said. "Sometimes everything goes through her like a sieve."

"*Oh!*" Stella was furious. "I can't talk to you. You're as bad as she is!" Stella picked up her pocketbook and flounced out of there, right past Earlene playing the piano and Floyd and Bobby wrestling in the hall and her mother all shrunk up to nothing in the sunlight on the sofa in the east parlor; Stella sailed straight out the front door just as Earl Junior hollered "Hike!"

So Miss Bett lived with Florrie and Earl until she died of heart failure, and when she did, it was all Stella could do to persuade Florrie to let them bury her mama decently. Florrie wanted Miss Bett put in a pine box, of all things, where the worms could get in. Then Florrie revealed that in fact this was the way she and Earl Mingo had buried Paul, the baby who had died so long ago. Stella and Florrie had a big argument about all of this in front of everybody, right there in the funeral home, but since Earl Mingo was out of town and Earlene had gone off to college, Florrie had no one to take her side and finally Claude just gave Mr. Morrow a check and that settled it, or seemed to, since Florrie did not mention the pine box or the worms again though she cried for three solid weeks, despite the fact that Miss Bett had left her the whole house out of pity.

Lord knows where Florrie got such ideas in the first place, although you can be sure she passed them along to Earlene, who turned into a hippie beatnik and won a full scholarship to the North Carolina School of the Arts while she was still in high school and went there, too, came home for vacations wearing purple tights and turtleneck sweaters and necklaces made out of string. Turned into a vegetarian and went away to college up North, where she majored in drama. Now that was Earlene.

Earl Junior was a horse of a different color. No brains to speak of, a big wide grin like his daddy, always wrecking a car or getting a girl in trouble. Earl Junior got a football scholarship to N.C. State where he played second string until his knee gave out, and then he quit school and got a job as some kind of salesman, nothing you would be proud of. But Earl Junior liked to travel, just like Earl. You would have thought Earl Junior owned all of North Carolina,

South Carolina, Virginia, and Tennessee, the way he called it his "territory."

Bobby Joe and Floyd were boys that anybody would be proud of, though, in the Boy Scouts and on the Junior High basketball team for instance, boys with brushed-back sandy hair and steady gray eyes, who mowed everybody's grass on Saturdays. Stella was glad to see that those two were turning out so well in spite of the way they were raised with no advantages to speak of, and as years drew into years and it became perfectly clear who had succeeded and who had not, she pitied Florrie, and tried to be extra nice to her sometimes—bringing them a country ham just before Christmas, for instance, or having oranges sent—things that Florrie often failed to notice, scatterbrained as she was. Because there is a kind of flyaway manner that might be fetching in a young girl, but goes sour when the years mount up, and Florrie was pushing forty. She should have known how to say "thank you" by then. Bobby Joe and Floyd were almost through with high school the year that the worst thing that *could* happen, *did*.

Earlene had always been Florrie's favorite, in a way, her being the only girl, and this made it that much worse all the way around: Earlene was the *last* one, the very last person you would pick to be the agent of her mother's doom. But you know how Earlene changed when she went off to school, so you can imagine what her friends would be like: tall skinny girls with wild curly hair or long drooping hair and big eyes, like those pictures of foreign children you see in the drugstore, and of course Earlene was exactly like the rest of Florrie's children—sooner or later, she brought every one of them home.

Elizabeth Blackwell was the daughter of two Duke professors, Dr. Blackwell and Dr. Blackwell, of the History Department. You would never have guessed what was going to happen if you had ever seen her or heard her name, which sounded so well-bred and nice. But Elizabeth Blackwell wore blue jeans day in and day out when she was visiting Earlene, and she had light red hair so long she could sit on it if it hadn't been braided in one long thick plait down the back of her lumberjack shirt. Whenever Elizabeth came to visit Earlene, all she wanted to do was go hiking up on the mountain with Earlene and Floyd and Bobby Joe, and sometimes Earl went too, if he was home. Elizabeth Blackwell wore big square boots from the army-navy store, boots exactly like a man's, and no makeup at all on her pale freckled face, which would have been pretty if she had known what to do with it, especially those big eyes that were such an unusual color, no color really, something in between green and gray. She was not feminine at all, so when she and Earl Mingo ran away together it was the biggest shock in the world to everybody.

Except Earlene, who urged everybody not to feel harsh toward her friend because, she said, Elizabeth Blackwell was pregnant, and furthermore it was Earl Mingo's child. Earl Mingo must have been almost fifty by then, and Elizabeth Blackwell was nineteen years old. Now who can understand a thing like that? Not Bobby Joe, who shot out the new streetlight on the corner of Lambert and Pine with his daddy's Remington pump shotgun and then threw the shotgun itself in the river; not Floyd, who got a twitch in one eye, clammed up in all his classes at the high school, and started studying so hard he beat out Louise Watson for valedictorian of the class; not even Earlene, who took a week off from college to come home and cry and tell everybody it was all her fault. Nobody could understand it except possibly Florrie herself, who of course had known Earl Mingo better than anyone else and did not seem all that surprised. It made you wonder what else had gone on through all those years, and exactly what other crosses Florrie had had to bear.

"I would just die if it was Claude," Stella said several days after it happened, one night when she had come over to commiserate with her sister and find out more details if she could. "But of course Claude would never do anything like that," Stella added. "It would never enter Claude's mind."

Florrie stood back from the wedding cake she was working on and looked at Stella. "You never know what's going to happen in this world," she said. Florrie sounded like she knew a secret, which made her sister mad.

"Well, I know! Claude and I have been married for twenty-six years, and I guess I ought to know by now."

Florrie smiled. Her smile was still as pretty as ever, like there might be a giggle coming right along behind it, but she had aged a lot around the eyes, and that night her eyes were all red. Her hair had a lot of gray mixed in with the blond by that time, and she wore it chopped off just any old way. Florrie had six different-sized layers of white cake already baked, and she was building them up, pink icing between each layer. Floyd sat in the corner in his daddy's chair, reading a library book.

"Who's that cake for?" Stella asked.

"Jennifer Alley and Mark Priest," Florrie said. "Look here what they got in Raleigh for me to put on the top." She showed Stella the bride and groom in cellophane wrapping, a little couple so lifelike they might have been real, the bride in a satin dress.

"Lord, I wish you'd look at that," Stella said. "Look at that little old veil."

Florrie smiled. "Real seed pearls," she said.

"But Florrie—" Stella looked at her watch. "Isn't the wedding to-morrow?" Stella *knew* it was, actually, because she and Claude had been invited, but of course Florrie had not.

"Noon," Florrie said. She rubbed her hand across her forehead, leaving a white streak of flour.

"Are you going to get it done in time?" Stella asked as Florrie spread the smooth white icing over the whole thing and then mixed up more pink and put it in her pastry tube.

"Sure," Florrie said.

"If I were you, I'd just go to bed and get up in the morning and finish it," Stella said.

"I like to make my wedding cakes at night," Florrie said. "You know I always do it this way."

"That's going to take you all night, though."

"Well." Florrie started on the tiny top layer, making pink bows all around the edge. "Light me a cigarette, honey, will you?" she said to Floyd, who did.

Stella sat up straight in the kitchen chair and put her mouth together in a line, but she kept it shut until Bobby Joe came in the kitchen for a Coke and told her hello, and then she said, "Listen, that's another reason I came over here tonight. Claude said for me to tell you that if you want to go off to school next year, Bobby Joe, you just let us know and we'll take care of it." Stella had been against this when Claude first brought it up, but now she was glad she had it to say, since everything was so pathetic over here at Florrie's. Floyd had a scholarship, of course, already. Floyd was a brain. "If you want to go to college, that is," Stella said for emphasis, since Bobby Joe was just standing there in the middle of the kitchen like he hadn't heard her right.

Bobby Joe stared at his aunt and then he popped off his pop top real loud. "Thanks but no thanks," he said.

Well! Bobby Joe took a long drink out of the can and Stella stood up. "If that's how you feel about it," she said, *"all right."*

Florrie was crying again without seeming to notice it, the tears leaking out as slow as Christmas, her blue eyes filling while she shaped three little red roses above each pink bow on the cake, crying right in front of her sons without a bit of shame.

Stella, who knew when she wasn't wanted, left. But the next day at Jennifer and Mark Priest's wedding reception, Stella couldn't eat *one bite* of that cake; it stuck fast in her throat, and thinking about Florrie gave her indigestion anyway, Florrie bent hunchbacked over that great huge cake the night before, making those tiny red roses.

And Lord knows whatever happened to Earl Mingo, or to Elizabeth Blackwell, or to that baby she either did or did not have. Nobody ever saw or heard from them again except for four postcards that Earl sent back over the next couple of years, from Disney World, from Mammoth Cave, from Death Valley, from Las Vegas—like that. He didn't write a thing on any of them except "Love, Earl Mingo." Florrie kept each one around for a while and then she threw it away, and kept on with her business, living hand-to-mouth some way, nobody knew quite how except that she had made some money when she sold off most of the backyard to Allstate Insurance, which tore up the gazebo and the fish pond and built a three-story brick office building on it right jam-up against that fine old house, and then Claude dropped by and did little odd jobs around the house that needed doing, and that was a savings, too. Other people came by all the time to see her. It seemed like there was always somebody in that kitchen having coffee with Florrie if it was winter, or Coke if it was summer, but then of course she had Earlene's children, Dolly and Bill, to take care of too, while Earlene was having a nervous breakdown after her divorce. Florrie took them in without a word and they lived with her for three years, which is how long it took Earlene to get

her feet back on the ground, give up art, and get her license in real
estate. Floyd is gone for good: he teaches at the college in Greensboro.
Bobby Joe has never amounted to much, like Earl Junior who runs
a Midget Golf in Myrtle Beach now. Bobby Joe is still in town. He
lives in an apartment near the country club and works in a men's
store at the mall, all dressed up like a swinging single in open-neck
shirts and gold neck chains, still coming over to see his mama every
day or so, breezing in through the screen porch door. Earl Junior's
ex-wife, Johnnie Sue, came to visit about two years ago and brought
their little boy, Chip, and she has stayed with Florrie ever since, leaving
Chip with his grandmother while she teaches tap dancing at Arthur
Murray's studio in Raleigh.

Johnnie Sue is not even related to Florrie, so who ever heard of
such an arrangement? Stella shakes her head, thinking about it, and
smokes a Silva Thin in the car as she drives across town from Belk's
to Florrie's house through the fine October day, the leaves all red
and golden, swirling down with the wind against the windshield of
Stella's new car. Florrie's house is almost the only one left standing
on Lambert Street since it has been zoned commercial, and it looks
so funny now with the Allstate Building rising up behind it and the
Rexall Drugstore next door.

"It's real convenient," Florrie says when Stella mentions the Rexall,
again, as tactfully as possible. "I just send Chip right over whenever
there's something we need."

Stella sighs. This will be harder than she thought. She had hoped
to find Florrie by herself, for one thing, but Chip is home with a
cold and she can hear him upstairs right now, banging things around
and singing in his high, thin voice. Chip is a hyperactive child who
has to take pills every day of his life. Not a thing like Stella's own
well-behaved grandchildren, who unfortunately live so far away. Well.
At least nobody else is here, even though the table is littered with
coffee cups and there's a strong smell of smoke, like pipe smoke, in
the air. Florrie, who doesn't keep up with a thing, probably doesn't
even know about room deodorizer sprays. Or no-wax wax, obviously,
since the floor has clearly not been touched in ages. Stella sighs,
taking a kitchen chair, at the memory of how this floor used to shine
and how the sun coming in that kitchen window through the starched

white curtains just gleamed on the white windowsill. Now the window-sill is blue and you can't even see it for the mess of African violets up there, and the windows have no curtains at all. It gives Stella a start. It's funny how you can be in a place for years and stop really noticing anything, and then one day suddenly you see it all, plain as day, before your face: things you haven't thought to see for years. She looks around Florrie's kitchen and notices Chip's Lego blocks all piled up in the corner, a pile of laundry in Earl's chair, the sink full of dirty dishes, a crack in the pane of the door—and then Stella's eyes travel back to the kitchen table and she sees what she must have seen when she first came in, or what she saw and didn't notice: smack in the middle of the table, on an ironstone platter, sits Florrie's weirdest cake yet.

This cake is shaped like a giant autumn leaf and it looks like a real leaf exactly, with icing that starts off red in the center and changes from flame to orange, to yellow, to gold. It's hard to tell where one color leaves off and turns into another, the way they flow together in the icing, and the icing itself seems to crinkle up, like a real leaf does, at all the edges of the cake.

"Mercy!" Stella says.

"I just made that this morning," Florrie remarks. She pushes the ironstone platter across the table so Stella can get a better look, but Stella scoots farther back in her chair. She can hear Chip coming down the stairs now, making a terrible racket, dragging something along behind him on his way.

"You want to know how I did it?" Florrie says. "I just thought it up today. What I did was, I made one big square cake, that's the middle of the leaf only you can't tell under all the icing, and a couple of little square cakes, and then I cut those all up to get the angles, see, for all the points of the leaves. Come here, honey," she says to Chip. "Let me blow your nose in this napkin. Now blow."

Stella looks away from them but there is no place for her to look in this kitchen, nothing her eye can light on without pain.

"Pretty!" Chip points at the cake. Chip is skinny, too small for his age, with thin light brown hair that sticks up on his head like straw.

"You should have seen what I made for his class," Florrie says to

Stella. "It was back when they were doing their science projects about volcanos, and I made them a cake like Mount St. Helen's and took it over there and you should have seen them, they got the biggest kick out of it! Didn't you, Chip?"

"Va-ROOM!" Chip acts like a volcano. Then he falls down on the floor.

Florrie smiles down at him, then up at Stella. "Aren't you off early?" she asks.

"Well, yes, I am," Stella begins. "I certainly am. But as a matter of fact I came over here for a special reason, Florrie, there's something I wanted to talk to you about. If you could maybe—" Stella raises her eyebrows and looks hard at Chip.

"Why don't you go over there and play some Legos?" Florrie asks him, pointing.

"No," Chip says. He starts singing again in his high little voice.

"I bet you could make a submarine," Florrie says, "like you were telling me about."

"No," Chip says, kicking the floor, but then he looks up and says he might like to go outside.

"I thought he had a cold," Stella says.

"He does. But I guess one little bike ride wouldn't make it any worse than it is already. OK," Florrie tells Chip. "Go on. But I want you back here in fifteen minutes."

Chip gives a whoop and runs out the door without a jacket; it will be a wonder if he lives to grow up at all.

"Now then." Florrie folds her hands in her lap and yawns and looks at Stella. "What is it?"

"Well, I've been thinking," Stella says, "about you living over here in this big old house with not even any real relatives to speak of, living with strangers, and how this property is zoned commercial now and we could make a pretty penny if we went ahead and sold it while the real estate market is so high—"

"This is my house," Florrie interrupts.

"Well, I know it is," Stella says, "but it's just so much for you to try to keep up, and if you sold it and moved in with Claude and me, why we could pool all our resources so to speak and none of us would ever have to worry about a thing."

"*Moved in with Claude and you?*" For some reason Florrie is grinning and then she's laughing out loud. It gives Stella a chill to see her; she knows that her suspicions are all true and Florrie's gone mental at last.

"*Moved in with Claude and you?*" Florrie keeps saying this over and over, and laughing.

"Now this is serious," Stella tells her. "I don't see anything funny here at all. When I think of you over here with strangers—"

"They're not strangers," Florrie says. "Chip is my very own grandson as you very well know, and Johnnie Sue is Earl Junior's ex-wife."

"You might as well be running a boardinghouse!"

"Now there's an idea," Florrie says, and it's hard to tell from her face whether she's serious or not, the way her eyes are shining so blue and crinkling up like that at the corners. "I hadn't thought of a boardinghouse." She smiles.

"Oh Florrie!" Stella bursts out. "Don't you see? If you came to live with us you wouldn't have to make these ridiculous cakes and drag them all over town . . ."

"I like making cakes," Florrie says.

"Well, I know you do, but that's neither here nor there. The fact is, Florrie, and I might as well just tell you, the fact is you are going around here acting like a crazy old woman, whether you know it or not, and it's just real embarrassing for everybody in this family, and I'm telling you how you can stop. We can sell this house, you can come to live with us. You're just a spectacle of yourself, Florrie, whether you know it or not."

"Does Claude know you came over here to tell me this?"

"Claude!" Stella bristles. "What does Claude have to do with anything?" Then Stella squints through her frosted eyelids, and drums her long red nails on the kitchen table. "Oh! I get it!" she said. "You're still jealous, aren't you? And I came over here prepared to let bygones be bygones."

"What bygones?" Florrie's eyes are bright, bright blue, and she has a deep spot of color, like rouge, on each cheek. "What bygones?" she repeats.

"Well," Stella says, "I guess the dog is out of the bag now! I mean I know exactly how you feel. Don't you think for one minute I don't know. I know you are jealous of me and always have been. You are jealous of my position at Belk's and my house and you resent our place in the community, mine and Claude's, and don't try to deny it. You always have. Don't try to tell me. I know you resent how Robert and Dawn Elizabeth have turned out so well, and all of that, but mainly I know you're still mad that you never got Claude in the first place, that Claude picked me over you."

"What?" Florrie says. "That Claude what?"

"You know what," Stella says.

Florrie sits looking at Stella for one long minute as the wind picks up again outside and rattles the kitchen window. Florrie looks at Stella with her mouth open, and then her mouth curves up and she's laughing, laughing to beat the band. "Lord, Stella!" Florrie is wiping her eyes.

Stella stands up and puts on her coat. "If that's how you feel about it," she says.

"I can't move over there," Florrie finally manages to say. "It would never work out, Stella, believe me." Then she's laughing again—it's clear just how mental she is.

Some people are beyond help. So Stella says, "Well," almost to herself. "Nobody can say I didn't try." This ought to give her some satisfaction, but it does not. She stands on one side of the table and Florrie stands on the other, with that crazy cake between them.

"Who'd you make *that* for, anyway?" Stella asks, jerking her head toward it.

"Why, nobody," Florrie tells her. "Just nobody at all."

Stella shakes her head.

"But you can have it if you want it," Florrie says. "Go on, take it, you and Claude can have it for dinner."

"What kind is it?"

"Carrot cake." Florrie picks up the ironstone platter like she's fixing to wrap it up.

"You know I can't touch roughage." Stella sighs, leaving, but Florrie follows her out to the car still holding that cake while Chip rides by on a bike that used to be Floyd's, trailing his high wordless song out behind him in the wind, and real leaves fall all around them. Stella doesn't doubt for one minute that if Johnny Sue and Chip don't cut a piece of that cake within the next few hours, Florrie will go right out in the street and give it to the very next person who

40

happens along. Chip puts his feet up on the handlebars, and waves both hands in the air. Stella turns her collar up against the wind: the first signs of a woman's age may be found around her eyes, on her hands, and at her throat.

Stella gets in her car and decides to drive back over to Belk's for a little while, to put out her new Venetian Court Colors display beneath the twinkling lights of her beautiful chandelier; while Claude, out driving his boat around and around in big slow circles at Kerr Lake, doesn't even pretend to fish but stares back at the long smooth trail of the wake on the cold blue water, with a little smile on his face as he thinks of Florrie; and Florrie stands out in the patchy grass of her front yard with the leaf cake still cradled in her bare arms, admiring the way the sunlight shines off the icing, thinking about Earl Mingo and thinking too about Earl's child off someplace in this world, that child related to her by more than blood it seems to Florrie, that child maybe squinting out at the sky right now like Earl did, through God knows what color of eyes.

Flannery O'Connor

Revelation

THE DOCTOR'S WAITING ROOM, which was very small, was almost full when the Turpins entered and Mrs. Turpin, who was very large, made it look even smaller by her presence. She stood looming at the head of the magazine table set in the center of it, a living demonstration that the room was inadequate and ridiculous. Her little bright black eyes took in all the patients as she sized up the seating situation. There was one vacant chair and a place on the sofa occupied by a blond child in a dirty blue romper who should have been told to move over and make room for the lady. He was five or six, but Mrs. Turpin saw at once that no one was going to tell him to move over. He was slumped down in the seat, his arms idle at his sides and his eyes idle in his head; his nose ran unchecked.

Mrs. Turpin put a firm hand on Claud's shoulder and said in a voice that included anyone who wanted to listen, "Claud, you sit in that chair there," and gave him a push down into the vacant one. Claud was florid and bald and sturdy, somewhat shorter than Mrs. Turpin, but he sat down as if he were accustomed to doing what she told him to.

Mrs. Turpin remained standing. The only man in the room besides Claud was a lean stringy old fellow with a rusty hand spread out on each knee, whose eyes were closed as if he were asleep or dead or pretending to be so as not to get up and offer her his seat. Her gaze settled agreeably on a well-dressed grey-haired lady whose eyes met hers and whose expression said: if that child belonged to me, he would have some manners and move over—there's plenty of room there for you and him too.

Claud looked up with a sigh and made as if to rise.

"Sit down," Mrs. Turpin said. "You know you're not supposed to stand on that leg. He has an ulcer on his leg," she explained.

Claud lifted his foot onto the magazine table and rolled his trouser leg up to reveal a purple swelling on a plump marble-white calf.

"My!" the pleasant lady said. "How did you do that?"

"A cow kicked him," Mrs. Turpin said.

"Goodness!" said the lady.

Claud rolled his trouser leg down.

"Maybe the little boy would move over," the lady suggested, but the child did not stir.

"Somebody will be leaving in a minute," Mrs. Turpin said. She could not understand why a doctor—with as much money as they made charging five dollars a day to just stick their head in the hospital door and look at you—couldn't afford a decent-sized waiting room. This one was hardly bigger than a garage. The table was cluttered with limp-looking magazines and at one end of it there was a big green glass ash tray full of cigaret butts and cotton wads with little blood spots on them. If she had had anything to do with the running of the place, that would have been emptied every so often. There were no chairs against the wall at the head of the room. It had a rectangular-shaped panel in it that permitted a view of the office where the nurse came and went and the secretary listened to the radio. A plastic fern in a gold pot sat in the opening and trailed its fronds down almost to the floor. The radio was softly playing gospel music.

Just then the inner door opened and a nurse with the highest stack of yellow hair Mrs. Turpin had ever seen put her face in the crack and called for the next patient. The woman sitting beside Claud grasped the two arms of her chair and hoisted herself up; she pulled her dress free from her legs and lumbered through the door where the nurse had disappeared.

Mrs. Turpin eased into the vacant chair, which held her tight as a corset. "I wish I could reduce," she said, and rolled her eyes and gave a comic sigh.

"Oh, *you* aren't fat," the stylish lady said.

"Ooooo I am too," Mrs. Turpin said. "Claud he eats all he wants to and never weighs over one hundred and seventy-five pounds, but me I just look at something good to eat and I gain some weight," and her stomach and shoulders shook with laughter. "You can eat all you want to, can't you, Claud?" she asked, turning to him.

Claud only grinned.

"Well, as long as you have such a good disposition," the stylish lady said, "I don't think it makes a bit of difference what size you are. You just can't beat a good disposition."

Next to her was a fat girl of eighteen or nineteen, scowling into a thick blue book which Mrs. Turpin saw was entitled *Human Development.* The girl raised her head and directed her scowl at Mrs. Turpin as if she did not like her looks. She appeared annoyed that anyone should speak while she tried to read. The poor girl's face was blue with acne and Mrs. Turpin thought how pitiful it was to have a face like that at that age. She gave the girl a friendly smile but the girl only scowled the harder. Mrs. Turpin herself was fat but she had always had good skin, and, though she was forty-seven years old, there was not a wrinkle in her face except around her eyes from laughing too much.

Next to the ugly girl was the child, still in exactly the same position, and next to him was a thin leathery old woman in a cotton print dress. She and Claud had three sacks of chicken feed in their pump house that was in the same print. She had seen from the first that the child belonged with the old woman. She could tell by the way they sat—kind of vacant and white-trashy, as if they would sit there until Doomsday if nobody called and told them to get up. And at right angles but next to the well-dressed pleasant lady was a lank-faced woman who was certainly the child's mother. She had on a yellow sweat shirt and wine-colored slacks, both gritty-looking, and the rims of her lips were stained with snuff. Her dirty yellow hair was tied behind with a little piece of red paper ribbon. Worse than niggers any day, Mrs. Turpin thought.

The gospel hymn playing was, "When I looked up and He looked down," and Mrs. Turpin, who knew it, supplied the last line mentally, "And wona these days I know I'll we-eara crown."

Without appearing to, Mrs. Turpin always noticed people's feet. The well-dressed lady had on red and grey suede shoes to match her dress. Mrs. Turpin had on her good black patent leather pumps.

The ugly girl had on Girl Scout shoes and heavy socks. The old woman had on tennis shoes and the white-trashy mother had on what appeared to be bedroom slippers, black straw with gold braid threaded through them—exactly what you would have expected her to have on.

Sometimes at night when she couldn't go to sleep, Mrs. Turpin would occupy herself with the question of who she would have chosen to be if she couldn't have been herself. If Jesus had said to her before he made her, "There's only two places available for you. You can either be a nigger or white-trash," what would she have said? "Please, Jesus, please," she would have said, "just let me wait until there's another place available," and he would have said, "No, you have to go right now and I have only those two places so make up your mind." She would have wiggled and squirmed and begged and pleaded but it would have been no use and finally she would have said, "All right, make me a nigger then—but that don't mean a trashy one." And he would have made her a neat clean respectable Negro woman, herself but black.

Next to the child's mother was a red-headed youngish woman, reading one of the magazines and working a piece of chewing gum, hell for leather, as Claud would say. Mrs. Turpin could not see the woman's feet. She was not white-trash, just common. Sometimes Mrs. Turpin occupied herself at night naming the classes of people. On the bottom of the heap were most colored people, not the kind she would have been if she had been one, but most of them; then next to them— not above, just away from—were the white-trash; then above them were the home-owners, and above them the home-and-land owners, to which she and Claud belonged. Above she and Claud were people with a lot of money and much bigger houses and much more land. But here the complexity of it would begin to bear in on her, for some of the people with a lot of money were common and ought to be below she and Claud and some of the people who had good blood had lost their money and had to rent and then there were colored people who owned their homes and land as well. There was a colored dentist in town who had two red Lincolns and a swimming pool and a farm with registered white-face cattle on it. Usually by the time she had fallen asleep all the classes of people were moiling

45

and roiling around in her head, and she would dream they were all crammed in together in a box car, being ridden off to be put in a gas oven.

"That's a beautiful clock," she said and nodded to her right. It was a big wall clock, the face encased in a brass sunburst.

"Yes, it's very pretty," the stylish lady said agreeably. "And right on the dot too," she added, glancing at her watch.

The ugly girl beside her cast an eye upward at the clock, smirked, then looked directly at Mrs. Turpin and smirked again. Then she returned her eyes to her book. She was obviously the lady's daughter because, although they didn't look anything alike as to disposition, they both had the same shape of face and the same blue eyes. On the lady they sparkled pleasantly but in the girl's seared face they appeared alternately to smolder and to blaze.

What if Jesus had said, "All right, you can be white-trash or a nigger or ugly!"

Mrs. Turpin felt an awful pity for the girl, though she thought it was one thing to be ugly and another to act ugly.

The woman with the snuff-stained lips turned around in her chair and looked up at the clock. Then she turned back and appeared to look a little to the side of Mrs. Turpin. There was a cast in one of her eyes. "You want to know wher you can get you one of themther clocks?" she asked in a loud voice.

"No, I already have a nice clock," Mrs. Turpin said. Once somebody like her got a leg in the conversation, she would be all over it.

"You can get you one with green stamps," the woman said. "That's most likely wher he got hisn. Save you up enough, you can get you most anythang. I got me some joo'ry."

Ought to have got you a wash rag and some soap, Mrs. Turpin thought.

"I get contour sheets with mine," the pleasant lady said.

The daughter slammed her book shut. She looked straight in front of her, directly through Mrs. Turpin and on through the yellow curtain and the plate glass window which made the wall behind her. The girl's eyes seemed lit all of a sudden with a peculiar light, an unnatural light like night road signs give. Mrs. Turpin turned her head to see if there was anything going on outside that she should see, but she could not see anything. Figures passing cast only a pale shadow

46

through the curtain. There was no reason the girl should single her out for her ugly looks.

"Miss Finley," the nurse said, cracking the door. The gum-chewing woman got up and passed in front of her and Claud and went into the office. She had on red high-heeled shoes.

Directly across the table, the ugly girl's eyes were fixed on Mrs. Turpin as if she had some very special reason for disliking her.

"This is wonderful weather, isn't it?" the girl's mother said.

"It's good weather for cotton if you can get the niggers to pick it," Mrs. Turpin said, "but niggers don't want to pick cotton any more. You can't get the white folks to pick it and now you can't get the niggers—because they got to be right up there with the white folks."

"They gonna *try* anyways," the white-trash woman said, leaning forward.

"Do you have one of those cotton-picking machines?" the pleasant lady asked.

"No," Mrs. Turpin said, "they leave half the cotton in the field. We don't have much cotton anyway. If you want to make it farming now, you have to have a little of everything. We got a couple of acres of cotton and a few hogs and chickens and just enough white-face that Claud can look after them himself."

"One thang I don't want," the white-trash woman said, wiping her mouth with the back of her hand. "Hogs. Nasty stinking things, a-gruntin and a-rootin all over the place."

Mrs. Turpin gave her the merest edge of her attention. "Our hogs are not dirty and they don't stink," she said. "They're cleaner than some children I've seen. Their feet never touch the ground. We have a pig-parlor—that's where you raise them on concrete," she explained to the pleasant lady, "and Claud scoots them down with the hose every afternoon and washes off the floor." Cleaner by far than that child right there, she thought. Poor nasty little thing. He had not moved except to put the thumb of his dirty hand into his mouth.

The woman turned her face away from Mrs. Turpin. "I know I wouldn't scoot down no hog with no hose," she said to the wall.

You wouldn't have no hog to scoot down, Mrs. Turpin said to herself.

"A-gruntin and a-rootin and a-groanin," the woman muttered.

47

"We got a little of everything," Mrs. Turpin said to the pleasant lady. "It's no use in having more than you can handle yourself with help like it is. We found enough niggers to pick our cotton this year but Claud he has to go after them and take them home again in the evening. They can't walk that half a mile. No they can't. I tell you," she said and laughed merrily, "I sure am tired of buttering up niggers, but you got to love em if you want em to work for you. When they come in the morning, I run out and I say, 'Hi yawl this morning?' and when Claud drives them off to the field I just wave to beat the band and they just wave back." And she waved her hand rapidly to illustrate.

"Like you read out of the same book," the lady said, showing she understood perfectly.

"Child, yes," Mrs. Turpin said. "And when they come in from the field, I run out with a bucket of icewater. That's the way it's going to be from now on," she said. "You may as well face it."

"One thang I know," the white-trash woman said. "Two thangs I ain't going to do: love no niggers or scoot down no hog with no hose." And she let out a bark of contempt.

The look that Mrs. Turpin and the pleasant lady exchanged indicated they both understood that you had to *have* certain things before you could *know* certain things. But every time Mrs. Turpin exchanged a look with the lady, she was aware that the ugly girl's peculiar eyes were still on her, and she had trouble bringing her attention back to the conversation.

"When you got something," she said, "you got to look after it." And when you ain't got a thing but breath and britches, she added to herself, you can afford to come to town every morning and just sit on the Court House coping and spit.

A grotesque revolving shadow passed across the curtain behind her and was thrown palely on the opposite wall. Then a bicycle clattered down against the outside of the building. The door opened and a colored boy glided in with a tray from the drug store. It had two large red and white paper cups on it with tops on them. He was a tall, very black boy in discolored white pants and a green nylon shirt. He was chewing gum slowly, as if to music. He set the tray down in the office opening next to the fern and stuck his head through to look for the secretary. She was not in there. He rested his arms on the ledge and waited, his narrow bottom stuck out, swaying slowly to the left and right. He raised a hand over his head and scratched the base of his skull.

"You see that button there, boy?" Mrs. Turpin said. "You can punch that and she'll come. She's probably in the back somewhere."

"Is thas right?" the boy said agreeably, as if he had never seen the button before. He leaned to the right and put his finger on it. "She sometime out," he said and twisted around to face his audience, his elbows behind him on the counter. The nurse appeared and he twisted back again. She handed him a dollar and he rooted in his pocket and made the change and counted it out to her. She gave him fifteen cents for a tip and he went out with the empty tray. The heavy door swung to slowly and closed at length with the sound of suction. For a moment no one spoke.

"They ought to send all them niggers back to Africa," the white-trash woman said. "That's wher they come from in the first place."

"Oh, I couldn't do without my good colored friends," the pleasant lady said.

"There's a heap of things worse than a nigger," Mrs. Turpin agreed. "It's all kinds of them just like it's all kinds of us."

"Yes, and it takes all kinds to make the world go round," the lady said in her musical voice.

As she said it, the raw-complexioned girl snapped her teeth together. Her lower lip turned downwards and inside out, revealing the pale pink inside of her mouth. After a second it rolled back up. It was the ugliest face Mrs. Turpin had ever seen anyone make and for a moment she was certain that the girl had made it at her. She was looking at her as if she had known and disliked her all her life—all of Mrs. Turpin's life, it seemed too, not just all the girl's life. Why, girl, I don't even know you, Mrs. Turpin said silently.

She forced her attention back to the discussion. "It wouldn't be practical to send them back to Africa," she said. "They wouldn't want to go. They got it too good here."

"Wouldn't be what they wanted—if I had anythang to do with it," the woman said.

"It wouldn't be a way in the world you could get all the niggers back over there," Mrs. Turpin said. "They'd be hiding out and lying down and turning sick on you and wailing and hollering and raring and pitching. It wouldn't be a way in the world to get them over there."

"They got over here," the trashy woman said. "Get back like they got over."

"It wasn't so many of them then," Mrs. Turpin explained.

The woman looked at Mrs. Turpin as if here was an idiot indeed but Mrs. Turpin was not bothered by the look, considering where it came from.

"Nooo," she said, "they're going to stay here where they can go to New York and marry white folks and improve their color. That's what they all want to do, every one of them, improve their color."

"You know what comes of that, don't you?" Claud asked.

"No, Claud, what?" Mrs. Turpin said.

Claud's eyes twinkled. "White-faced niggers," he said with never a smile.

Everybody in the office laughed except the white-trash and the ugly girl. The girl gripped the book in her lap with white fingers. The trashy woman looked around her from face to face as if she thought they were all idiots. The old woman in the feed sack dress continued to gaze expressionless across the floor at the high-top shoes of the man opposite her, the one who had been pretending to be asleep when the Turpins came in. He was laughing heartily, his hands still spread out on his knees. The child had fallen to the side and was lying now almost face down in the old woman's lap.

While they recovered from their laughter, the nasal chorus on the radio kept the room from silence.

> "You go to blank blank
> And I'll go to mine
> But we'll all blank along
> To-geth-ther,
> And all along the blank
> We'll hep eachother out
> Smile-ling in any kind of
> Weath-ther!"

Mrs. Turpin didn't catch every word but she caught enough to agree with the spirit of the song and it turned her thoughts sober. To help anybody out that needed it was her philosophy of life. She never spared herself when she found somebody in need, whether they were white or black, trash or decent. And of all she had to be thankful for, she was most thankful that this was so. If Jesus had said, "You can be high society and have all the money you want and be thin and svelte-like, but you can't be a good woman with it," she would have had to say, "Well don't make me that then. Make me a good woman and it don't matter what else, how fat or how ugly or how poor!" Her heart rose. He had not made her a nigger or white-trash or ugly! He had made her herself and given her a little of everything. Jesus, thank you! she said. Thank you thank you thank you! Whenever she counted her blessings she felt as buoyant as if she weighed one hundred and twenty-five pounds instead of one hundred and eighty.

"What's wrong with your little boy?" the pleasant lady asked the white-trashy woman.

"He has a ulcer," the woman said proudly. "He ain't give me a minute's peace since he was born. Him and her are just alike," she said, nodding at the old woman, who was running her leathery fingers through the child's pale hair. "Look like I can't get nothing down them two but Co'Cola and candy."

That's all you try to get down em, Mrs. Turpin said to herself. Too lazy to light the fire. There was nothing you could tell her about people like them that she didn't know already. And it was not just that they didn't have anything. Because if you gave them everything, in two weeks it would all be broken or filthy or they would have chopped it up for lightwood. She knew all this from her own experience. Help them you must, but help them you couldn't.

All at once the ugly girl turned her lips inside out again. Her eyes were fixed like two drills on Mrs. Turpin. This time there was no mistaking that there was something urgent behind them.

Girl, Mrs. Turpin exclaimed silently, I haven't done a thing to you! The girl might be confusing her with somebody else. There was no need to sit by and let herself be intimidated. "You must be in college," she said boldly, looking directly at the girl. "I see you reading a book there."

The girl continued to stare and pointedly did not answer.

Her mother blushed at this rudeness. "The lady asked you a question, Mary Grace," she said under her breath.

"I have ears," Mary Grace said.

The poor mother blushed again. "Mary Grace goes to Wellesley College," she explained. She twisted one of the buttons on her dress. "In Massachusetts," she added with a grimace. "And in the summer she just keeps right on studying. Just reads all the time, a real book worm. She's done real well at Wellesley; she's taking English and Math and History and Psychology and Social Studies," she rattled on, "and I think it's too much. I think she ought to get out and have fun."

The girl looked as if she would like to hurl them all through the plate glass window.

"Way up north," Mrs. Turpin murmured and thought, well, it hasn't done much for her manners.

"I'd almost rather to have him sick," the white-trash woman said, wrenching the attention back to herself. "He's so mean when he ain't. Look like some children just take natural to meanness. It's some gets bad when they get sick but he was the opposite. Took sick and turned good. He don't give me no trouble now. It's me waitin to see the doctor," she said.

If I was going to send anybody back to Africa, Mrs. Turpin thought, it would be your kind, woman. "Yes, indeed," she said aloud, but looking up at the ceiling, "it's a heap of things worse than a nigger." And dirtier than a hog, she added to herself.

"I think people with bad dispositions are more to be pitied than anyone on earth," the pleasant lady said in a voice that was decidedly thin.

"I thank the Lord he has blessed me with a good one," Mrs. Turpin said. "The day has never dawned that I couldn't find something to laugh at."

"Not since she married me anyways," Claud said with a comical straight face.

Everybody laughed except the girl and the white-trash.

Mrs. Turpin's stomach shook. "He's such a caution," she said, "that I can't help but laugh at him."

The girl made a loud ugly noise through her teeth.

Her mother's mouth grew thin and tight. "I think the worst thing in the world," she said, "is an ungrateful person. To have everything and not appreciate it. I know a girl," she said, "who has parents who would give her anything, a little brother who loves her dearly, who is getting a good education, who wears the best clothes, but who can never say a kind word to anyone, who never smiles, who just criticizes and complains all day long."

"Is she too old to paddle?" Claud asked.

The girl's face was almost purple.

"Yes," the lady said, "I'm afraid there's nothing to do but leave her to her folly. Some day she'll wake up and it'll be too late."

"It never hurt anyone to smile," Mrs. Turpin said. "It just makes you feel better all over."

"Of course," the lady said sadly, "but there are just some people you can't tell anything to. They can't take criticism."

"If it's one thing I am," Mrs. Turpin said with feeling, "it's grateful. When I think who all I could have been besides myself and what all I got, a little of everything, and a good disposition besides, I just feel like shouting, 'Thank you, Jesus, for making everything the way it is!' It could have been different!" For one thing, somebody else could have got Claud. At the thought of this, she was flooded with gratitude and a terrible pang of joy ran through her. "Oh thank you, Jesus, Jesus, thank you!" she cried aloud.

The book struck her directly over her left eye. It struck almost at the same instant that she realized the girl was about to hurl it. Before she could utter a sound, the raw face came crashing across the table toward her, howling. The girl's fingers sank like clamps into the soft flesh of her neck. She heard the mother cry out and Claud shout, "Whoa!" There was an instant when she was certain that she was about to be in an earthquake.

All at once her vision narrowed and she saw everything as if it were happening in a small room far away, or as if she were looking at it through the wrong end of a telescope. Claud's face crumpled and fell out of sight. The nurse ran in, then out, then in again. Then the gangling figure of the doctor rushed out of the inner door. Magazines flew this way and that as the table turned over. The girl fell with a thud and Mrs. Turpin's vision suddenly reversed itself and she saw everything large instead of small. The eyes of the white-trashy woman were staring hugely at the floor. There the girl, held down on one side by the nurse and on the other by her mother, was wrenching and turning in their grasp. The doctor was kneeling astride her, trying to hold her arm down. He managed after a second to sink a long needle into it.

Mrs. Turpin felt entirely hollow except for her heart which swung from side to side as if it were agitated in a great empty drum of flesh.

"Somebody that's not busy call for the ambulance," the doctor said in the off-hand voice young doctors adopt for terrible occasions.

Mrs. Turpin could not have moved a finger. The old man who had been sitting next to her skipped nimbly into the office and made the call, for the secretary still seemed to be gone.

"Claud!" Mrs. Turpin called.

He was not in his chair. She knew she must jump up and find him but she felt like some one trying to catch a train in a dream, when everything moves in slow motion and the faster you try to run the slower you go.

"Here I am," a suffocated voice, very unlike Claud's, said.

He was doubled up in the corner on the floor, pale as paper, holding his leg. She wanted to get up and go to him but she could not move. Instead, her gaze was drawn slowly downward to the churning face on the floor, which she could see over the doctor's shoulder.

The girl's eyes stopped rolling and focused on her. They seemed a much lighter blue than before, as if a door that had been tightly closed behind them was now open to admit light and air.

Mrs. Turpin's head cleared and her power of motion returned. She leaned forward until she was looking directly into the fierce brilliant eyes. There was no doubt in her mind that the girl did know her, knew her in some intense and personal way, beyond time and place and condition. "What you got to say to me?" she asked hoarsely and held her breath, waiting, as for a revelation.

The girl raised her head. Her gaze locked with Mrs. Turpin's. "Go back to hell where you came from, you old wart hog," she whispered. Her voice was low but clear. Her eyes burned for a moment as if she saw with pleasure that her message had struck its target.

Mrs. Turpin sank back in her chair.

After a moment the girl's eyes closed and she turned her head wearily to the side.

The doctor rose and handed the nurse the empty syringe. He leaned over and put both hands for a moment on the mother's shoulders, which were shaking. She was sitting on the floor, her lips pressed together, holding Mary Grace's hand in her lap. The girl's fingers were gripped like a baby's around her thumb. "Go on to the hospital," he said. "I'll call and make the arrangements."

"Now let's see that neck," he said in a jovial voice to Mrs. Turpin. He began to inspect her neck with his first two fingers. Two little moon-shaped lines like pink fish bones were indented over her windpipe. There was the beginning of an angry red swelling above her eye. His fingers passed over this also.

"Lea' me be," she said thickly and shook him off. "See about Claud. She kicked him."

"I'll see about him in a minute," he said and felt her pulse. He was a thin grey-haired man, given to pleasantries. "Go home and have yourself a vacation the rest of the day," he said and patted her on the shoulder.

Quit your pattin me, Mrs. Turpin growled to herself.

"And put an ice pack over that eye," he said. Then he went and squatted down beside Claud and looked at his leg. After a moment he pulled him up and Claud limped after him into the office.

Until the ambulance came, the only sounds in the room were the tremulous moans of the girl's mother, who continued to sit on the floor. The white-trash woman did not take her eyes off the girl. Mrs. Turpin looked straight ahead at nothing. Presently the ambulance drew up, a long dark shadow, behind the curtain. The attendants came in and set the stretcher down beside the girl and lifted her expertly onto it and carried her out. The nurse helped the mother gather up her things. The shadow of the ambulance moved silently away and the nurse came back into the office.

"That ther girl is going to be a lunatic, ain't she?" the white-trash woman asked the nurse, but the nurse kept on to the back and never answered her.

"Yes, she's going to be a lunatic," the white-trash woman said to the rest of them.

"Po' critter," the old woman murmured. The child's face was still in her lap. His eyes looked idly out over her knees. He had not moved during the disturbance except to draw one leg up under him.

"I thank Gawd," the white-trash woman said fervently, "I ain't a lunatic."

Claud came limping out and the Turpins went home.

As their pick-up truck turned into their own dirt road and made the crest of the hill, Mrs. Turpin gripped the window ledge and looked out suspiciously. The land sloped gracefully down through a field dotted with lavender weeds and at the start of the rise their small yellow frame house, with its little flower beds spread out around it like a fancy apron, sat primly in its accustomed place between two giant hickory trees. She would not have been startled to see a burnt wound between two blackened chimneys.

Neither of them felt like eating so they put on their house clothes and lowered the shade in the bedroom and lay down, Claud with his leg on a pillow and herself with a damp washcloth over her eye. The instant she was flat on her back, the image of a razor-backed hog with warts on its face and horns coming out behind its ears snorted into her head. She moaned, a low quiet moan.

"I am not," she said tearfully, "a wart hog. From hell." But the denial had no force. The girl's eyes and her words, even the tone of her voice, low but clear, directed only to her, brooked no repudiation. She had been singled out for the message, though there was trash in the room to whom it might justly have been applied. The full force of this fact struck her only now. There was a woman there who was neglecting her own child but she had been overlooked. The message had been given to Ruby Turpin, a respectable, hard-working, church-going woman. The tears dried. Her eyes began to burn instead with wrath.

She rose on her elbow and the washcloth fell into her hand. Claud was lying on his back, snoring. She wanted to tell him what the girl had said. At the same time, she did not wish to put the image of herself as a wart hog from hell into his mind.

"Hey, Claud," she muttered and pushed his shoulder.

Claud opened one pale baby blue eye.

She looked into it warily. He did not think about anything. He just went his way.

"Wha, whasit?" he said and closed the eye again.

"Nothing," she said. "Does your leg pain you?"

"Hurts like hell," Claud said.

"It'll quit terreckly," she said and lay back down. In a moment Claud was snoring again. For the rest of the afternoon they lay there. Claud slept. She scowled at the ceiling. Occasionally she raised her fist and made a small stabbing motion over her chest as if she was defending her innocence to invisible guests who were like the comforters of Job, reasonable-seeming but wrong.

About five-thirty Claud stirred. "Got to go after those niggers," he sighed, not moving.

She was looking straight up as if there were unintelligible handwriting on the ceiling. The protuberance over her eye had turned a greenish-blue. "Listen here," she said.

"What?"

"Kiss me."

Claud leaned over and kissed her loudly on the mouth. He pinched her side and their hands interlocked. Her expression of ferocious concentration did not change. Claud got up, groaning and growling, and limped off. She continued to study the ceiling.

She did not get up until she heard the pick-up truck coming back with the Negroes. Then she rose and thrust her feet in her brown oxfords, which she did not bother to lace, and stumped out onto the back porch and got her red plastic bucket. She emptied a tray of ice cubes into it and filled it half full of water and went out into the back yard. Every afternoon after Claud brought the hands in, one of the boys helped him put out hay and the rest waited in the back of the truck until he was ready to take them home. The truck was parked in the shade under one of the hickory trees.

"Hi yawl this evening?" Mrs. Turpin asked grimly, appearing with the bucket and the dipper. There were three women and a boy in the truck.

"Us doin nicely," the oldest woman said. "Hi you doin?" and her gaze stuck immediately on the dark lump on Mrs. Turpin's forehead.

"You done fell down, ain't you?" she asked in a solicitous voice. The old woman was dark and almost toothless. She had on an old felt hat of Claud's set back on her head. The other two women were younger and lighter and they both had new bright green sun hats. One of them had hers on her head; the other had taken hers off and the boy was grinning beneath it.

Mrs. Turpin set the bucket down on the floor of the truck. "Yawl hep yourselves," she said. She looked around to make sure Claud had gone. "No. I didn't fall down," she said, folding her arms. "It was something worse than that."

"Ain't nothing bad happen to you!" the old woman said. She said it as if they all knew that Mrs. Turpin was protected in some special way by Divine Providence. "You just had you a little fall."

"We were in town at the doctor's office for where the cow kicked Mr. Turpin," Mrs. Turpin said in a flat tone that indicated they could leave off their foolishness. "And there was this girl there. A big fat girl with her face all broke out. I could look at that girl and tell she was peculiar but I couldn't tell how. And me and her mama were just talking and going along and all of a sudden WHAM! She throws this big book she was reading at me and . . ."

"Naw!" the old woman cried out.

"And then she jumps over the table and commences to choke me."

"Naw!" they all exclaimed, "naw!"

"Hi come she do that?" the old woman asked. "What ail her?"

Mrs. Turpin only glared in front of her.

"Somethin ail her," the old woman said.

"They carried her off in an ambulance," Mrs. Turpin continued, "but before she went she was rolling on the floor and they were trying to hold her down to give her a shot and she said something to me." She paused. "You know what she said to me?"

"What she say?" they asked.

"She said," Mrs. Turpin began, and stopped, her face very dark and heavy. The sun was getting whiter and whiter, blanching the sky overhead so that the leaves of the hickory tree were black in the face of it. She could not bring forth the words. "Something real ugly," she muttered.

"She sho shouldn't said nothin ugly to you," the old woman said. "You so sweet. You the sweetest lady I know."

"She pretty too," the one with the hat on said.

"And stout," the other one said. "I never knowed no sweeter white lady."

"That's the truth befo' Jesus," the old woman said. "Amen! You des as sweet and pretty as you can be."

Mrs. Turpin knew just exactly how much Negro flattery was worth and it added to her rage. "She said," she began again and finished this time with a fierce rush of breath, "that I was an old wart hog from hell."

There was an astounded silence.

"Where she at?" the youngest woman cried in a piercing voice.

"Lemme see her. I'll kill her!"

"I'll kill her with you!" the other one cried.

"She b'long in the sylum," the old woman said emphatically. "You the sweetest white lady I know."

"She pretty too," the other two said. "Stout as she can be and sweet. Jesus satisfied with her!"

"Deed he is," the old woman declared.

Idiots! Mrs. Turpin growled to herself. You could never say anything intelligent to a nigger. You could talk at them but not with them. "Yawl ain't drunk your water," she said shortly. "Leave the bucket in the truck when you're finished with it. I got more to do than just stand around and pass the time of day," and she moved off and into the house.

She stood for a moment in the middle of the kitchen. The dark protuberance over her eye looked like a miniature tornado cloud which might any moment sweep across the horizon of her brow. Her lower lip protruded dangerously. She squared her massive shoulders. Then she marched into the front of the house and out the side door and started down the road to the pig parlor. She had the look of a woman going single-handed, weaponless, into battle.

The sun was a deep yellow now like a harvest moon and was riding westward very fast over the far tree line as if it meant to reach the hogs before she did. The road was rutted and she kicked several good-sized stones out of her path as she strode along. The pig parlor was on a little knoll at the end of a lane that ran off from the side of the barn. It was a square of concrete as large as a small room, with a board fence about four feet high around it. The concrete floor sloped slightly so that the hog wash could drain off into a trench where it was carried to the field for fertilizer. Claud was standing on the outside, on the edge of the concrete, hanging onto the top board, hosing down the floor inside. The hose was connected to the faucet of a water trough nearby.

Mrs. Turpin climbed up beside him and glowered down at the hogs inside. There were seven long-snouted bristly shoats in it—tan with liver-colored spots—and an old sow a few weeks off from farrowing. She was lying on her side grunting. The shoats were running about shaking themselves like idiot children, their little slit pig eyes searching the floor for anything left. She had read that pigs were the most intelligent animal. She doubted it. They were supposed to be smarter than dogs. There had even been a pig astronaut. He had performed his assignment perfectly but died of a heart attack afterwards because they left him in his electric suit, sitting upright throughout his examination when naturally a hog should be on all fours.

A-gruntin and a-rootin and a-groanin.

"Gimme that hose," she said, yanking it away from Claud. "Go on and carry them niggers home and then get off that leg."

"You look like you might have swallowed a mad dog," Claud observed, but he got down and limped off. He paid no attention to her humors.

Until he was out of earshot, Mrs. Turpin stood on the side of the pen, holding the hose and pointing the stream of water at the hind quarters of any shoat that looked as if it might try to lie down. When he had had time to get over the hill, she turned her head slightly and her wrathful eyes scanned the path. He was nowhere in sight. She turned back again and seemed to gather herself up. Her shoulders rose and she drew in her breath.

"What do you send me a message like that for?" she said in a low fierce voice, barely above a whisper but with the force of a shout in its concentrated fury. "How am I a hog and me both? How am I saved and from hell too?" Her free fist was knotted and with the other she gripped the hose, blindly pointing the stream of water in and out of the eye of the old sow whose outraged squeal she did not hear.

The pig parlor commanded a view of the back pasture where their twenty beef cows were gathered around the hay-bales Claud and the boy had put out. The freshly cut pasture sloped down to the highway. Across it was their cotton field and beyond that a dark green dusty wood which they owned as well. The sun was behind the wood, very red, looking over the paling of trees like a farmer inspecting his own hogs.

"Why me?" she rumbled. "It's no trash around here, black or white, that I haven't given to. And break my back to the bone every day working. And do for the church."

She appeared to be the right size woman to command the arena before her. "How am I a hog?" she demanded. "Exactly how am I like them?" and she jabbed the stream of water at the shoats. "There was plenty of trash there. It didn't have to be me.

"If you like trash better, go get yourself some trash then," she railed. "You could have made me trash. Or a nigger. If trash is what you wanted why didn't you make me trash?" She shook her fist with the hose in it and a watery snake appeared momentarily in the air. "I could quit working and take it easy and be filthy," she growled. "Lounge about the sidewalks all day drinking root beer. Dip snuff and spit in every puddle and have it all over my face. I could be nasty.

"Or you could have made me a nigger. It's too late for me to be a nigger," she said with deep sarcasm, "but I could act like one. Lay down in the middle of the road and stop traffic. Roll on the ground."

In the deepening light everything was taking on a mysterious hue. The pasture was growing a peculiar glassy green and the streak of highway had turned lavender. She braced herself for a final assault and this time her voice rolled out over the pasture. "Go on," she yelled, "call me a hog! Call me a hog again. From hell. Call me a wart hog from hell. Put that bottom rail on top. There'll still be a top and bottom!"

A garbled echo returned to her.

A final surge of fury shook her and she roared, "Who do you think you are?"

The color of everything, field and crimson sky, burned for a moment with a transparent intensity. The question carried over the pasture and across the highway and the cotton field and returned to her clearly like an answer from beyond the wood.

She opened her mouth but no sound came out of it.

A tiny truck, Claud's, appeared on the highway, heading rapidly out of sight. Its gears scraped thinly. It looked like a child's toy. At any moment a bigger truck might smash into it and scatter Claud's and the niggers' brains all over the road.

Mrs. Turpin stood there, her gaze fixed on the highway, all her muscles rigid, until in five or six minutes the truck reappeared, returning. She waited until it had had time to turn into their own road. Then like a monumental statue coming to life, she bent her head slowly and gazed, as if through the very heart of mystery, down into the pig parlor at the hogs. They had settled all in one corner around the old sow who was grunting softly. A red glow suffused them. They appeared to pant with a secret life.

Until the sun slipped finally behind the tree line, Mrs. Turpin remained there with her gaze bent to them as if she were absorbing some abysmal life-giving knowledge. At last she lifted her head. There was only a purple streak in the sky, cutting through a field of crimson and leading, like an extension of the highway, into the descending dusk. She raised her hands from the side of the pen in a gesture hieratic and profound. A visionary light settled in her eyes. She saw the streak as a vast swinging bridge extending upward from the earth through a field of living fire. Upon it a vast horde of souls were rumbling toward heaven. There were whole companies of white-trash, clean for the first time in their lives, and bands of black niggers in white robes, and battalions of freaks and lunatics shouting and clapping and leaping like frogs. And bringing up the end of the procession was a tribe of people whom she recognized at once as those who, like herself and Claud, had always had a little of everything and the God-given wit to use it right. She leaned forward to observe them closer. They were marching behind the others with great dignity, accountable as they had always been for good order and common sense and respectable behavior. They alone were on key. Yet she could see by their shocked and altered faces that even their virtues were being burned away. She lowered her hands and gripped the rail of the hog pen, her eyes small but fixed unblinkingly on what lay ahead. In a moment the vision faded but she remained where she was, immobile.

At length she got down and turned off the faucet and made her slow way on the darkening path to the house. In the woods around her the invisible cricket choruses had struck up, but what she heard were the voices of the souls climbing upward into the starry field and shouting hallelujah.

Barry Hannah

Horning In—A.

TONNIE RAY WAS passionately busy all her days at Dream of
Pines High. In junior high she was one of those neutral-looking
skinnies very much concerned with the concept *personality*, because
she didn't think she had any, and she was right. So she got together
with small groups of like spirits and went around telling, keeping,
and betraying incredibly inconsequential secrets, and that was about
it, for Tonnie Ray Reese. She changed skirts every day, and was
generally clean, and could be counted on to be scandalized by a shady
joke or bad word. When "John was home" the first time, that is,
when she had her first menstrual period, she missed a day of school.
A girl actually asked about her when she came back. So she missed
school every first day of her period for a while. She liked to create
that mystery, and liked to reply in coy ways to anybody that asked
about her absence—like she would say "I was with John," which was
sort of romantic too. She and her group were the giggling poultry
of the recess yard, huddling here and there with their little egg-secrets.
But in high school she was very busy; she had gotten desperate. The
only boy who'd ever asked her out was an absolute grub. Tonnie
Ray wanted to get into a good crowd so badly; she wanted in with
the popular crowd. And now she'd quit her old crowd and was really
of no crowd. All she thought of was emulating the popular set and
it kept her busy and extremely nervous. She would sit by the popular
cuties in the cafeteria and listen to all the recent anecdotes on parties
and dates, and then laugh along knowledgeably at them. There were
several girls like Tonnie Ray at Dream of Pines. They were all equally

frantic. Frantic to please, if you were the right person. We called them roaches, mainly, I guess, because they were as addled as maimed insects, and sucked up to such social crumbs as were offered.

I and the couple of guys I ran with paid a bitter kind of attention to Tonnie Ray and her type. We'd watch her collar some cheerleader, or class officer, or football player and start chattering away with them, making out to have crucial deals going with the honchos of the school. The guys and I winked at each other as her nervous voice rose in cries when she spotted somebody important in the hall. I don't know why Tonnie Ray and all the roaches rubbed us so raw. But we despised them from a special place of hatred in our hearts. We hated them so much that we'd skip lunch and loiter out in the hall in hopes of seeing one of them in the act.

"Look at Tonnie Ray leach up to that cheerleader babe," I said to a guy.

"I know. Wouldn't you love to put a shotgun down her throat and let it off coupla times?"

"It wouldn't be enough."

I confess that the guys and I, who weren't really hoodlums at all, talked theoretically on and off of assassinating Tonnie Ray. We had a prolonged deliberation over this idea throughout the rest of high school, but never could imagine anything quite excruciating enough for her. And we beheld with agony the fact that Tonnie Ray *was* making friends, she *was* getting in with the popular set; she became stylish and finally, to our horror, was one of the "Personalities of the Week" in the student newspaper.

"I say once a roach, always a roach," one guy said.

"Damn right." We were a bereaved consensus of three.

"Wouldn't you like to pick up a pair of ice tongs and just . . ."

"Not good enough."

We had the mill girls at Dream of Pines, too. These were the daughters of anybody who held a position below master foreman at one of the paper mills. Some of these gals were twenty-one and had given birth. *These* girls didn't roach or advertise themselves. They even seemed to resent being spoken to by students above their class. Of course you noticed them right off; their clothes were not terribly sharp and they tended to be a bit bruised around the legs. They swarmed in at lunch from another building where vocational arts were taught. They'd look at you straightforwardly with either lust or disdain, and you could pick up on unknown swear words by just hanging back in a locker and listening to them crowd into the cafeteria line. We liked them. We looked studiously at their bosoms and hips and had nothing to say when they disappeared.

I fell hard for one of them, under the influence of a dream I had of her. In the dream she was completely charming, said nothing, and was lusciously red-haired, and just before I awoke, she coyly threw her wrap aside and was milk naked. It was one of those dreams that mesmerizes your waking life. I waited in torture to see her again. When she came in with them, I tried to get her attention but couldn't. Her name was Ann. She had fine orangish hair and passable skin. Her hair was actually her best feature, but she peroxided her bangs so her hair went into toasted yellow around her face. Ann never wore a dress to school—always pants, with a raincoat like dirty beach sand thrown over her and a tee shirt underneath. The raincoat had a habit of draping on one nipple to one side and exposing the other slightly, the way it dropped. Ann dear, with that unamused face of an operatic slut, gave the impression that she wouldn't have cared if she had a burning sparkler on both nipples.

I already knew she worked at the old man's mattress factory in the afternoons. Her father worked there too, in another shop. He was a legendary wino who'd probably vomited or slept on every square foot of the pavement in Dream of Pines at one time or another. But he could cure himself for periods reaching to a year. Her mother was some species of obese dwarf who wore a swath of garbage for a dress and black high-top tennis shoes. I'd seen the mother before on the porch of a two-room plank house hard by the biggest Sink mill. Ann's old man used to work at the mill until he lucked into a place with the mattress factory. The mother waited for them sitting on the porch and just being a slum unto herself. God knows what she fixed them to eat. I often thought about that. I could see Ann, who by the family standard was Helen of Troy, being slowly destroyed by some monotonous supper of grease and cornmeal wads.

Three days a week she skipped lunch because, I guess, she didn't want to pay the quarter. She'd sit in the Film Room, right outside the cafeteria, and wait for her friends. While as for me, I always had a bunch of dollar bills in my wallet. She needed me; I knew she did. In my dream she'd been so happy to please, and the body which she had let me see I loved and pitied too for its helplessness. My feeling for her threw me. It got me in soft places I didn't know I had. I was a fool over some rare idea like taking her out to my house and giving her a shower and letting her sit on the edge of my bed in a towel and holding her face in my hands.

There was a story about Ann. Back in the tenth grade she was rumored to have given birth to a dead child. She was known to be a follower of the Dream of Pines basketball team, and some boy on the varsity was supposed to be the father. I saw her on the front row at the gym several times, sitting in her raincoat, alone, smiling out at the court as if enchanted by the game in a calm way. She didn't clap, or cheer, and was otherwise placid—not strictly a fan—except for the fixed smile. I used to think she was an idiot or a gypsy. She looked a little like the woman on a package of Muriel cigars. She smoked in the gym while she sat there. This was not allowed; there were signs up all over the place, and I saw her get called down for it several times. She never hid her cigarettes and in a minute she'd have another one going strong and have to be spoken to again by somebody officious like the scorekeeper, who was also a Baptist preacher. Well, about the third time he walked over to her, I thought she was just clearly insane. But she finally quit smoking when he told her she'd have to leave the gym if she didn't. And she remained transfixed to the game with the smile getting dimmer and dimmer as the game neared a close. Nowadays she never smiled, that I knew of. She ran with a crowd of girls that looked like hicks, lady wrestlers and carnival women. I wondered if it was true about her baby. Maybe having it had hurt her, and maybe she was pregnant again, and maybe eating made her sick. No wonder she looked right through me when I said hello and called her name in the hall.

Dear Ann you need me, need me, I beckoned to her mentally. My good looks, my sympathy, my $800 checking account. What do I care if you're in trouble again? You haven't ever met anybody like me before. I don't run. I know what life's about. I believe in my dream about you. I'll watch you give birth, even in Mexico if that's what it takes. I know life, honey. The ins and outs: no sweat. I'll watch the baby *come out,* dearest, and kiss your lips when it's over. I know it'll hurt and you've been hurt so much already. And about other matters that might come up: I won't expect marital privileges with you. I mean not until a whole lot of soft talking between you and me. I imagined us together in a modest cottage overlooking the Pacific Ocean at Malibu, California, by this time. I would be a fisherman and bring back natural things to eat from the hills. *National Geographic* illuminations of blue, green, and wheaten shades, with rocks, surf, and coves as private as the planet Mars, took over my head and carried me sleepily down all the roads of color-photograph geography. I did feel sleepy throughout all this thinking about Ann and me. I'm the sort of fellow, anyway, who isn't inclined to ever bring himself fully awake. I have a tremendous respect for people who *do* meet life with eyes wide-awake—like Ann, for example—but I've always been a coward that way; I think that if I ever did wake up completely, life would be too harsh and would lead me to suicide. Whereas, at the borders of sleep, I've usually adored life and could take down every breakfast bowl of thorns that came along.

Where my passionately imaginative kindness for Ann came from must have been the dream. I'd never been this way before. I wasn't ordinarily even courteous to folks I didn't know. For two weeks I was miserable over her. Aw, that she ignored me, that she maybe wasn't even conscious enough of me to be doing even that. I tried hard to dream about her again and get her to give me some message in the dream, but I couldn't. The memory of her in the dream was waning, and I got in a desperate funk. I made a fool out of myself when she came by one day. I started singing a song, "I've got the money, honey, if you've got the time," loud, putting myself directly in front of her face and doing a little hazardous bop stop. Ann looked at me worriedly, she did notice me, and then drew in her lip while glancing around in her crowd and deciding it was only her I was trying to entertain. Oh yeah, it was embarrassing as hell for me to have to do this. I was probably red in the face and silly as a sheik in drag, but I thought music might get her. She looked back at me once as she went on to the cafeteria. I was sure I had something moving now.

But no. I decided she was extremely shy. I couldn't wait any longer, though. Next day I found her sitting in the Film Room by herself. I stepped up to the wall and printed out a note, went in and put it on the desk she was sitting on, then fled. The note read: "I dreamed about you and I like you very much. If you're in trouble I want to help out. Do you know, want to know what I dreamed about you (us)? Even though you might of thought it was stupid of me singing in the hall yesterday I meant it, *I Have The Money Honey* as in the song I was singing. I know I don't have a very good voice. You know who my father is don't you. I have $1000 in my bank account. Please call me at 212-5037 at Pierre Hills soon. You know that song 'You Send Me'? I listen to it on the radio and think, You Send Me. Cares, Harry Monroe."

She never called. I went out to the mattress factory in the afternoons and watched her from my old man's glass office. It wrecked him with curiosity that I came down and watched the work. Ann worked behind a sewing machine in the shop just below us. She knew I was watching her. Then one day I noticed with a shock that she was violating the smoking ordinance. A great careless cloud boiled out of her mouth and floated up in the rafters. The old man chose this moment to rise out of his chair behind the desk and walk over to the shop window beside me, meaning, I think, to put his arm around my shoulder in a father-chum gesture. I knew he'd see Ann smoking. I could think of nothing very smart to distract him, but moved wildly, looking for some trick. There were several piles of job tickets on a table near me, and so I just dashed my hand through them and knocked them all over the floor. Sure enough, the old man stopped. He bent down and picked up a couple of handfuls, then rose up and stared at me.

"It was an accident. Let me help you," I said.

"I worked on those tickets all morning," the old man spoke, very dry. "It looked like you just . . . *knocked* them, son."

"Something nervous happened to me."

"That was *crazy.*" His face meant something deeper than this. I felt sorry for him; he started hopping from ticket to ticket on the floor.

"Let me help."

"You *can't* help. You go on home and . . . get well, boy. Sometimes you scare us. You know what? Donna says you close up your room

69

in the afternoons and lie on the bed listening to the phonograph in the dark. What does that mean?"

The only answer to that was I liked to do it. Hell—kick a guy because he favors salt in his beer, peanuts in his soft drink, dark with his music: he happens to be a guy who likes to grip the sheets and close his eyes until greenish movies featuring him as the hero appear, changing scenes and milieux with the changing climes of music—Harry happy, Harry sad, Harry bitter or melancholic, Harry truculent, but always Harry marvelous, Harry celebrated by the high-class babes of Paris, Berlin, London, Rome, New York, Baton Rouge, New Orleans, and of such shady places as Vicksburg, Natchez, Biloxi, Mobile, Savannah, and Charleston, twentieth-century holdouts of the romantic Southland, where it would be all magnolias, swamps and bayous, Spanish moss, cigarillos, piers, catfish, subtly brewed Bourbon drinks, and extravagantly well-dressed, complex, historic vagina, for Harry suave. Caving in a pier by his sheer presence. And lately, dreams of Malibu, California, in the simple cottage with Ann. Kick in a fellow's head for wanting the dark, and the evocative phonograph. Very well.

I suffered in behalf of Ann and in behalf of, really, myself, the way I happened to be. I had enough pride to be proud of it, though. Times were when I felt like God's special friend, I was suffering so much. Like the Jews. We were reading about the unspeakable persecution of the Jews under Hitler in history about that time. Of course I had dug into all that lore years ago. The old teacher was married to a Jewish woman from Chicago. He held forth on the sins against the Jews as if he suffered a chronic nightmare one week a year about it. The atrocity photographs he showed were the only attraction of the year's history class. He'd bring them out of an old cardboard folder and just sigh pitifully as he passed around the pictures. Guys would take his class for reason for the photographs alone. The pictures they were really awesome and sordid, showing open mouths and exposed pubes. The year I was under the old boy, a girl in my class threw up, and the principal came in the next day to say he couldn't show those pictures around any more. So right in front of us the old boy got his folder together, put on his overcoat, caught up his briefcase, and quit the school, giving us some kind of hopeless salute.

So what? everybody says. The only thing he was good at was telling about the Jews and about how time flies—tempus fugit, and all that, with a few other Latin phrases that seemed to grip him personally but never affected any of us. The principal read to us out of the textbook the rest of the year. And let me take this opportunity to say that this man, the principal, had a acute breath problem; air like from a cavern full of dead men came out of his mouth, and I caught it all, being on the front row, attempting as a sort of last ditch effort to create a scholarly air around myself by sitting there. I was doing so mediocrely at Dream of Pines, and my parents wanted me to get in such a mighty college. They had the money. They wanted me at Harvard, or Princeton, or better yet, Columbia, in New York City. As I said, my old man was partial to New York because it had all that unimaginable money.

Another time I came to the factory to see Ann. I had managed to force myself into another dream about her. This time she was a kind of puppet that said, "I love you. I need you. I love you. I need you." She'd taken off her clothes again and revealed a painted-doll type of nudity, showing two red dots and a black V that seemed varnished and inaccessible. The old man happened to be out of the office. I waved at her vigorously at the office window. She was talking to a stumpy fellow in gray coveralls and smoking a cigarette. When the fellow saw me, he hiked off instantly to another shop. Ann kept her eyes on me. Then she lifted up her hand and gave me the finger. I couldn't believe it. But the familiarity of the old signal somehow gave me some hope.

I followed her home. She was in some smoky car of the women's car pool and I was in the black station wagon of old. They let her out at her slum-pocket and she walked rapidly over her lawn toward the house. I say lawn, but what it was was a soil flat that looked beaten out by a goon whose duty it was to let no sprig grow. I drove up with her and began calling her name. She seemed to be ignoring me and was almost running into her house, thinking to be rid of me in there. What a dump to run to for safety. I saw her doing this, and I could not believe the story about her having a baby. This was a furiously shy girl I was dealing with.

I lay down on the car horn. I had quite a horn. It was loud, and by some accident at General Motors, played a whole harmonic chord, like C against E and G. It sounded like a band tuning up. It pierced, was rather regal, and could not be ignored except by the deaf. All right. Ann gave up and walked back to my car and got in, leaving her door open. She was the first girl I'd had in the car.

"Ann. Why aren't I good enough for you?" I said right off. I knew good and well that wasn't the issue. All the signs were that I was too good for *her* and was bending down to her heroically.

"You do *talk*, don't you?" I asked her further.

"I know a guy that would kill both of us if he knew we were to-gether," she said. God, she'd spoken to me. She looked beautiful in the sunset at five-thirty—that was when I was talking to her. Her raincoat came apart.

"You don't wear a brassiere, do you, Ann?"

"Don't you talk like that." Her voice was steady. It had a low harsh music in it. That pleased me.

"I'm sorry, Ann."

"Don't write me notes. Don't follow me around. You're not big enough or old enough. You wouldn't want me if you knew you might get killed for wanting me."

"I heard you had a baby. Did you?"

"That's for me to know and you to find out."

"You did, didn't you? I don't care. I had a dream about us. You liked me and took off your clothes . . ." I stuttered this out.

"Oh yeah?" she took it up. "What'd you do in this dream?"

"I just stared. Looked at you."

"You see. You're not ready to do anything yet, you see." She looked away from me toward the sunset, and then all around at the scraggly pines growing outside her lawn; she seemed to be inspecting the whole globe. It was just a minute before night, and very red in the sky. "You know I'm the best piece of ass at Dream of Pines that has ever been, don't you, Harry?"

"No, mam," I got out. No, I didn't know she was anything as deluxe as that. Ann laughed.

"They say I am. I am the girl whose butt don't often hit the mattress, they say. Some guy was looking in a window and observed that when I didn't know it."

While she was saying that she was taking me all in, probably for

72

the first time. I was exhausted by all I'd found out about her. I'd always thought of her as my private discovery.

"You come back around when you grow up some," Ann said. "I haven't got anything against you." She got out of the car.

"What do you think of Malibu, California? I've got love for you. I've got *money!*" I yelled when she seemed to be leaving the car. She came back and put her red-haired head in the window.

"Don't think I ain't dreamed of all that money with you . . . Harry . . . Everybody knows *love* is the loveliest word there is, also. Don't throw it around like you do."

She went in. By God, I wanted her more than ever. She had a little intelligence, which surprised the daylights out of me. You bet I'd wait around and grow until I was man enough for her. I'd grow hair all over. I'd seen what a woman she was when I talked to her. All set. Ann and I would wait on each other. An enormously profitable way to spend your spare time, waiting, growing, for Ann.

Two weeks later I drove the car up in the garage and there was the old man. It was twilight. He was sitting on the hood of his Buick. I knew by his weak smile that he was after me.

"That's the way to park that old caroobie," he yelled. I knew something was on his mind, like a ton of bricks. The old man gets friendlier than a faggot Japanese when he approaches me on bad trouble. He wants to establish that all is normal except one tiny thing, and that thing is the business at hand.

"Guess what Mr. Mick told me the other day?" he says. No relation to anything. I am alarmed. Mr. Mick is Ann's wino father. Her name is Ann Mick.

"He said the reason he gave up wine the last time was that the air from the paper mills in Dream of Pines was so bad it cut into his wine and ruined it the minute he pulled the cap off. It was like mixing wine with raccoon dung, he said." Big laughing in the garage. I'm struggling toward the house but the old man has got a great humorous cuff on me.

"It's a shame about Mr. Mick," I say. Let me go, old man.

"His daughter goes to your high school," says my father. His voice has the crisp delight of profundity in it. What am I supposed to do? Deny that she attends the school? "She works for me on the sewing machines. She's the worst worker I have. She smokes in the shop.

73

Somebody told me she does something worse than that with somebody else back of the stacks at coffee break. I'm thinking of letting her go."

"You know I have a crush on her," I admit.

"I'll say a crush. With dreams abut her, and singing songs to her." He lifted out of his vest pocket the very note I gave her in the Film Room. It was the blue-lined notebook paper with ripped ringer holes, and by then it was very crumpled and folded and almost yellow. "You don't want me to read it, do you?"

I snatched it out of the old man's fingers.

"You put our phone number in there," he mused.

"Did Ann give this to you?" I asked.

"No. It's been through several people before it got to me. You'll be happy to know that. First, she gave it to her father, and he thought it was such a precious joke that he handed it over to Harley Butte, his foreman. Then Harley kept it a week, thinking about it, and finally decided I ought to see it. He gave it to me. He said he thought I wouldn't think it was very funny, and he was right. I don't think this note's very funny. With all the fine girls you could be interested in . . ."

He had me down. He began accusing me of trying to embarrass him. He said he didn't need that, and that my mother Donna, who was a very fine lady, didn't need that. He said it was a slander to her name that Ann Mick was the first girl I chose to show any interest in, because (he whispered) Ann Mick was a little "harlot" that everybody knew about. He finally got so upset, saying we wouldn't mention any of this to Mother, and that this matter was "Closed. Closed, you hear?" I couldn't understand him. I'd agreed to everything he said long ago, out of sheer fright and humiliation. But he was forcing himself into a nervous panic, still holding onto my arm, and looking out into the dark back yard as if there was some specter there which yet threatened his life and family. I do believe he was holding to me protectively and not just to keep me from running in the house. I'd seen the old man nervous and full of clamor before, but never like this.

The old man was a converted Presbyterian and was occasionally flooded by the idea of being morally circumspect. He'd quit smoking and use up a bottle of Listerine in one week trying to expunge every hint of the weed within and without his body. He'd begin drinking worlds of milk and throw out the one bottle of sherry in the house, which he and my mother touched only about twice a year anyway. He'd walk to work and back, a distance over all of five miles, with his hair combed neat and slick and a modest pin-on bow tie at his throat—other days he despised bow ties as menial-looking—and he would have some book in his hands: a dictionary, or a book of poems by a Presbyterian missionary to China, what did it matter. He never cracked it, but made sure to have his name signed gloriously on the flyleaf, and all he wanted out of it was the sober sanction that a piece of literature in the hands gives one. He'd get home drunk on sunshine, goodness, and his own sweat. He would be concerned about his family name, which meant that he was concerned about me. He called me into the kitchen, where he'd have two glasses waiting. There he began, "Well. Tell me what you've been doing," and engaged me in a sort of contest at milk-drinking while we waited for the answers to come out. It all ended with our drinking so much milk we were ready to puke; the old man churning himself into a dull butter of meditation about my life. Not one understandable sentence having passed between us.

So I thought after I left him in the garage that he was only being a Presbyterian again, with all this business about the family name and so on, but that was not it. Or that was only partly it. I think I saw into this matter later.

I went to his office again one afternoon to look at Ann. He did not see me come in. The old man was sitting on a stool near the shop window and peering down at someone very concentratedly. I walked over—I suppose quietly—and looked past his shoulder. There was Ann bent down at her machine. I know he wasn't looking at the middle-aged women around her.

"You didn't fire her, did you?"

He jerked around coming out of a very soulful smile. Then he seemed to become concerned over what he was doing. He squirmed around right-face on the stool. He bit his lips, closed his eyes, and failed once at crossing his arms.

"Who?" he said weakly.

Oh, Daddy, oh, Ode Elann Dupont. You've been in love with her too, haven't you? Or at least you like to look at her very much, don't you? I do not think I was wrong about it. The fishiest grin I've ever seen popped out on his mouth. I looked past his shoulder down to Ann on the floor, and seeing her, blooming heavily forward, unbrassiered, under her tee shirt as I'd never seen her before, her legs crossed, her hairstrands falling over into her eyes like wispy copper as she bent to the machine doing her little bit, I knew she was too much woman for me, for one thing, and for another, no man could look on her without becoming a slobbering kind of rutting boar; she did not enchant you: she put you in heat. You thought of a pig-run alley full of hoofmarks running between you and her—lots of hoofmarks, dried deep in the clay—for after all, she was known to have mated with others. She was at the edge of a water hole, bending down for a drink with her feminine parts up in the air. I thought of the old man looking at her.

He seemed depraved and perverse, this old boy who should've been out of the running years ago. I didn't like him. I suspected him of really having tried something with Ann, of maybe keeping her in some kind of wagebondage lust. I thought of the old boy naked, using her like a trampoline. I'm sure he never did anything but look, like me, but uncertainty in me has always bred a phantasmagoric imagination.

Well, to the credit of his honesty, the old man instantly gave up the sham and said, "She's quite a slut, isn't she?"

We broke out laughing when he said that. The old man and I are both amused by the concept of a whore. The idea of women being gored for lucre by some poor man has always been a joke to bring down the house between us. We heard it called the oldest profession, and then thought of a cavewoman doing it for a glowing coal, a piece of fire from his cracking wealthy bonfire; an Egyptian woman doing it for a leek; a Hebrew woman doing it for water; a Roman woman doing it for an acre of German tundra; a World War II woman doing it for a radio. The only contact the old man and I had for years was whispering whore jokes to each other. We started giggling when the word *whore* was first mentioned. The worst of them all was told by me during a terrible period of my college life. It was about a seventy-year-old whore thrusting a bag into a dark closet where her lover was hidden; he thought they were potato chips, but they were actually the scabs off her own body. The old man closed his eyes and edged away after I told that one, not knowing his own flesh and blood son all over again. I really hadn't wanted to tell it, but it had gone around for bowelish laughs among the terribly unhappy crowd I ran with at college. My resources were low; in my crowd, whatever gagged a maggot passed for humor. After I'd told the old man that joke, the whore jokes between us stopped completely, and there was, as a matter of fact, no further communication between us. I did us in as father and son when I told that last rotten one.

However, now we laughed together. I forgot all the vile imaginings about the old man. I forgot everything and laughed with him till I cried. I do believe it was all because of the pleasure of finally forgetting Ann. He'd called her a slut, and I at last believed him. She was a comic whore. I told her goodbye. You'll be waiting a long time for me to grow up enough for you, Ann, I thought. The old man and I got out our handkerchiefs and wiped the tears off our cheeks. He reached over and held my shoulder. Too bad for you, Ann, I thought, looking at her still, past him. She looked up and saw us in the office and her mouth fell open with some surprise. That's the most I ever evoked from her. Too bad you don't get to go to that cottage in Malibu with me, Ann. What kind of gimp did you think I was? You whore. How dare you?

What a farce! I had come to the office with my suitcase packed and in the bed of my station wagon. I was intending to draw out the $800 in my account that afternoon. I had come to the factory for no other reason than picking up Ann, persuading her, and driving straight to Malibu with her. I thought I'd drop in and see her through the glass window again, and see the old man too, for sentimental reasons. I was laughing over the ruins of my first dream. The facts were of course that Ann was not strictly a whore. She never took money, that I had heard of. She did it with mature athletes because she liked it. I knew that. But it was somehow less humbling to the old ego to think of her as a whore than as a woman of pleasure. There were too many muscles involved in that.

And sometimes things are so monstrous you can't do anything else

77

but laugh. The old man liked to have her around him; he liked to look at her and think of her putting out; he liked to think of that tee shirt rolled up to her chin and of that red hair writhing and of her yellow teeth biting her underlip and of her shut eyes and smile when she was getting her paroxysms. Great God, he was the same as me, and that was what was monstrous. He could not bear to be picturing the same woman that his son was. He thought it was depraved. All that he knew of Presbyterian decorum was brought into question. That's why he got so upwrought at me in the garage.

There was a light rap on the office door, and then the door opened and in stepped that devil Harley Butte. Don't think I hadn't been thinking of this man for a couple of weeks. I'd never heard of such an officious nigger. I just couldn't figure him, the man who handed my note to Ann to my old man. Mainly what I couldn't figure was what the old man had said about Harley *thinking* for a week before he decided to hand the note over. I didn't know anything about a thinking nigger at the time. I knew of wild niggers, romantic niggers, lazy niggers, comic niggers, fishing niggers, foxy niggers, even rich niggers, but I knew nothing about yellow thinking niggers.

Harley was colored more toward white than I'd imagined him. He was my size and handsome, with points of brown at the brows and eyes, and stiff hair; he had an orange pretty face. His eyes closed every other breath he drew. He was a baby bursting forth with dark points of maturity and had on his face a sort of amazement that all this growth had come to him so suddenly. He looked toward me, immediately shut his eyes, and talked only to the old man.

"I'm afraid they've scheduled another game on Friday afternoon. I'll have to have Friday off again, Mr. Monroe. I can't help it. I'm the director of the band, and there isn't any way I can get out of it."

The old man looked to me.

"Have you met Mister Butte, Harry?" The *Mister* threw me. Especially as used toward a man whose parents you wondered about first thing when you saw him. Yellow man. I made a point out of despising him as a mixed breed. I became an authority and a prophet about his certain doom. I gave him no more chances than the chances a child begat of human sperm and sheep egg had. I knew there were special laws against doing it with sheep, because something would produce—something unspeakable. I thought, Butte, you'll probably die at thirty at the latest, of simple natural causes. Go ahead and be a foreman for the old man, be the band director out at Grell, hand in notes I wrote, kick around a few more years, then you'll be *gone,* buddy. You look too strange to make it, my friend. It satisfied me to think such thoughts.

"I don't think you're going to get much out of him. Your boy doesn't like me," said Harley. He and the old man laughed.

"But now, Harry and I know each other from way back. I and he were introduced one evening he was throwing firecrackers. He was having lots of fun."

The old man bent his brows impishly. I couldn't tell whether he knew what Butte was talking about. It's among the old man's habits of snobbery to make out like nothing is unknown to him. I began feeling watched, or worse, spied upon, and went home.

Butte is a spy in the old man's hire, I thought. I was outraged. What else has the yellow son of a bitch seen? How long has he been watching? Then I imagined that unlikely scene with the old man and Ann again, such things as his saying, "Come here, my pet, and sit on my lap," with him sitting in nothing but an underwear shirt, and Harley Butte smiling cynically at the window, every now and then lifting up binoculars to spy out for me. It all a depraved inside joke on me.

Put some shotgun holes in that yellow son of a bitch, then he can sigh and play his intestines like a flute, I thought. Then I regretted dismally that the old man had been able to make me give up Ann so easily. Something filthy has been going on against me.

I went to bed and lay there. I had the phonograph way up loud on an old record of marimba music. *Looble Loo Loo Loooble Boooble Looooo Loo Pi Pi Looble!* "Catch a falling star and put it in your pocket . . . !" was the tune. Ordinarily I detested this record, but now it evoked bereft, dispossessed emotions in me. I imagined that it was the musical version of the cliffs and seascape of Malibu, California, where I had wanted to take Ann. I saw the *National Geographic* picture flood out of its frame in thick gorgeous colors of blue, wheat, and green, and I saw the cottage sag into rivulets of white. It was dripping

away, all gone: *Loo Looble!* And I was left floating on this bed somewhere between Dream of Pines and Malibu, alone, Harry tragic. The
suitcase was still in the car, the silver ballpoint which would have
signed for the release of my money was in my hands.

Ann, I whispered. Ann, Ann, Ann. You were going to be so sweet
at Malibu. You were going to have a clean white tee shirt and be
always just coming out of the bath. You and I were going to wait
until your red bangs grew out and there wasn't any more of that
yellow peroxide in your hair. We would have gone swimming and
one day I would give you a mild kiss on the foot and love would
grow gradually from there. Maybe one day you would come in with
your tee shirt rolled up coy so I could see your navel. Another day
I might come in mistakenly and see your bare breasts. I know they
look like crushed ice with rubies on top. Another day I would acciden-
tally get in the shower when you were already in there and you would
say, "Oh, you silly thing," and then we would have love, with you
moaning against the shower wall and water droplets on our faces.
We could not help it, all the forces said "Love." But you had been
my legal wife for all this time and I had held back like a shy hero.
Ann. I loved you.

But I did not love her any more. She was a whore in the comic
strips. She probably took money from beasts who smelled of the locker
room and the paper mills.

Thank the old man for reminding me of that. I hated him. I saw
him in his undershirt having his way. Vomit fumes came up in my
throat. And I thought I could taste in my mouth the body of a yellow
nigger; he was standing, pressing spread-eagled against my esophagus
walls; his eyeballs boiled out a rancid muck which dripped down to
my lungs. He had the rubbery smile of a minstrel entertainer from
the old days.

I didn't know I was taking the flu that night. At around five in
the morning, one eye seeped out a tear, and then the other began
raining down my cheek. I thought it must be sadness over Ann, so
I just let go and let the disease of my world have me.

John Kennedy Toole

from A Confederacy of Dunces

A GREEN HUNTING CAP squeezed the top of the fleshy balloon of a head. The green earflaps, full of large ears and uncut hair and the fine bristles that grew in the ears themselves, stuck out on either side like turn signals indicating two directions at once. Full, pursed lips protruded beneath the bushy black moustache and, at their corners, sank into little folds filled with disapproval and potato chip crumbs. In the shadow under the green visor of the cap Ignatius J. Reilly's supercilious blue and yellow eyes looked down upon the other people waiting under the clock at the D. H. Holmes department store, studying the crowd of people for signs of bad taste in dress. Several of the outfits, Ignatius noticed, were new enough and expensive enough to be properly considered offenses against taste and decency. Possession of anything new or expensive only reflected a person's lack of theology and geometry; it could even cast doubts upon one's soul.

Ignatius himself was dressed comfortably and sensibly. The hunting cap prevented head colds. The voluminous tweed trousers were durable and permitted unusually free locomotion. Their pleats and nooks contained pockets of warm, stale air that soothed Ignatius. The plaid flannel shirt made a jacket unnecessary while the muffler guarded exposed Reilly skin between earflap and collar. The outfit was acceptable by any theological and geometrical standards, however abstruse, and suggested a rich inner life.

Shifting from one hip to the other in his lumbering, elephantine fashion, Ignatius sent waves of flesh rippling beneath the tweed and flannel, waves that broke upon buttons and seams. Thus rearranged, he contemplated the long while that he had been waiting for his mother. Principally he considered the discomfort he was beginning to feel. It seemed as if his whole being was ready to burst from his swollen suede desert boots, and, as if to verify this, Ignatius turned his singular eyes toward his feet. The feet did indeed look swollen. He was prepared to offer the sight of those bulging boots to his mother as evidence of her thoughtlessness. Looking up, he saw the sun beginning to descend over the Mississippi at the foot of Canal Street. The Holmes clock said almost five. Already he was polishing a few carefully worded accusations designed to reduce his mother to repentance or, at least, confusion. He often had to keep her in her place.

She had driven him downtown in the old Plymouth, and while she was at the doctor's seeing about her arthritis, Ignatius had bought some sheet music at Werlein's for his trumpet and a new string for his lute. Then he had wandered into the Penny Arcade on Royal Street to see whether any new games had been installed. He had been disappointed to find the miniature mechanical baseball game gone. Perhaps it was only being repaired. The last time that he had played it the batter would not work and, after some argument, the management had returned his nickel, even though the Penny Arcade people had been base enough to suggest that Ignatius had himself broken the baseball machine by kicking it.

Concentrating upon the fate of the miniature baseball machine, Ignatius detached his being from the physical reality of Canal Street and the people around him and therefore did not notice the two eyes that were hungrily watching him from behind one of D. H. Holmes' pillars, two sad eyes shining with hope and desire.

Was it possible to repair the machine in New Orleans? Probably so. However, it might have to be sent to some place like Milwaukee or Chicago or some other city whose name Ignatius associated with efficient repair shops and permanently smoking factories. Ignatius hoped that the baseball game was being carefully handled in shipment, that none of its little players was being chipped or maimed by brutal railroad employees determined to ruin the railroad forever with damage claims from shippers, railroad employees who would subsequently go on strike and destroy the Illinois Central.

As Ignatius was considering the delight which the little baseball game afforded humanity, the two sad and covetous eyes moved toward him through the crowd like torpedoes zeroing in on a great woolly tanker. The policeman plucked at Ignatius' bag of sheet music.

"You got any identification, mister?" the policeman asked in a voice that hoped that Ignatius was officially unidentified.

"What?" Ignatius looked down upon the badge on the blue cap. "Who are you?"

"Let me see your driver's license."

"I don't drive. Will you kindly go away? I am waiting for my mother."

"What's this hanging out your bag?"

"What do you think it is, stupid? It's a string for my lute."

"What's that?" The policeman drew back a little. "Are you local?"

"Is it the part of the police department to harass me when this city is a flagrant vice capital of the civilized world?" Ignatius bellowed over the crowd in front of the store. "This city is famous for its gamblers, prostitutes, exhibitionists, anti-Christs, alcoholics, sodomites, drug addicts, fetishists, onanists, pornographers, frauds, jades, litterbugs, and lesbians, all of whom are only too well protected by graft. If you have a moment, I shall endeavor to discuss the crime problem with you, but don't make the mistake of bothering *me.*"

The policeman grabbed Ignatius by the arm and was struck on his cap with the sheet music. The dangling lute string whipped him on the ear.

"Hey," the policeman said.

"Take that!" Ignatius cried, noticing that a circle of interested shoppers was beginning to form.

Inside D. H. Holmes, Mrs. Reilly was in the bakery department pressing her maternal breast against a glass case of macaroons. With one of her fingers, chafed from many years of scrubbing her son's mammoth, yellowed drawers, she tapped on the glass case to attract the saleslady.

"Oh, Miss Inez," Mrs. Reilly called in that accent that occurs south of New Jersey only in New Orleans, that Hoboken near the Gulf of Mexico. "Over here, babe."

"Hey, how you making?" Miss Inez asked. "How you feeling, darling?"

"Not so hot," Mrs. Reilly answered truthfully.

"Ain't that a shame." Miss Inez leaned over the glass case and forgot about her cakes. "I don't feel so hot myself. It's my feet."

"Lord, I wisht I was that lucky. I got arthuritis in my elbow."

"Aw, no!" Miss Inez said with genuine sympathy. "My poor old poppa's got that. We make him go set himself in a hot tub fulla berling water."

"My boy's floating around in our tub all day long. I can't hardly get in my own bathroom no more."

"I thought he was married, precious."

"Ignatius? Eh, la la," Mrs. Reilly said sadly. "Sweetheart, you wanna gimme two dozen of them fancy mix?"

"But I thought you told me he was married," Miss Inez said while she was putting the cakes in a box.

"He ain't even got him a prospect. The little girl friend he had flew the coop."

"Well, he's got time."

"I guess so," Mrs. Reilly said disinterestedly. "Look, you wanna gimme half a dozen wine cakes, too? Ignatius gets nasty if we run outta cake."

"Your boy likes his cake, huh?"

"Oh, Lord, my elbow's killing me," Mrs. Reilly answered.

In the center of the crowd that had formed before the department store the hunting cap, the greed radius of the circle of people, was bobbing about violently.

"I shall contact the mayor," Ignatius was shouting.

"Let the boy alone," a voice said from the crowd.

"Go get the strippers on Bourbon Street," an old man added. "He's a good boy. He's waiting for his momma."

"Thank you," Ignatius said haughtily. "I hope that all of you will bear witness to this outrage."

"You come with me," the policeman said to Ignatius with waning self-confidence. The crowd was turning into something of a mob, and there was no traffic patrolman in sight. "We're going to the precinct."

"A good boy can't even wait for his momma by D. H. Holmes." It was the old man again. "I'm telling you, the city was never like this. It's the communiss."

84

"Are you calling me a communiss?" the policeman asked the old man while he tried to avoid the lashing of the lute string. "I'll take you in, too. You better watch out who you calling a communiss."

"You can't arress me," the old man cried. "I'm a member of the Golden Age Club sponsored by the New Orleans Recreation Department."

"Let that old man alone, you dirty cop," a woman screamed. "He's prolly somebody's grampaw."

"I am," the old man said. "I got six granchirren all studying with the sisters. Smart, too."

Over the heads of the people Ignatius saw his mother walking slowly out of the lobby of the department store carrying the bakery products as if they were boxes of cement.

"Mother!" he called. "Not a moment too soon. I've been seized."

Pushing through the people, Mrs. Reilly said, "Ignatius! What's going on here? What you done now? Hey, take your hands off my boy."

"I'm not touching him, lady," the policeman said. "Is this here your son?"

Mrs. Reilly snatched the whizzing lute string from Ignatius.

"Of course I'm her child," Ignatius said. "Can't you see her affection for me?"

"She loves her boy," the old man said.

"What you trying to do my poor child?" Mrs. Reilly asked the policeman. Ignatius patted his mother's hennaed hair with one of his huge paws. "You got plenty business picking on poor chirren with all the kind of people they got running in this town. Waiting for his momma and they try to arrest him."

"This is clearly a case for the Civil Liberties Union," Ignatius observed, squeezing his mother's drooping shoulder with the paw. "We must contact Myrna Minkoff, my lost love. She knows about those things."

"It's the communiss," the old man interrupted.

"How old is he?" the policeman asked Mrs. Reilly.

"I am thirty," Ignatius said condescendingly.

"You got a job?"

"Ignatius hasta help me at home," Mrs. Reilly said. Her initial courage was failing a little, and she began to twist the lute string with the cord on the cake boxes. "I got terrible arthuritis."

"I dust a bit," Ignatius told the policeman. "In addition, I am at the moment writing a lengthy indictment against our century. When my brain begins to reel from my literary labors, I make an occasional cheese dip."

"Ignatius makes delicious cheese dips," Mrs. Reilly said.

"That's very nice of him," the old man said. "Most boys are out running around all the time."

"Why don't you shut up?" the policeman said to the old man.

"Ignatius," Mrs. Reilly asked in a trembling voice, "what you done, boy?"

"Actually, Mother, I believe that it was he who started everything." Ignatius pointed to the old man with his bag of sheet music. "I was simply standing about, waiting for you, praying that the news from the doctor would be encouraging."

"Get that old man outta here," Mrs. Reilly said to the policeman. "He's making trouble. It's a shame they got people like him walking the streets."

"The police are all communiss," the old man said.

"Didn't I say for you to shut up?" the policeman said angrily.

"I fall on my knees every night to thank my God we got protection," Mrs. Reilly told the crowd. "We'd all be dead without the police. We'd all be laying in our beds with our throats cut open from ear to ear."

"That's the truth, girl," some woman answered from the crowd.

"Say a rosary for the police force." Mrs. Reilly was now addressing her remarks to the crowd. Ignatius caressed her shoulder wildly, whispering encouragement. "Would you say a rosary for a communiss?"

"No!" several voices answered fervently. Someone pushed the old man.

"It's true, lady," the old man cried. "He tried to arrest your boy. Just like in Russia. They're all communiss."

"Come on," the policeman said to the old man. He grabbed him roughly by the back of the coat.

"Oh, my God!" Ignatius said, watching the wan little policeman try to control the old man. "Now my nerves are totally frayed."

"Help!" the old man appealed to the crowd. "It's a takeover. It's a violation of the Constitution!"

"He's crazy, Ignatius," Mrs. Reilly said. "We better get outta here, baby." She turned to the crowd. "Run, folks. He might kill us all. Personally, I think maybe *he's* the communiss."

"You don't have to overdo it, Mother," Ignatius said as they pushed through the dispersing crowd and started walking rapidly down Canal Street. He looked back and saw the old man and the bantam policeman grappling beneath the department store clock. "Will you please slow down a bit? I think I'm having a heart murmur."

"Oh, shut up. How you think I feel? I shouldn't haveta be running like this at my age."

"The heart is important at any age, I'm afraid."

"They's nothing wrong with your heart."

"There will be if we don't go a little slower." The tweed trousers billowed around Ignatius' gargantuan rump as he rolled forward. "Do you have my lute string?"

Mrs. Reilly pulled him around the corner onto Bourbon Street, and they started walking down into the French Quarter.

"How come that policeman was after you, boy?"

"I shall never know. But he will probably be coming after us in a few moments, as soon as he has subdued that aged fascist."

"You think so?" Mrs. Reilly asked nervously.

"I would imagine so. He seemed determined to arrest me. He must have some sort of quota or something. I seriously doubt that he will permit me to elude him so easily."

"Wouldn't that be awful! You'd be all over the papers, Ignatius. The disgrace! You musta done something while you was waiting for me, Ignatius. I know you, boy."

"If anyone was ever minding his business, it was I," Ignatius breathed. "Please. We must stop. I think I'm going to have a hemorrhage."

"Okay," Mrs. Reilly looked at her son's reddening face and realized that he would very happily collapse at her feet just to prove his point. He had done it before. The last time that she had forced him to accompany her to mass on Sunday he had collapsed twice on the way to the church and had collapsed once again during the sermon about sloth, reeling out of the pew and creating an embarrassing disturbance. "Let's go in here and sit down."

She pushed him through the door of the Night of Joy bar with one of the cake boxes. In the darkness that smelled of bourbon and cigarette butts they climbed onto two stools. While Mrs. Reilly arranged her cake boxes on the bar, Ignatius spread his expansive nostrils and said, "My God, Mother, it smells awful. My stomach is beginning to churn."

"You wanna go back on the street? You want that policeman to take you in?"

Ignatius did not answer; he was sniffing loudly and making faces. A bartender, who had been observing the two, asked quizzically from the shadows, "Yes?"

"I shall have a coffee," Ignatius said grandly. "Chicory coffee with boiled milk."

"Only instant," the bartender said.

"I can't possibly drink that," Ignatius told his mother. "It's an abomination."

"Well, get a beer, Ignatius. It won't kill you."

"I may bloat."

"I'll take a Dixie 45," Mrs. Reilly said to the bartender.

"And the gentleman?" the bartender asked in a rich, assumed voice. "What is his pleasure?"

"Give him a Dixie, too."

"I may not drink it," Ignatius said as the bartender went off to open the beers.

"We can't sit in here for free, Ignatius."

"I don't see why not. We're the only customers. They should be glad to have us."

"They got strippers in here at night, huh?" Mrs. Reilly nudged her son.

"I would imagine so," Ignatius said coldly. He looked quite pained. "We might have stopped somewhere else. I suspect that the police will raid this place momentarily anyway." He snorted loudly and cleared his throat. "Thank God my moustache filters out some of the stench. My olfactories are already beginning to send out distress signals."

After what seemed a long time during which there was much tinkling of glass and closing of coolers somewhere in the shadows, the bartender appeared again and set the beers before them, pretending to knock Ignatius' beer into his lap. The Reillys were getting the Night of Joy's worst service, the treatment given unwanted customers.

"You don't by any chance have a cold Dr. Nut, do you?" Ignatius asked.

"No."

"My son loves Dr. Nut," Mrs. Reilly explained. "I gotta buy it by the case. Sometimes he sits himself down and drinks two, three Dr. Nuts at one time."

"I am sure that this man is not particularly interested," Ignatius said.

"Like to take that cap off?" the bartender asked.

"No, I wouldn't!" Ignatius thundered. "There's a chill in here."

"Suit yourself," the bartender said and drifted off into the shadows at the other end of the bar.

"Really!"

"Calm down," his mother said.

Ignatius raised the earflap on the side next to his mother.

"Well, I will lift this so that you won't have to strain your voice. What did the doctor tell you about your elbow or whatever it is?"

"It's gotta be massaged."

"I hope you don't want me to do that. You know how I feel about touching other people."

"He told me to stay out the cold as much as possible."

"If I could drive, I would be able to help you more, I imagine."

"Aw, that's okay, honey."

"Actually, even riding in a car affects me enough. Of course, the worst thing is riding on top in one of those Greyhound Scenicruisers. So high up. Do you remember the time that I went to Baton Rouge in one of those? I vomited several times. The driver had to stop the bus somewhere in the swamps to let me get off and walk around for a while. The other passengers were rather angry. They must have had stomachs of iron to ride in that awful machine. Leaving New Orleans also frightened me considerably. Outside of the city limits the heart of darkness, the true wasteland begins."

89

"I remember that, Ignatius," Mrs. Reilly said absently, drinking her beer in gulps. "You was really sick when you got back home."

"I felt better *then*. The worst moment was my arrival in Baton Rouge. I realized that I had a round-trip ticket and would have to return on the bus."

"You told me that, babe."

"The taxi back to New Orleans cost me forty dollars, but at least I wasn't violently ill during the taxi ride, although I felt myself beginning to gag several times. I made the driver go very slowly, which was unfortunate for him. The state police stopped him twice for being below the minimum highway speed limit. On the third time that they stopped him they took away his chauffeur's license. You see, they had been watching us on the radar all along."

Mrs. Reilly's attention wavered between her son and the beer. She had been listening to the story for three years.

"Of course," Ignatius continued, mistaking his mother's rapt look for interest, "that was the only time that I had ever been out of New Orleans in my life. I think that perhaps it was the lack of a center of orientation that might have upset me. Speeding along in that bus was like hurtling into the abyss. By the time we had left the swamps and reached those rolling hills near Baton Rouge, I was getting afraid that some rural rednecks might toss bombs at the bus. They love to attack vehicles, which are a symbol of progress, I guess."

"Well, I'm glad you didn't take the job," Mrs. Reilly said automatically, taking *guess* as her cue.

"I couldn't possibly take the job. When I saw the chairman of the Medieval Culture Department, my hands began breaking out in small white bumps. He was a totally soulless man. Then he made a comment about my not wearing a tie and made some smirky remark about the lumber jacket. I was appalled that so meaningless a person would dare such effrontery. That lumber jacket was one of the few creature comforts to which I've ever been really attached, and if I ever find the lunatic who stole it, I shall report him to the proper authorities."

Mrs. Reilly saw again the horrible, coffee-stained lumber jacket that she had always secretly wanted to give to the Volunteers of America along with several other pieces of Ignatius' favorite clothing.

"You see, I was so overwhelmed by the complete grossness of that spurious 'chairman' that I ran from his office in the middle of one of his cretinous ramblings and rushed to the nearest bathroom, which turned out to be the one for 'Faculty Men.' At any rate, I was seated in one of the booths, having rested the lumber jacket on top of the door of the booth. Suddenly I saw the jacket being whisked over the door. I heard footsteps. Then the door of the restroom closed. At the moment, I was unable to pursue the shameless thief, so I began to scream. Someone entered the bathroom and knocked at the door of the booth. It turned out to be a member of the campus security force, or so he said. Through the door I explained what had just happened. He promised to find the jacket and went away. Actually, as I have mentioned to you before, I have always suspected that he and the 'chairman' were the same person. Their voices sounded somewhat similar."

"You sure can't trust nobody nowadays, honey."

"As soon as I could, I fled from the bathroom, eager only to get away from that horrible place. Of course, I was almost frozen standing on that desolate campus trying to hail a taxi. I finally got one that agreed to take me to New Orleans for forty dollars, and the driver was selfless enough to lend me his jacket. By the time we arrived here, however, he was quite depressed about losing his license and had grown rather surly. He also appeared to be developing a bad cold, judging by the frequency of his sneezes. After all, we were on the highway for almost two hours."

"I think I could drink me another beer, Ignatius."

"Mother! In this forsaken place?"

"Just one, baby. Come on, I want another."

"We're probably catching something from these glasses. However, if you're quite determined about the thing, get me a brandy, will you?"

Mrs. Reilly signaled to the bartender, who came out of the shadows and asked, "Now what happened to you on that bus, bud? I didn't get the end of the story."

"Will you kindly tend the bar properly?" Ignatius asked furiously. "It is your duty to silently serve when we call upon you. If we had wished to include you in our conversation, we would have indicated it by now. As a matter of fact, we are discussing rather urgent personal matters."

"The man's just trying to be nice, Ignatius. Shame on you."

91

"That in itself is a contradiction in terms. No one could possibly be nice in a den like this."

"We want two more beers."

"One beer and one brandy," Ignatius corrected.

"No more clean glasses," the bartender said.

"Ain't that a shame," Mrs. Reilly said. "Well, we can use the ones we got."

The bartender shrugged and went off into the shadows.

In the precinct the old man sat on a bench with the others, mostly shoplifters, who composed the late afternoon haul. He had neatly arranged along his thigh his Social Security card, his membership card in the St. Odo of Cluny Holy Name Society, a Golden Age Club badge, and a slip of paper identifying him as a member of the American Legion. A young black man, eyeless behind spaceage sunglasses, studied the little dossier on the thigh next to his.

"Whoa!" he said, grinning. "Say, you mus belong to everthin."

The old man rearranged his cards meticulously and said nothing.

"How come they draggin in somebody like you?" The sunglasses blew smoke all over the old man's cards. "Them po-lice mus be gettin desperate."

"I'm here in violation of my constitutional rights," the old man said with sudden anger.

"Well, they not gonna believe that. You better think up somethin else." A dark hand reached for one of the cards. "Hey, wha this mean, 'Colder Age'?"

The old man snatched the card and put it back on his thigh.

"Them little card not gonna do you no good. They throw you in jail anyway. They throw everbody in jail."

"You think so?" the old man asked the cloud of smoke.

"Sure." A new cloud floated up. "How come you here, man?"

"I don't know."

"You don know? Whoa! That crazy. You gotta be here for somethin. Plenty time they pickin up color peoples for nothin, but, mister, you gotta be here for somethin."

"I really don't know," the old man said glumly. "I was just standing in a crowd in front of D. H. Holmes."

"And you lif somebody wallet."

"No, I called a policeman a name."

"Like wha you callin him?"

" 'Communiss.' "

"Cawmniss! Ooo-woo. If I call a po-lice a cawnmiss, my ass be in Angola right now for sure. I like to call one of them mother a cawmniss, though. Like this afternoon I standin aroun in Woolsworth and some cat steal a bag of cashew nuts out the 'Nut House' star screamin like she been stab. Hey! The nex thing, a flo'walk grabbin me, and then a police mother draggin me off. A man ain got a chance. Whoa!" His lips sucked at the cigarette. "Nobody findin them cashews on me, but that po-lice still draggin me off. I think that flo'walk a cawmniss. Mean motherfucker."

The old man cleared his throat and played with his cards.

"They probly let you go," the sunglasses said. "Me, they probly gimma a little talk think it scare me, even though they know I ain got them cashews. They probly try to prove I got them nuts. They probly buy a bag, slip it in my pocket. Woolsworth probly try to send me up for life."

The Negro seemed quite resigned and blew out a new cloud of blue smoke that enveloped him and the old man and the little cards. Then he said to himself, "I wonder who lif them nuts. Probly that flo'walk hisself."

A policeman summoned the old man up to the desk in the center of the room where a sergeant was seated. The patrolman who had arrested him was standing there.

"What's your name?" the sergeant asked the old man.

"Claude Robichaux," he answered and put his little cards on the desk before the sergeant.

The sergeant looked over the cards and said, "Patrolman Mancuso here says you resisted arrest and called him a communiss."

"I didn't mean it," the old man said sadly, noticing how fiercely the sergeant was handling the little cards.

"Mancuso says you says all policemen are communiss."

"Oo-wee," the Negro said across the room.

"Will you shut up, Jones?" the sergeant called out.

"Okay," Jones answered.

"I'll get to you next."

"Say, I didn call nobody no cawmniss," Jones said. "I been frame by that flo'walk in Woolsworth. I don even like cashews."

"Shut your mouth up."

"Okay," Jones said brightly and blew a great thundercloud of smoke.

"I didn't mean anything I said," Mr. Robichaux told the sergeant. "I just got nervous. I got carried away. This policeman was trying to arress a poor boy waiting for his momma by Holmes."

"What?" the sergeant turned to the wan little policeman. "What were you trying to do?"

"He wasn't a boy," Mancuso said. "He was a big fat man dressed funny. He looked like a suspicious character. I was just trying to make a routine check and he started to resist. To tell you the truth, he looked like a big prevert."

"A pervert, huh?" the sergeant asked greedily.

"Yes," Mancuso said with new confidence. "A great big prevert."

"How big?"

"The biggest I ever saw in my whole life," Mancuso said, stretching his arms as if he were describing a fishing catch. The sergeant's eyes shone. "The first thing I spotted was this green hunting cap he was wearing."

Jones listened in attentive detachment somewhere within his cloud.

"Well, what happened, Mancuso? How come he's not standing here before me?"

"He got away. This woman came out the store and got everything mixed up, and she and him run around the corner into the Quarter."

"Oh, two Quarter characters," the sergeant said, suddenly enlightened.

"No, sir," the old man interrupted. "She was really his momma. A nice, pretty lady. I seen them downtown before. This policeman frightened her."

"Oh, listen, Mancuso," the sergeant screamed. "You're the only guy on the force who'd try to arrest somebody away from his mother. And why did you bring in grampaw here? Ring up his family and tell them to come get him."

"Please," Mr. Robichaux pleaded. "Don't do that. My daughter's busy with her kids. I never been arrested in my whole life. She can't come get me. What are my granchirren gonna think? They're all studying with the sisters."

"Get his daughter's number, Mancuso. That'll teach him to call us communiss!"

"Please!" Mr. Robichaux was in tears. "My granchirren respect me."

"Jesus Christ!" the sergeant said. "Trying to arrest a kid with his momma, bringing in somebody's grampaw. Get the hell outta here, Mancuso, and take grampaw with you. You wanna arrest suspicious characters? We'll fix you up."

"Yes, sir," Mancuso said weakly, leading the weeping old man away.

"Ooo-wee!" Jones said from the secrecy of his cloud.

Twilight was settling around the Night of Joy bar. Outside, Bourbon Street was beginning to light up. Neon signs flashed off and on, reflecting in the streets dampened by the light mist that had been falling steadily for some time. The taxis bringing the evening's first customers, midwestern tourists and conventioneers, made slight splashing sounds in the cold dusk.

A few other customers were in the Night of Joy, a man who ran his finger along a racing form, a depressed blonde who seemed connected with the bar in some capacity, and an elegantly dressed young man who chainsmoked Salems and drank frozen daiquiris in gulps.

"Ignatius, we better go," Mrs. Reilly said and belched.

"What?" Ignatius bellowed. "We must stay to watch the corruption. It's already beginning to set in."

The elegant young man spilled his daiquiri on his bottle-green velvet jacket.

"Hey, bartender," Mrs. Reilly called. "Get a rag. One of the customers just spilled they drink."

"That's *quite* all right, darling," the young man said angrily. He arched an eyebrow at Ignatius and his mother. "I think I'm in the wrong bar anyway."

"Don't get upset, honey," Mrs. Reilly counseled. "What's that you drinking? It looks like a pineapple snowball."

"Even if I described it to you, I doubt whether you'd understand what it is."

"How dare you talk to my dear, beloved mother like that!"

"Oh, hush, you big thing," the young man snapped. "Just look at my jacket."

"It's totally grotesque."

"Okay, now. Let's be friends," Mrs. Reilly said through foamy lips. "We got enough bombs and things already."

"And your son seems to delight in dropping them, I must say."

"Okay, you two. This is the kinda place where everybody oughta have themselves some fun." Mrs. Reilly smiled at the young man. "Let me buy you another drink, babe, for the one you spilled. And I think I'll take me another Dixie."

"I really must run," the young man sighed. "Thanks anyway."

"On a night like this?" Mrs. Reilly asked. "Aw, don't pay no mind to what Ignatius says. Why don't you stay and see the show?"

The young man rolled his eyes heavenward.

"Yeah." The blonde broke her silence. "See some ass and tits."

"Mother," Ignatius said coldly. "I do believe that you are encouraging these preposterous people."

"Well, you're the one wanted to stay, Ignatius."

"Yes, I did want to stay as an observer. I am not especially anxious to mingle."

"Honey, to tell you the truth, I can't listen to that story about that bus no more tonight. You already told it four times since we got here."

Ignatius looked hurt.

"I hardly suspected that I was boring you. After all, that bus ride was one of the more formative experiences of my life. As a mother, you should be interested in the traumas that have created my world-view."

"What's with the bus?" the blonde asked, moving to the stool next to Ignatius. "My name's Darlene. I like good stories. You got a spicy one?"

The bartender slammed the beer and the daiquiri down just as the bus was starting off on its journey in the vortex.

"Here, have a clean glass," the bartender snarled at Mrs. Reilly.

"Ain't that nice. Hey, Ignatius, I just got a clean glass."

But her son was too preoccupied with his arrival in Baton Rouge to hear her.

"You know, sweetheart," Mrs. Reilly said to the young man, "me and my boy was in trouble today. The police tried to arress him."

"Oh, my dear. Policemen are always so adamant, aren't they?"

"Yeah, and Ignatius got him a master's degree and all."

"What in the world was he doing?"

"Nothing. Just standing waiting for his poor, dear momma."

"His outfit is a little bizarre. I thought he was a performer of some sort when I first came in, although I tried not to imagine the nature of his act."

"I keep on telling him about his clothes, but he won't listen." Mrs. Reilly looked at the back of her son's flannel shirt and at the hair curling down the back of his neck. "That's sure pretty, that jacket you got."

"Oh, this?" the young man asked, feeling the velvet on the sleeve. "I don't mind telling you it cost a fortune. I found it in a dear little shop in the Village."

"You don't look like you from the country."

"Oh, my," the young man sighed and lit a Salem with a great click of his lighter. "I meant Greenwich Village in New York, sweetie. By the way, where did you ever get that hat? It's truly fantastic."

"Aw, Lord, I had this since Ignatius made his First Communion."

"Would you consider selling it?"

"How come?"

"I'm a dealer in used clothing. I'll give you ten dollars for it."

"Aw, come on. For this?"

"Fifteen?"

"Really?" Mrs. Reilly removed the hat. "Sure, honey."

The young man opened his wallet and gave Mrs. Reilly three five dollar bills. Draining his daiquiri glass, he stood up and said, "Now I really must run."

"So soon?"

"It's been perfectly delightful meeting you."

"Take care out in the cold and wet."

The young man smiled, placed the hat carefully beneath his trench coat, and left the bar.

"The radar patrol," Ignatius was telling Darlene, "is obviously rather foolproof. It seems that the cab driver and I were making small dots on their screen all the way from Baton Rouge."

"You was on radar," Darlene yawned. "Just think of that."

"Ignatius, we gotta go now," Mrs. Reilly said. "I'm hungry."

She turned toward him and knocked her beer bottle to the floor where it broke into a spray of brown, jagged glass.

"Mother, are you making a scene?" Ignatius asked irritably. "Can't you see that Miss Darlene and I are speaking? You have some cakes with you. Eat those. You're always complaining that you never go anywhere. I would have imagined that you would be enjoying your night on the town."

Ignatius was back on radar, so Mrs. Reilly reached in her boxes and ate a brownie.

"Like one?" she asked the bartender. "They nice. I got some nice wine cakes, too."

The bartender pretended to be looking for something on his shelves.

"I smell wine cakes," Darlene cried, looking past Ignatius.

"Have one, honey," Mrs. Reilly said.

"I think that I shall have one, too," Ignatius said. "I imagine that they taste rather good with brandy."

Mrs. Reilly spread the box out on the bar. Even the man with the racing form agreed to take a macaroon.

"Where you bought these nice wine cakes, lady?" Darlene asked Mrs. Reilly. "They're nice and juicy."

"Over by Holmes, sugar. They got a good selection. Plenty variety."

"They are rather tasty," Ignatius conceded, sending out his flabby pink tongue over his moustache to hunt for crumbs. "I think that I shall have a macaroon or two. I have always found coconut to be good roughage."

He picked around in the box purposefully.

"Me, I always like some good cake after I finish eating," Mrs. Reilly told the bartender, who turned his back on her.

"I bet you cook good, huh?" Darlene asked.

"Mother doesn't cook," Ignatius said dogmatically. "She burns."

"I use to cook too when I was married," Darlene told them. "I sort of used a lot of that canned stuff, though. I like that Spanish rice they got and that spaghetti with the tomato gravy."

"Canned food is a perversion," Ignatius said. "I suspect that it is ultimately very damaging to the soul."

"Lord, my elbow's starting up again," Mrs. Reilly sighed.

"Please. I am speaking," her son told her. "I never eat canned food. I did once, and I could feel my intestines starting to atrophy."

"You got a good education," Darlene said.

"Ignatius graduated from college. Then he stuck around there for four more years to get him a master's degree. Ignatius graduated smart."

" 'Graduated smart,' " Ignatius repeated with some pique. "Please define your terms. Exactly what do you mean by 'graduated smart.'"

"Don't talk to your momma like that," Darlene said.

"Oh, he treats me bad sometimes," Mrs. Reilly said loudly and began to cry. "You just don't know. When I think of all I done for that boy . . ."

"Mother, what are you saying?"

"You don't appreciate me."

"Stop that right now. I'm afraid that you've had too much beer."

"You treat me like garbage. I been good," Mrs. Reilly sobbed. She turned to Darlene. "I spent all his poor Grammaw Reilly's insurance money to keep him in college for eight years, and since then all he's done is lay around the house watching television."

"You oughta be ashamed," Darlene said to Ignatius. "A big man like you. Look at your poor momma."

Mrs. Reilly had collapsed, sobbing, on the bar, one hand clenched around her beer glass.

"This is ridiculous. Mother, stop that."

"If I knew you was so crool, mister, I wouldna listened to your crazy story about that Greyhound bus."

"Get up, Mother."

"You look like a big crazyman anyway," Darlene said. "I shoulda known. Just look how that poor woman's crying."

Darlene tried to push Ignatius from his stool but sent him crashing into his mother, who suddenly stopped crying and gasped, "My elbow!"

"What's going on here?" a woman asked from the padded chartreuse leatherette door of the bar. She was a statuesque woman nearing middle age, her fine body covered with a black leather overcoat that glistened with mist. "I leave this place for a few hours to go shopping and look what happens. I gotta be here every minute, I guess, to watch out you people don't ruin my investment."

"Just two drunks," the bartender said. "I've been giving them the cold shoulder since they come in, but they've been sticking like flies."

"But you, Darlene," the woman said. "You're big friends with them, huh? Playing games on the stools with these two characters?"

"This guy's been mistreating his momma," Darlene explained.

"Mothers? We got mothers in here now? Business already stinks."

"I beg your pardon," Ignatius said.

The woman ignored him and looked at the broken and empty cake box on the bar, saying, "Somebody's been having a picnic in here. Goddamit. I already told you people about ants and rats."

"I beg your pardon," Ignatius said again. "My mother is present."

"It's just my luck to have this crap broken all over here just when I'm looking for a janitor." The woman looked at the bartender. "Get these two out."

"Yes, Miss Lee."

"Don't you worry," Mrs. Reilly said. "We're leaving."

"We certainly are," Ignatius added, lumbering toward the door, leaving his mother behind to climb off her stool. "Hurry along, Mother. This woman looks like a Nazi commandant. She may strike us."

"Wait!" Miss Lee screamed, grabbing Ignatius' sleeve. "How much these characters owe?"

"Eight dollars," the bartender said.

"This is highway robbery!" Ignatius thundered. "You will hear from our attorneys."

Mrs. Reilly paid with two of the bills the young man had given her and, as she swayed past Miss Lee, she said, "We know when we not wanted. We can take our trade elsewheres."

"Good," Miss Lee answered. "Beat it. Trade from people like you is the kiss of death."

After the padded door had closed behind the Reillys, Miss Lee said, "I never liked mothers. Not even my own."

"My mother was a whore," the man with the racing form said, not looking up from his paper.

"Mothers are full of shit," Miss Lee observed and took off her leather coat. "Now let's you and me have a little talk, Darlene."

Outside, Mrs. Reilly took her son's arm for support, but, as much as they tried, they moved forward very slowly, although they seemed to move sideward more easily. Their walking had developed a pattern: three quick steps to the left, pause, three quick steps to the right, pause.

"That was a terrible woman," Mrs. Reilly said.

"A negation of all human qualities," Ignatius added. "By the way, how far is the car? I'm very tired."

"On St. Ann, honey. Just a few blocks."

"You left your hat in the bar."

"Oh, I sold it to that young man."

"You sold it? Why? Did you ask me whether I wanted it to be sold? I was very attached to that hat."

"I'm sorry, Ignatius. I didn't know you liked it so much. You never said nothing about it."

"I had an unspoken attachment to it. It was a contact with my childhood, a link with the past."

"But he gave me fifteen dollars, Ignatius."

"Please. Don't talk about it anymore. The whole business is sacrilegious. Goodness knows what degenerate uses he will find for that hat. Do you have the fifteen dollars on you?"

"I still got seven left."

"Then why don't we stop and eat something?" Ignatius pointed to the cart at the corner. It was shaped like a hot dog on wheels. "I believe that they vend foot-long hot dogs."

"Hot dogs? Honey, in all this rain and cold we gonna stand outside and eat weenies?"

"It's a thought."

"No," Mrs. Reilly said with somewhat beery courage. "Let's get home. I wouldn't eat nothing outta one of them dirty wagons anyway. They all operated by a bunch of bums."

"If you insist," Ignatius said, pouting. "Although I am rather hungry, and you have, after all, just sold a memento of my childhood for thirty pieces of silver, so to speak."

They continued their little pattern of steps along the wet flagstones of Bourbon Street. On St. Ann they found the old Plymouth easily.

101

Its high roof stood above all the other cars, its best feature. The Plymouth was always easy to find in supermarket parking lots. Mrs. Reilly climbed the curb twice trying to force the car out of the parking place and left the impression of a 1946 Plymouth bumper in the hood of the Volkswagon in the rear.

"My nerves!" Ignatius said. He was slumped down in the seat so that just the top of his green hunting cap appeared in the window, looking like the tip of a promising watermelon. From the rear, where he always sat, having read somewhere that the seat next to the driver was the most dangerous, he watched his mother's wild and inexpert shifting with disapproval. "I suspect that you have effectively demolished the small car that someone innocently parked behind this bus. You had better succeed in getting out of this spot before its owner happens along."

"Shut up, Ignatius. You making me nervous," Mrs. Reilly said, looking at the hunting cap in the rear view mirror.

Ignatius got up on the seat and looked out of the rear window.

"That car is a total wreck. Your driver's license, if you do indeed have one, will doubtlessly be revoked. I certainly wouldn't blame them."

"Lay down there and take a nap," his mother said as the car jerked back again.

"Do you think that I could sleep now? I'm afraid for my life. Are you sure that you're turning the wheel the right way?"

Suddenly the car leaped out of the parking spot and skidded across the wet street into a post supporting a wrought-iron balcony. The post fell away to one side, and the Plymouth crunched against the building.

"Oh, my God!" Ignatius screamed from the rear. "What have you done now?"

"Call a priest!"

"I don't think that we're injured, Mother. However, you have just ruined my stomach for the next few days." Ignatius rolled down one of the rear windows and studied the fender that was pressed against the wall. "We shall need a new headlight on this side, I imagine."

"What we gonna do?"

"If I were driving, I would put the auto in reverse and back gracefully away from the scene. Someone will certainly press charges. The people who own this wreck of a building have been waiting for an opportunity like this for years. They probably spread grease on the street after nightfall hoping that motorists like you will spin toward their hovel." He belched. "My digestion has been destroyed. I think that I am beginning to bloat!"

Mrs. Reilly shifted the worn gears and inched slowly backward. As the car moved, the splintering of wood sounded over their heads, a splintering that changed into splitting of boards and scraping of metal. Then the balcony was falling in large sections, thundering on the roof of the car with the dull, heavy thud of grenades. The car, like a stoned human, stopped moving, and a piece of wrought-iron decoration shattered a rear window.

"Honey, are you okay?" Mrs. Reilly asked wildly after what seemed to be the final bombardment.

Ignatius made a gagging sound. The blue and yellow eyes were watering.

"Say something, Ignatius," his mother pleaded, turning around just in time to see Ignatius stick his head out of a window and vomit down the side of the dented car.

Patrolman Mancuso was walking slowly down Chartres Street dressed in ballet tights and a yellow sweater, a costume which the sergeant said would enable him to bring in genuine, bona fide suspicious characters instead of grandfathers and boys waiting for their mothers. The costume was the sergeant's punishment. He had told Mancuso that from now on he would be strictly responsible for bringing in suspicious characters, that police headquarters had a costume wardrobe that would permit Mancuso to be a new character every day. Forlornly, Patrolman Mancuso had put on the tights before the sergeant, who had pushed him out of the precinct and told him to shape up or get off the force.

In the two hours that he had been cruising the French Quarter, he had captured no one. Twice things had looked hopeful. He had stopped a man wearing a beret and asked for a cigarette, but the man had threatened to have him arrested. Then he accosted a young man in a trench coast who was wearing a lady's hat, but the young man had slapped him across the face and dashed away.

103

As Patrolman Mancuso walked down Chartres rubbing his cheek, which still smarted from the slap, he heard what seemed to be an explosion. Hoping that a suspicious character had just thrown a bomb or shot himself, he ran around the corner onto St. Ann and saw the green hunting cap emitting vomit among the ruins.

Lee K. Abbott, Jr.

A Modern Story of Woe and Lovecraft

ALMOST THE DAY he returned from Nam, still LURP-eyed and loosey-goosey, he roared into Coach Frank's office, his face a hive of twitches, jerks, and hinky-do's. You could tell Fleece'd come from, say, Venus or Fort Apache, someplace vile and wonderful.

"Dig it, Coach," he was saying, hopping and slapping himself on the chest, "I am a definite possible. My heart's on edge, Señor. You looking for prime meat, that's me. I'm 22, blessed."

You could see Coach Frank's forebrain light up and start smoking with hope. It was '71, not a promising year for the Razorbacks; what Coach needed, see, was a star, someone cut from whole Jesus cloth, or a Lone Ranger type, or a glorious fool like Audie Murphy.

"You mean?" Coach said, "angry, vicious, etc.?"

"Indeed and so true," Fleece said. "I could bring you prominence and lasting fame."

With a yip, Fleece diddled through some watusi footwork—mostly knee action and breathtaking thighcraft—settling with a growl into a three-point stance that Coach later swore was the very get-go of Terror, Doom, and Bone-crunching Fear.

"I see myself as an end," Fleece said, "independent and high-minded, the proper stuff of slo-mo and instant replay."

"I see you as a strong safety," Coach said, "numb and a heartbreak to receivers."

"I prefer catching," Fleece said, "zigging and dancing to glory. I'm tough and understand how the world works."

Coach Frank's heart went up his neck like a horned frog, all warts and slime. Courage, Foolhardiness, Pride—this boy was it!

"I ain't a ravisher," Fleece was saying. "I respect order and right thinking. I'm an orphan, too."

In a jiffy, they were on the practice field, Fleece going one-on-two with Bobo and Scooter, Coach at the QB. "I'm a fan of beauty," Fleece told 'em, "I read Spinoza and Dear Abby. Pink's my favorite color." Watching that boy was like laying in the tender arms of Abstract Pleasure and knowing whole libraries of ancient and perdurable truths. He was slick. First time out, he did a Mondo Cane dazzle on Bobo that hurried that Prairie Grove grit back into his ignorant soul for warmth and coddling. "Bye-bye," Fleece called, slipping by him, "you're slow and an embarrassment. I see slackness in your jaw, and waste." His gig was nearly sex—somewhere between, on the one hand, Burly-Q and Tease, and, on the other hand, Self-Worship and Crime.

Scooter was next.

"Listen," Fleece said, lining up while Coach barked out the hut-huts. "I can hear you thinking. I'm getting truly offensive vibes from you."

Scooter was a former Little Rock vandal who believed, honest, in Kryptonite and spies and understanding but contrary vegetable gods. "I'm thinking about breaking your arms," he said, "and stealing your wallet."

But Fleece had already vamoosed, his feet a blur, shooting under the arc of that pigskin as if fleeing gloom and other hard feelings. "My secret is Pez candy and Nehi," he told Scooter. "I smoke, too. Cheroots and dope. You're looking at a perfected man!"

All that summer you could watch him working out with the team, sliding and spinning and doing inspired dipsy-doodles—moves with names like Sin and Coy Humiliation and Suffering—slicing through defenses like slaughter and necessity. He was a poem, someone said, tense with joy and purpose, springing to the lips of an eloquent and hopeful man. "I'm a thinker, I'm deep," he said one day, afterwards lecturing the defensive line about the Planes of Space and Curies, ending the conversation on a high and spooky note by saying that, on account of genes and inguinal juices and microscopic do-dahs, everybody—slope, low-rider, King of Siam—everybody was the same weak, raunchy and partly noble dude!

He was a leaper, too. Up he'd go, eternal and gleeful, quoting

Andrew Marvell and General Westmoreland—gents with smudged but faithful hearts—and you could look down, lace up your Keds, loop a loogie into the bleachers, smear on Tuff-Skin, by God anything but nap; and when you'd look up, there he'd be, suspended and grinning, his eyes thyroid, his face glazed, his voice pure and ever-lasting: "Look out, Texas, you Horned Frogs of TCU, you Owls of Rice," he'd be hollering, "I, Fleece Dee Monroe, am in the world for keeps. I am your destiny and your peril. Oooooooiiieee!"

Then he fell in love.

Her name was April May Bates and she was, Fleece said on the eve of the opener with Rice, Miss Dreamboat Incarnate—uptown, mayonnaise white, poised, close-pored, moist and slim, deep, and quote probably one of the truly potent forces of nature herself un-quote. "Man," Fleece said, his eyes flashing with frantic and various lights, "she is Virtue and Patience and Nose-Rubbed-Into Facts. She makes my hair melt."

Coming out of the Colonel Potts Reading Room at the Library, he'd spied her. There she was, in the History section, in the aisle, bent in the close pursuit of war and the causes thereof, accounts of ruined Europe and zapped Troy open at her feet. Fleece felt he'd been whanged with a shovel.

"Hot shit and amen," he said, seizing her in a Texas whizzer. "I love you." He had the program planned: polite talk, friendly kisses, light petting, then sleeping together forever. A primo moth-to-flame romance.

"Let's go to my place," he whispered. "I have records and party games."

April was flabbergasted but resourceful. She was a recent graduate of Ida M'Toy's School of Self-Defense in Nablus, Arkansas. "No," she said, dealing a forearm shiver into Fleece's blood-engorged neck.

He teetered.

"Son," she declared, "I could handicap you with all my anatomy—tongue, elbows, even my hair. Plus I know special words which could warp you forever."

Fleece went over like a log.

Flattened, he heard the hope-inspired chitty-chat of his entire lymph

107

system: Fleece, his glands were saying, this be the one, she is your sunlit future, your Baby Love, your jackpot and sweepstakes, the mother of your unborn babies.

"Oooooiiiieee!" he told those cats at the training table that night, "she is my be-all and end-all: my main veins, my memory and primitive hurts." Then he ripped into an ear-splitting paragraph of Cong talk that Associate Professor Hong Li in zoology later noted was angst-fed Commie-Frenchy agitprop for Human Need, Sacrifice, and Eternal Toil.

As it happened, April was liberal, a Bill Fulbright Democrat, soft for anguished boys and well-read in the literature of Despair and Failure. "I am engaged," she told Fleece. Her fiancé was a Tulane law student named Lewis L. Percy. "He's tall and dresses well. I think he will make a fine Senator."

Fleece would not be dissuaded. Didn't she understand? This was Love he was talking about! This was smooching and mutual interests and Bliss!

"He's skillful with his hands and has a nimble mind."

Fleece had her by the ankles. "I'm complex," he said. "I've been a villain."

"Me and Lewis," she said, "we're as natural as dish and spoon. We're harmonized and cool."

"I been good, too," Fleece said. "You ought to see me with animals and blind folks."

It went on this way for minutes.

"I gave her my whole bio," he told the boys afterwards, "everything, details of my birth, my first words, puberty, confidential comments from my Brownfield High transcripts, the high and low spots of my war records in Hua Ningh Province, and a songful description of my ideals and aspirations."

April was touched. "I will allow myself to be tempted," she said. It was a classic moment of 19th century sentiment. Fleece said he could hear bells and violins and the profound swell of heartcraft.

"I am wooing her," he told Coach that night. "I intend to be happy."

Everybody heard sooner or later. Even those high-achieving Owls from Rice. "I have forsaken human dirts," Fleece told the free safety who came up to cover him the first play of the game. "Before, I was sullen and heavy into hurt. Now, I am in love."

"Me, too," that Rice sophomore said, "I believe in physics and the reachable frontiers of knowledge."

The ball was hiked and Fleece started cooking up some secret Bombs Away science of his own, something involving guile and darkness. "Adios," he told that Rice boy, "I am gone and fulfilled."

It was like going toe-to-toe with a ghost.

A week later, in College Station, a prideful A & M Aggie tried to take away the outside. He had a face that said, *smack it, my idols are Monster Zero and Satan, let's eat dogs and be fierce.*

"My April does not approve," Fleece said, showing his foe arms and legs and a disturbing moil of fakes and possibilities. "She subscribes to ruggedness and free will. Plus, she can dance."

That Aggie was dumbfounded, his face blank with wonder. "You haven't kissed her, right?"

Fleece heard the snap-count and hurtled forward. "Not yet," he hollered, "but I have held her warm hand and sat with her in the dark."

Back in Fayetteville, he accelerated his courting. After practice, in the autumn evening, you'd see him parading outside the Zeta house, in weenie jeans and a DeMolay sportcoat, a citizen of Squaresville with a CYO hair-do. "I am abandoning the weak mental life," he announced after the TCU game. All the sisters were looking at him from April's second-story window. "I am taking up the beat of simplicity and action," he was saying. "C'mon down, April, you are my main lady."

She couldn't, she said. The straight and lasting skinny was this: Lewis L. Percy was divinely handsome and witty and well up the ladder of success. "My Daddy loves him," she said, "my little brother Marvin loves him, my step-momma Dorene loves him, and I love him as well."

Next night, undaunted, Fleece was back, reciting verse that spoke to Woe and Lovecraft and Alp-like Desire. "I plan to outflank your heart," he declared, "by appealing to your round and well-folded brain." He charged into the first stanza at full tilt, eyes lit with zeal, then stumbled out, two beats later, like he'd seen the Boogey Man.

"Fleece," she said, "I do not respond to pain and disappointment."

On Wednesday, he was back with a carnal and Beatnik God. Fleece mentioned Cunning, Lively Punishments, The Roiling of This'un and the Throes of That'un, Redemption and sexy mysteries.

"Fleece," she said, "I am agnostic and so believe in selfhood and mortality."

Thursday evening, he arrived with a Green Stamp guitar. "How 'bout this?" he said, sending up cowpoke and tonk lyrics that left his face, like Big Joe Turner's, blazing with rue.

"I prefer aliens," she said, "especially Frenchmen, and Spanish melancholy. You know anything haunting and wicked?"

Friday, before the squad left for Waco, he appeared with idealism and a list of personal goals. "I want to own a home," he said, "and a Pontiac convertible. I will be a millionaire, honest, skillful in all things and a friend to the unfortunate."

"Fleece," she said, "me and Lewis L., we aim to cut corners and be expedient."

"She weakening," Fleece told Bobo during the Baylor game. "By Homecoming, she will be mine."

Coach Frank said later it was during the Tech game that the strain began to show. "I am moving in the extreme regions of the human spirit," Fleece said. "I am in touch with my nerves and small cells." They were telling him one thing: Persevere. He'd drag-ass to the huddle like a numero uno Army loser, moody and brilliant.

"X-39-Ford," the QB Ronnie Tipton said. It was a post pattern, the normalest route to Victory.

"I see myself flying," Fleece said, "an example to youngsters everywhere." He came to the line hopping and twitching.

"What's that you're doing?" the TT corner back said. This Tech boy had a common face, full of the soft life and cheap insights.

"That's Jealousy," Fleece said, his cheeks dark. "And Revenge and Steadfastness."

Tipton shouted "Go!" and Fleece went off like a two-dollar alarm clock.

"What's that?" the TT grunt said.

110

Fleece was doing an anal hootchy-koo near the sideline, tippy-toeing and skulking into the secondary. "That's Hope," he said, "and Wishful Thinking." The effect was grim. He gave that boy hips and shoulders, then dipped inside.

"Why not a theater major or a potter?" the TT boy yelled. "They have big hearts. Take up books, my Daddy says, and hard work."

On the films, you noticed Fleece hesitate, grow weary in an instant. He rose lazily, the zip clearly gone the moment two thoroughbred linebackers, both 100% mindless meat, converged on him.

"What's that?" Fleece hollered, going down in a swirl of legs.

"Pain," the Tech boy said, "and an Incomplete Forward Pass."

That week he limped to class, his eyeballs adrenal. He sent April a drawing from Art 101, Life Figures. "Art improves the mind," he told Scooter. (They were friends now, Scooter knowing the value of a gifted man.) The drawing came back in a flash, a note attached: "Dear Fleece Dee Monroe, I am not impressed by lust. I prefer color anyway, and apples or grapes."

"I wrote an essay for her," he told Scooter that night in their room. For twenty minutes he read, touching the familiar and profound themes of Passion and Dread. He compared her eyes to pools, her skin to alabaster, and her personality to a rare and velvety flower.

It came back, too: "Fleece, do not drool on your manuscripts. Spit blurs the ink and makes your Latin words fatal to read."

He did her Econ 211 lessons, working out a scheme that made everybody—Chinaman, Wop, Swiss, etc.—tall and rich and free.

"My Prof disagrees," April said, "he cleaves to bullion and hard times."

At last, he wrote a letter to Lewis L. Percy, which he high-balled to the PO, telling the dude behind the counter to hurry that letter along and not mess up 'cause things like love and true happiness depended on its safe receipt.

"It mentions Triumph for me and tough luck for him." Fleece told Bobo. "It says April is nearly mine and he can be our friend if he likes. He should buck up and not cry."

Within days, an answer: "Mr. Monroe, Esq.: At this second I am overburdened with torts and judicial history, so I can only briefly reply. I know everything about you, from your Beatle boots to your string tie and Arab nose. I hope you will be happy when April and I marry. See you at Homecoming."

"Hot damn!" Fleece shouted at the training table that night. "She's mine, she's mine, she's mine."

You could see his mood much improved. "Look here," he told Bobo in practice, lifting his sweat shirt, exposing his hairless and sleek chest. "Two Florida ladies paid cash money to see my sternum. They thought I was fine statuary come alive." He eased through a series of moves as complex and recondite as liquid intelligence. "I am a Scorpio," he said, "I cannot be touched by defeat," Coach Frank said that watching that wholesome redneck steal through the Hog defense was like Springtime, human birth and world peace.

"Wait'll those Texas hombres see this," Fleece said, demonstrating a new move, one pulled from the dark waters of his imagination. It involved wit, he said, and equal parts of grace and grief.

The boys from the *Gazette* and the *Northwest Arkansas Times* couldn't get their minds around it. "I am fully evolved," Fleece told them in one interview. "I am what everybody will look like in three, maybe four generations. You want to touch my fingers?" And the stories coming out of practice that week said it was on account of love— not physiology or superior recruiting or fat-free foods. No, it was blind love. These stories, of course, got to April and her intended, Lewis L., and hovered over her when she went to the Homecoming game. "I am determined," she said, "to be rid of that singleminded Porker."

The folks from ABC-TV claimed it was a variant of the Tennessee System Single Wing that took the leather and thump out of Texas in the first half. Wrong. It was Fleece, jiving and twisting, his eyes radiant with glee.

"Look me in the face," he told his man in the first quarter. "Tell me I am not pretty and driven by a higher calling."

That Texas boy had distressed hair and an infant's naughty smile. Fleece wasn't doodley-squat to him.

"You have lofty ambitions, all right," he said, "but I am committed to your undoing."

112

The replay showed Fleece's face burning like a country at war. He did a kamikaze shuffle, a heartbreakingly persnickety zig-out, and vanished, high-stepping down the line, waving to April in the stands, and waiting for the ball to come to him and be his.

"Touchdown!" he hollered, sprinting into the end zone and pausing to wiggle over his achievement in what Maylene Le Duc, Professor of Dance, later wrote was a sanguine, innocent, broad-minded, genuine, and hair-curling interpretation of Heroism and the Modern Predicament.

The locker-room was Ozville. "Open up my head," Fleece yelled, "and you will see sunlight and clear air, I am happy." He went on for a while, talking about pine trees, romantic vistas, and quote a new continent unquote.

Coach Frank was pleased but fearful. Overconfidence was death, he said. You could go out there and in no time find yourself adrift in Squalor and Hardship for the good guys.

Fleece wouldn't hear of it. He was in a wiggy, critical place of his own. "Bring me children," he was singing while Trainer Mac taped him up, "and I will teach them. I am knowledge and a way in the world."

Fortune went in the dumper lickety-split. Immediately, Coach Royal of the Longhorns sicked two mean-eyed spades on Fleece. "Howdo, Twilight Time," they said, scurrying onto the field. It was that celebrated ding-dong of doom. These fellas were crypto-Panthers, in the sport for discipline and, eventually, moola. "We's killers, both of us," they said. "In another universe, we'd be rocks."

Bobo recalled how it was a touching sorrow to see Fleece trying to flee those dudes. Without success, he'd throw ruse and lie and vanity in their path. "This is winning," Fleece told them during one play, doing a special hokey-pokey in the flat. "This is losing," they said, pouncing on him.

Soon enough, the score was tied.

"I'm pulling out the A material now," he said. "This is a move called Plunder and Loot. Take notes."

He darted out, spun and whooped in dismay, finding those two fellas as near to him as shadow and memory. "You boys will tire and go off alone," he said. No way, they said. They were there for

113

the duration: Plague, Pestilence, Famine, Disease—take your pick.

By the fourth quarter, Fleece was calling names. "You boys been in jail?" he said. "You look like convicts to me." He picked on their pedigree and good intentions. "Which one of you is Unitarian?" he said. "My April is looking on and she expects me to triumph."

Everybody agrees where the end came.

"X-Reverse, on 4," Ronnie Tipton said, and Fleece stormed to the line with renewed faith. He could see April sitting with her family. "Hey there, sweet chips," he called. "Am I not gorgeous?" Beside her was Lewis L. Percy. "Hey there, Lewis L.," he hollered, "you have my sympathy and deep regard."

"Four!" shouted Tipton and Fleece leapt toward the scrimmage line.

"Banzai!" Fleece said. He took the ball on an end-around, doing a move called Prayer, and braked to an astonished, bone-rattling halt. In front of him were the Panthers and several Longhorn buddies, their faces gleaming with evil. "Uh-oh," Fleece said.

In a blink, he sped the other way, his moves speaking volumes about daring and panic. "Oh-no!" he squealed. Longhorns were everywhere. His face said *Condition Red* and *Bail Out, Mama* and *Take My Feet and Ears and Shiny Teeth but Leave Me My Still Stubborn Heart.*

For seconds, there was serious dashing, thundering feet and crunching, then you heard it—everybody, all 55,000 of them heard it—just as Fleece howled headlong into the aroused opposition: "I'M TIRED, LEWIS. LET'S NECK!"

You could see the shock rip through his face: April was going elsewhere for affection! Fleece was the picture of bad news. His mouth was working. *Holy moly,* he was yelling, and *Jumping Jesus,* and *I am crushed and spurned at the same moment,* and *Ain't this a rude end for a valiant man.*

Then, he was buried.

Coach Frank trotted out, after everyone untangled, to find his blue-chipper laying in heartache, all the love gone from his face. "Ooooommmppphhh," Fleece was sobbing. "Aaaarrrggghhh!"

Truth to tell, Fleece played a little after that, but he was using C material, shameful and routine. Then, after the season, he quit, stuffed his tricks in a bag and split. Scooter heard from him once. Fleece called, saying he was playing semi-pro for the quote Boogie-Woogie Industries of the Truly Damned unquote. It was a joke.

There were rumors, of course. You'd hear he'd changed his name, that he was calling himself Mr. Pitiful or Indian Charlie. You'd hear, too, that he was living in Florida with a woman named Libby and her two girls, both named Debbie-do. It was dire.

Then one day Coach Frank got a Polaroid. Fleece looked the same, but you could tell the juices were gone. On the back was scribbling: "I have given up loving the impossible," Fleece had written. His letters were cramped, like the writing had been the product of fever and bad humor, and you could tell—by the dark spots under his eyes and his arms hanging limp—you could tell that the good times were over and that he'd gone back, still mournful and funny, to the real world of trying and failing.

Mark Steadman

John Fletcher's Night of Love

SEAMAN WILLISTON. Seaman Williston. Seaman Williston." It wasn't just then that he hated the voice. Earlier, he had. And, later, he would. But this time—not yet. Somewhere under the mucous, adenoidal surface of the words there was a grace note, a musical quality, coming on toward the top. He homed in on it, letting the words float off down the windows of the ward.

He had an ear for grace notes.

"Time to take your temperature, Seaman Williston," she said.

"Up yours, Lieutenant," he thought, ". . . ma'am."

Her hand looked enormous. Man-heavy and freckled. The thermometer—like the kind banks put on billboards, as he would see it from a distance on a hot day. His eyes were squinting. Blurring the hand and the thermometer, and going on up behind them where the high ceilings of the ward receded into the vault of the roof. He could see patches where the plaster had fallen away. And gray continents of mold, like a grainy photograph of the moon. His head rolled sideways on the pillow, making him tighten the squint against the glare from the late-afternoon sun, banging in through the windows on the opposite wall of the ward, like a battery of lemon-yellow klieg lights. A sound of cymbals was in the color.

Still life on chipped porcelain table beside ward bed: Item—glass of water with bent, clear plastic straw leaning; Item—large metal spoon with

USN stamped on handle; Item—medicine bottle half full of purplish-pink liquid, handwritten label stuck on crooked.

He framed them in the squint. Watery vermilion of the medicine bottle and the bluish metal of the spoon on the white porcelain table-top. Part of the spoon handle jagged behind the water glass. The USN magnified through the glass on the offset part.

He moved his eyes toward the foot of the bed, picking up the projectile-shaped container, suspended upside down in a wire frame. Half full, the thick, clear liquid making runs on the sides as the level went down. Rubber tube connected to it underneath into the blocky metal cap. More plastic straws jointing the black rubber tube, with adhesive tape wrapped around the joints. Awkward. But efficient-looking. By tightening the squint he could see a foamy trace of bubbles moving down the clear plastic parts of the siphon into the black rubber tube. The tube falling straight down out of the heavy metal cap of the container, going out of sight toward the floor, then looping back beside the bed where he wasn't seeing it.

He moved his arm slightly, feeling the sting of the needle planted in the vein of his right arm. A vague pain, as if his arm were lying two or three beds away down the ward. He closed his eyes, listening to the sting of the needle in his arm.

"Seamanwillistonseamanwillistonseamanwilliston." Slimy membrane of words, with the grace note lifting and swelling underneath.

The hand and the thermometer came back into focus again. The thermometer looked too big—too big to lift. He was thinking that she might let it fall on him. It would hurt.

"Buh . . . buh . . . buh . . . ," he tried to tell her, pumping his tongue in his mouth aimlessly. A furry Ping-Pong ball he would have liked to spit out.

The thermometer rattled on his lower teeth, jabbing up into the soft, thin place under his tongue. He closed his mouth on it, to stop the jabbing.

His head rolled on the pillow, eyelids fluttering. Everything winging in and out of focus, until he was looking again at the projectile-shaped container hanging in the frame by the bed, and feeling the sting in his arm. A bulletlike container, still half full, with the clear runs down the sides, like a glass of Cointreau half-finished.

A bubble big enough to see by itself floated up from the liquid bottle, the bank of windows on the other side turning it yellow.

Yellow.

Yellow.

Now paling as the sun died, going away. Turning the liquid a pure, translucent lime.

He tightened the squint, moving inside the glass bullet of the container, inside the bubble. Rising and turning. Seeing only the pure, pale, green-yellow of the color itself.

. . . lime . . .
. . . lime . . .
. . . lyme . . .
. . . ROYALL LYME . . .
. . . Royall Lyme . . .
. . . Royall Lyme.

Not Mennen's. The usual.

Not Old Spice. For special occasions.

This, now. This was a *very* special occasion.

The shape of the bottle. Well, he didn't care much for the shape of the bottle. Too crude-looking where the seams met, and bigger than it should have been for the shape it was. He needed to be ten feet tall before he could use it. Something about the perspective made him feel his size. A small bottle. Better a small bottle, he thought.

And the crown cap looked dull, leadlike. Which worried him. For a crown.

But all the way from the Bahama Islands. He couldn't get over that it was made from limes in the Bahama Islands.

He unscrewed the cap and held the bottle to his nose. It wasn't like lemons at all.

He put the bottle into the carton and started the car. On the way out he stopped by Kose's sometime picture show—the Vanguard Theater—to get his passes signed by Floyd Wehatchett, the manager. The passes went with his usher's job—four a week. He thought that he would put them into the envelope with the money as a kind of bonus for Nettie. The idea of paying her at all worried him—the fact of it. He didn't want to just hand over the money to her—plain bills. So he decided to get around the problem by buying her a greeting card, something with an appropriate verse on it, and putting the money into that. It would make things seem less like a business transaction. The passes to the picture show would be a bonus. He knew she came there a good bit, since he saw her two or three times a week. Never by herself, it's true. But then, if she didn't need them herself, she could pass them on to John Henry as a kind of bonus to him for his part in arranging things.

Floyd's hair was reddish brown, long on the sides and ducktailed, but crew-cut on top. John Fletcher looked down into the pink shine of his scalp while he waited for him to sign the passes. The manager was thin in an unhealthy, cadaverous way, and to cover it up he bought his coats a size too large, with padded shoulders. If he had worn a big manila envelope, the effect would have been the same—like a two-button sandwich board. He had to walk kind of sideways, with one shoulder down and leading him—as if he couldn't move head-on because of the wind resistance. When he leaned over the desk to sign the passes, his buttoned coat hung away from him so John Fletcher could see right down to his belt buckle.

"Could a colored boy use them?" John Fletcher asked.

Floyd looked up at him from the other side of the desk that filled most of the tiny manager's office. He had a cast in one eye, so his glance forked all over the office. John Fletcher could never tell for sure which eye was doing the looking, and their conversations always made him nervous.

"I don't give a shit who uses them," he said. "Niggers sit in the balcony."

"Yes," said John Fletcher. "I just thought I'd ask."

Selecting the card had taken time. He had canvassed the drugstores in all the towns for twenty miles around. In the end he had gotten one of the first ones he'd looked at in Mr. Lane's Rexall store.

It was a large card with a stuffed red satin heart in an inset. With a good bit of lavender and some yellow, and a dusting of silver glitter scattered all over. Inside there was another heart. Not a stuffed one. There was also a cupid drawing a bow getting ready to shoot an arrow into it.

The verse started with a silver capital, then flowed on down the page in a liquid script. It read:

> Some girls remind me of mother,
> With loving hearts so true.
> Some girls remind me of sister,
> For the very sweet things they do.
> Some girls make me feel sadder
> Than a worn-out, discarded old shoe.
> Some girls make me feel "gladder"
> Than boys could ever do.
> There are girls of all stripes and colors
> Every kind of hue.
> But the girl who is everything to me,
> Is the girl who is known as YOU.

Across the bottom of the card, he had written in purple ink: *"July 3, 1956—A night I will ALWAYS remember."* He had signed it *"John Fletcher Williston."* The envelope he had addressed to: *"The Incompareably Lovely Miss Nettie Oatley."* He slipped the passes into the card, along with the check—he had thought a check more refined than cash money, and had written it out, also in purple ink, tearing up three checks before he got one on which the handwriting suited him just right. The card was in his inside coat pocket, along with the new black Swank wallet.

It was full dark by the time he got home. The headlights of his 1949 Studebaker swept the oaks lining the road. He got a good feeling looking out at the trees as they rushed into the beams of the lights over the nacelles of the hood and fenders which characterized that futuristic automobile. Driving it was like what he imagined it to have been to fly a P-38 in the war.

Some of the trees—the ones leaning out too far into the roadway— had white trunks. The county gang painted them as a warning to drivers. It was a narrow road anyway, and they were dangerous. Everywhere you went at night in McAfee County the low, spreading branches of the water oaks, with the moss hanging down, made you feel like you were driving in a cave. It was lonesome.

As he drove, he sang. ". . . Soooftly . . . as in a MORNNNing SUNNNrise . . ." He had learned it in the high-school glee club, but had never gotten to sing a solo because Mr. Forne, the director, had kept those to himself—except for the girls. It was his favorite song.

He pulled off the dirt road into his front yard, not swept, but intended to be—bare dirt, with two big oak trees flanking the entrance, and others here and there closing in on the house. He parked his car right up next to the porch, leaving enough room so the second car coming in wouldn't be cramped or have difficulty turning around.

His voice filled the darkness, ". . . SAAWFT—ly, as in an EEEVE—ning SUNNN—set, our love will faaaade aaaa—WAY." He was holding onto the "WAY," but going up the front steps he saw a shadow on the porch. He clipped off the note.

"Who's there?" he said.

"Is she with you, John Fletcher?" The voice out of the shadows of the porch was raspy and high-pitched. The voice of an old man with too few teeth. Slobbery and wet.

"Pa?" said John Fletcher.

"Is she with you?" he said, stepping out of the shadows and into the moonlight of the porch. A small, gnomelike man in overalls. His lower jaw hooked up, caving in his mouth where the teeth were missing—all the uppers. His hair was sparse and wispy, plastered down in sweaty, black tendrils, as if a small octopus was trying to climb over him from the back. His hands were folded inside the bib of his overalls.

"Why'd you have to come over here tonight, Pa?" he said.

"Is she coming on later?" said Pa.

"You got to go home, Pa," said John Fletcher.

John Fletcher and his pa didn't get along. Never had gotten along. Since he was ten years old John Fletcher had known there was some kind of unbridgeable gulf between them, but his pa never found it out. All he knew was that they were father and son—root and branch. "You and me's two of a kind," he would say. He didn't notice that

121

John Fletcher's mouth went tight, and that he always turned around and walked away whenever he said that to him. Most things he didn't notice. His son had been out of the house and gone for more than a week that summer before he missed him. "John Fletcher ain't here, is he?" he said.

No one had ever known Dorcus Williston to have a steady job, though he was pretty good at thinking up get-rich-quick schemes. Some of them were really good in an overall way. But all of them eventually fell through because Dorcus never could get around to working out the details. So it had been Minnie Williston—the mother—who had kept the family together, feeding them and putting clothes on their backs. The old man drove all of them to distraction from time to time. But John Fletcher *stayed* that way. Being the oldest, he had it harder than the other three boys. Dorcus was all the time meddling in his business and getting in the way, putting his arm around his shoulders and offering him homey but stupid advice that he had recognized as disastrous from the very beginning.

So when he got the usher's job at the picture show that summer he talked to Case Deering about the tenant house and moved into it to get some peace and rest.

"I wasn't going to get in the way or nothing," said Dorcus. "I just thought I would stay around and see what she looks like. You know. I had two nights with Maggie Poat once, and I wanted to see if Nettie was like her ma. Maggie was the best there is."

"Pa," said John Fletcher, "this is costing me money."

There was a silence.

"It ain't free, Pa," he said. "I got to pay for it."

"How much a girl like that cost?" said Dorcus.

"Enough," said John Fletcher. "Enough so I don't want you sitting around watching us like it was a picture show."

"I wouldn't do no more than just to watch," said Dorcus. "I just ain't never seen a girl like Nettie close to."

"You seen Nettie plenty of times," said John Fletcher.

"With her clothes on," said Dorcus. "I mean I ain't never *seen* her."

"You saw her ma, you said," said John Fletcher.

"Shit, John Fletcher," said Dorcus. "Twenty years ago. Ain't no piece of ass good enough a man is going to keep it in mind *that* long. I just wanted to see what Nettie looked like. You know . . . *tonight.*"

John Fletcher looked at him. "I ain't going to share my time with you, Pa," he said. "Get you some money and you can buy her to look at all you want to."

"How much?" said Dorcus.

John Fletcher looked at him. "Twenty dollars," he said.

Dorcus whistled. "Twenty dollars!" he said. "That must be *some* pussy. Maggie was five. I *got* to see what it looks like now."

"Not on *my* time," said John Fletcher.

"I wouldn't disturb nothing," he said.

"Yes, shit," said John Fletcher. "Go home, Pa."

"I ain't only just going to watch," said Dorcus.

"You ain't going to do nothing," said John Fletcher.

"Aw, son," he said.

"Aw, shit, Pa," said John Fletcher. "Save up your money. You can pay for it yourself."

"Twenty dollars?" said Dorcus. "Time I scratched me up that kind of a pile, I wouldn't give a shit no more. It always did take the lead out of my pencil—worrying about money."

John Fletcher didn't answer him.

"Maybe I could get took sick and drop dead tonight, John Fletcher," he said. "Then what?"

"I ain't never been that lucky," said John Fletcher.

"That's a hard thing to say, John Fletcher," he said. "I'm going to be took sometime. It might could be I'd be took this very night. Dead in the morning, and how would you feel then? You got to look at it every way you could. Might be it would happen. You'd be sorry as hell for it in the morning when I was done dead and gone. Too late then."

"Pa," said John Fletcher, "this ain't the kind of a thing that you go and share it with somebody. You sure as hell don't go and share it with your own pa."

There was a long silence.

"It'd be a piss-poor last thought to have of you anyway," said John Fletcher. "I wouldn't want to remember you horny."

"You'd be sorry just the same," he said.

"Go on, Pa," said John Fletcher. "Get the shit out of here. I ain't kidding."

"Jesus, son," said Dorcus. "You got a hard heart."

"I ain't kidding, Pa," said John Fletcher.

"Shit," said Dorcus.

"Pa . . . ," said John Fletcher.

There was a long pause.

"When you going in the navy, son?" he said.

"Jesus wept," said John Fletcher.

"I'm going on home now," he said, though he didn't make a move. "Your ma wants to know. She worries about you, son."

"We talked about it already. She's going to see me off at the bus when I go to Jacksonville."

"She worries about you, son," he said. "The only mother you got."

"Go on home, Pa," said John Fletcher.

"You want me to take a message, son?" he said. "To your ma?"

"Just go on, Pa," said John Fletcher. "I told her already."

For a minute he didn't say anything. "Is this your first time, son?" he said.

"Shit, Pa," said John Fletcher. "Just shit."

"It was just that I thought you might need some advice from an old experienced hand. Somebody to show you the ropes."

"Don't show me no ropes, Pa," said John Fletcher. "Don't show me nothing at all. Just please get the shit out of here."

"All right," he said. "I'm going. Going home right now."

He started down the steps, then paused, scratching his head. "I never told you nothing about none of this," he said, not looking at John Fletcher.

John Fletcher didn't answer him.

"One thing I always found worked for me pretty good. You should blow in her ear. That drives them right out of their mind. I done it to your ma when we was courting . . ."

"Pa," said John Fletcher, "I don't want to hear it about Ma."

". . . She chased me right up that chinaberry tree in her daddy's front yard . . ."

"Pa . . . ," said John Fletcher.

". . . chinaberry," he said. "Lucky. I wouldn't never have made it up no oak. Drove her right out of her mind."

"Pa . . . ," said John Fletcher.

"Just blow in her ear," he said. He tapped his ear with his finger.

"I'm *paying* for this, Pa," said John Fletcher. "I ain't going to have to blow in nothing."

"Yeah," he said. "I just thought you might like to know about it for some other time. In the navy." He paused, looking down off the porch into the yard. "Cigarette ashes," he said. "Cigarette ashes in Coca-Cola. That's high-powered stuff. You got to be careful with that. I knowed a girl torn herself up on a gearshift once." He looked at John Fletcher. "When you get real hard up you can try that. But you got to be careful." He stopped and scratched his head again. "Ain't none of the cars got floor shifts no more anyway," he said.

"Go on, Pa," said John Fletcher.

The old man walked down the steps slowly, putting both feet on each step. When he got to the bottom, he stood there a minute. "Anything you want me to tell your ma?" he said. "She's the only ma you got," he added.

"You going to tell her about this, I suppose," said John Fletcher.

"Jesus, son," he said. "You want me to tell her you're fucking Nettie Oatley?" He looked up at the porch. "I wouldn't of thought you'd of wanted her to find out about that."

"I just figured you was going to do it," said John Fletcher. "It's just about your idea of good news, ain't it?"

"I wouldn't never mention no names or nothing about a thing like that," he said. "I got some sense."

"When did that happen?" said John Fletcher.

"I know how to handle things," he said. "You don't need to worry about me none."

"Just tell her *one* of her sons is fucking Nettie Oatley?" he said.

"I ain't going to tell her nothing," he said.

"Come on, Pa," he said. "You try to hold that in and you'll blow up like a two-dollar tire."

The old man held his finger up to his mouth. "She ain't never going to know," he said.

John Fletcher looked at him standing in the yard at the bottom of the steps. "Just go on, Pa," he said. "Tell Ma I'll be over to see her tomorrow, or the next day."

"Okay, son," he said. "Never a word. Have you a good time." He turned to go, then turned back. "Wash yourself up real good after you finished," he said. "You don't want to go in the navy all clapped up."

"I'll tell you about it, Pa," he said. "Maybe I'll tell you about it."

The old man looked up into the shadows of the porch. "Yes," he said. "That would be nice."

John Fletcher stood looking down at him in the yard. "I might send you twenty dollars, Pa," he said. "After I get in the navy."

Dorcus looked up into the shadows. "You wouldn't really do that, would you, son?"

"You leave me alone tonight," said John Fletcher. "I might do it."

"You could do it with your navy money?" said Dorcus.

"I don't want to be spoiling my evening looking out the windows for you all night," said John Fletcher.

"You got the money?" he said.

"I'll get it," said John Fletcher.

"You figure you going to make you some money in the navy?" he said. "That picture-show job don't pay you enough so you could be taking out high-class whores like Nettie Oatley all the time."

"I'll do it," said John Fletcher.

"Nettie Oatley?" said Dorcus. "You talking about Nettie Oatley?" Not some flappy-twatted old fartbag out of one of them pineywoods roadhouses? I done already laid enough pipe in that kind of snatch to run a pissline from here to Daytona Beach."

"I'm talking about twenty dollars," said John Fletcher. "If I see hide or hair of you around this house tonight, you wouldn't get a nickel."

"You wouldn't fuck me up, would you, son?" said Dorcus. "You wouldn't fuck up your own father, would you?"

"You going to fuck *me* up?" said John Fletcher. "I'll do you as I'm done by."

They stood for a minute in silence.

"I don't know whether I'd be up to Nettie Oatley," he said.

"Pa," said John Fletcher, "get the hell out of here. *Now.* Will you, Pa? Before she comes?"

"I trust you, son," he said. He gave an imitation of a salute and began shuffling off toward the road.

"Hey, Pa!" said John Fletcher, shouting from the porch.

"Yeah?" he said, stopping in the yard and turning back toward the house.

"Pa, tell Ma I'll be over for supper tomorrow night, will you?"

"Yes," he said. He put his finger to his mouth again. "Not a word," he said. "Remember. Blow in her ear. Just to prove it works. Don't put no cigarette ashes in her Coca-Cola, though. You wouldn't believe what it would do."

"We ain't going to have no Coca-Colas," said John Fletcher.

"Just as well," he said. "Not the first time, anyways. You got to know what you're doing."

He saluted, then turned and shuffled out of the yard.

John Fletcher watched him out of sight, then turned and went into the house.

All the tenant houses were alike. Functional. This one wasn't in such bad condition, though it was warped over to the side, like it was beginning to want to lie down. Case Deering tried to keep up his houses. Most of the windowpanes were still in, and the front porch sagged only a little. By being just normally careful, you could avoid falling through the rotten planks.

It was built well up off the ground on brick pillars. High enough that a good-sized child could walk under it without stooping over. Outside, it was unpainted clapboard. Inside, the walls were covered with sheet rock, with wide taped joints showing under the paint—salmon pink in the front room, blue in the bedroom, green in the kitchen. All of the colors were pastel and pasty-looking, as though they had been worked into a base of vanilla ice cream. The walls were all furry with a coat of grease and dirt now, with patches here and there where the sheet rock had started to turn to powder and disintegrate. The floors were covered with linoleum rugs—bright yellow, with red and blue triangles that intersected each other. When all the lights were on the glare tended to get up back of your eyes and blind you. In one corner of the living room was a coal stove, painted salmon pink to match the walls. The pipe elbowed out through a flange. It was painted salmon pink too, with weeping black stains at the joints, and more black stains running out from under the flange and down the wall.

The furniture was plain and cast-off looking. An overstuffed couch of coarse cloth, gray with a green fleck in it. One overstuffed chair that looked like the next year's model from the rival company of the one that had made the couch. Darker gray with a brown fleck. End tables at the couch, veneered in some blond wood. One of them had a long sliver of veneer stripped away, leaving the glassy-brown glue showing beneath. Lamps on the end tables. One homemade, from a quart bourbon bottle filled with sand, the shade tan with red and blue ships on it. The other was a vanity lamp, of white plastic that looked like milk glass until you got close enough to see the line of flash along the seam. Potbellied and knobbed. With a white shade, gathered with a pink ribbon at the top. On the wall behind the couch was a large picture in a plastic frame. The lights from the end-table lamps bouncing off it made it difficult to see what it was. A landscape with big patches of blue in it.

John Fletcher had tried to fix the room up a little, though he couldn't afford to spend much money on it. He had draped a crocheted afghan over the back of the couch. His mother had made it, black-bordered squares sewed together, with bright-colored centers. It blotted out pretty much of the gray with green flecks. There were two pillows stuffed into the corners—red and blue satin—souvenirs from Stuckey's, with the "Welcome to Florida" turned to the back. Two ashtrays on the end tables—one from Stuckey's that was chocolate brown with gold lettering, part of the verse to "America the Beautiful," the other from the ten-cent store, a ceramic skull with places in the eye sockets to hold the cigarettes.

He had also added some pictures on the walls—a couple of three-sheet posters from the picture show. One was from a Marilyn Monroe picture that showed her getting her skirts blown up, and trying to hold them down. One was from a Rex Harrison movie, showing him

128

in a dressing gown, with one hand in the pocket, the thumb hooked out. And one was from a Japanese horror movie, showing a giant lizard stepping over a city that was on fire, holding a train over his head in his front paws, and kicking down a bridge with one of his feet. In the foreground a pretty Oriental girl was cringing and looking up at him. The lizard was looking down at her with the red whites of his eyes showing, and a kind of smile on his face. A rapy kind of look.

He had improved on the room as much as he could for this night. Brought a card table out and set it up in the living room for them to eat on, with two kitchen chairs—one straight-backed and wood, the other tubular with yellow formica seat and back—and a checkered tablecloth. He didn't like the color of the room and had decided to cover it up by eating by candlelight. He wanted a wine bottle to hold the candle, but didn't have one, except the wine for supper, which was full. So he used a syrup bottle that had something of the look of a wine bottle about it, he thought. It had a long neck. He soaked the label off, and it didn't look too bad with a red candle in it.

He had set out flowers, red zinnias and marigolds. But the marigolds smelled so bad he had to throw them out. Except for the pink walls, the zinnias looked pretty good. He had sprayed the room with Evening in Paris cologne that he had borrowed from his mother. To cover up the marigolds.

On the end tables he laid out magazines that he had collected for the occasion—*Time, Look, Life, The New Yorker,* and a *National Geographic* that he had found in a trash can behind the library. A couple of paperback books—*Rivers of Glory* by F. Van Wyck Mason and *Sangaree* by Frank Slaughter. Frank Yerby was his favorite, but his copy of *The Foxes of Harrow* had disintegrated and wouldn't make much of a show. On the couch he spread a Sunday edition of the Atlanta *Journal-Constitution,* turned to the book-review page. He had circled a review of a book on Chinese porcelain, making marginal notes like "very good" and "I agree."

He had debated about whether or not to leave the bedroom door open. It wasn't much of a room, and he couldn't afford to redecorate the whole house for just the one evening, but the blue was the best color of the three. Finally he decided against it, though he hedged by leaving the door cracked open just a little.

The supper menu had given him trouble. Finally he had decided on Salisbury-steak TV dinners. He liked the sound of "Salisbury steak." They would have wine with the meal—Roma burgundy—and coffee after. No dessert. He had a little speech about that. The third draft went: "Sweets I have in great abundance. Nettie Oatley, you are a sugar lump in my eye." He had bought a box of chocolate-covered cherries, in case she wanted something more substantial than the speech.

He lit the oven, then read the directions on the TV-dinner cartons and put them in.

Back in the living room he sat down on the sofa and smoked a cigarette. When he finished, he went into the kitchen and emptied the ashtray and rinsed it out. Then he put it back on the end table. He hadn't thought about it before, but he decided now that he should put out some cigarettes too, so he went and got a juice glass and emptied half of his pack of English Ovals into it, and put that on the end table too. He tuned his transistor until he got some slow music, then put it under the couch, thinking that would be a nice touch—to have the music coming from nowhere.

He lit another cigarette and looked at his watch. Nine-thirty. She had been due at nine o'clock. When he finished his cigarette, he took the ashtray out to the kitchen and washed it again. As he came back into the living room he heard the car and saw the lights sweep the front of the house. He put the ashtray back on the end table and turned off the lamps. Then he lit the candle. It took him two matches to get it burning. Before he finished, Nettie was knocking at the door. She knocked twice, then opened it and let herself in.

John Fletcher was in the middle of the room when she came in. He put his right hand into his coat pocket with the thumb hooked out, dropping the match on the floor and looking at her. He was trying to get a debonair expression onto his face. When Nettie first looked at him she thought he had probably cut a fart.

"Welcome," he said, speaking out of the corner of his mouth, "to my humble abode."

From where she stood at the door, she could see the Rex Harrison picture on the wall behind him. "It ain't so humble," she said, looking at the picture and then at John Fletcher. Her dress was blue. Filmy and low-cut. When she came close to him he smelled magnolias.

Nettie was a good-looking girl. Dark hair, almost black. Thick and long. Her eyes were yellow. Not brown, or light brown, but a golden honey color with sharp green flecks in it. Like a cat's eyes, but not quite as hard. The rest of her facial features were finely drawn, even a little sharp. In fact, her face seemed out of place on her body. Above the neck she was a kind of clingstone-peach soufflé; below it she was all meat and potatoes.

"Come in," he said, going over and closing the door, still keeping his hand in his pocket.

She walked over toward the sofa, pausing at the table for a moment and laying her fingers on it gently. "Very nice," she said.

"Have a seat," said John Fletcher. "And let me get you some wine."

"Wine too?" said Nettie, sweeping the papers into a corner of the couch and sitting down. "You *are* putting it on, ain't you?"

"There is nothing that is too good for a beautiful woman," he said. He didn't look at her when he said it. He looked at the candle. There was a rather long silence, during which he put his left hand into his pocket too, and rocked on his heels slightly, pulling his chin into his collar. "Nothing in this world," he said.

Nettie looked at him. "This is going to be one hell of a night," she said.

John Fletcher stopped rocking and smiled. "I'll get the wine," he said, going out to the kitchen. He still had both of his hands in his coat pockets.

He poured the wine into glasses that he had bought at the ten-cent store, and brought them back out to the living room. Nettie was sitting on the couch smoking one of the cigarettes when he returned.

"I like your coat," she said, taking the glass. "Is it real?"

"No," he said.

"It *looks* real," she said.

"Thank you," he said.

He handed her the glass in his left hand, then put the hand back

131

into his coat pocket. He looked at her for a minute, then raised his glass and toasted her. "To the beautifully . . . To the beautiful Nettie Oatley," he said. He looked down at her. His left eyebrow was raised slightly. She thought he had farted again.

"Shit I reckon," she said. "this is going to be one hell of a night."

She raised her glass to his, tapping it hard enough that some of the wine spilled down her arm. "You can lick it off later," she said, and laughed.

They sipped the wine.

Nettie smacked her lips. "Makes you pucker, don't it?" she said.

John Fletcher gave a number of short smacks. "A little persimmony," he said.

"It's wine right on," she said, taking another sip.

John Fletcher sipped his with his hand in his coat pocket. Every now and then he would take it out, but then he couldn't think of anything to do with it, so he would end up putting it back in again.

"Come on," said Nettie, giving the couch a slap, "sit down and let's us get started."

John Fletcher looked at her. "How about supper first?" he said.

Nettie looked at the table. "Well," she said. "I had me a steak just before I left to come over here. I hate to work on a empty stomach. I get gas something awful." She patted her stomach. "I'm afraid I couldn't eat nothing else. What you got?"

"Salisbury steaks," said John Fletcher. He pronounced it *Sal-is-berry*.

"What kind of a steak is that?" said Nettie. "Something fancy I bet."

"Not really," said John Fletcher. "I thought you might like to try them."

"I'll try anything once, buddy," she said, leaning over and slapping him hard on the thigh.

John Fletcher flinched, spilling wine in her lap.

"You can lick that off later, too," she said.

She reached out and felt his thigh where she had slapped him. "You ain't too solid, are you?" she said. "Kind of pony size."

John Fletcher didn't say anything. He took his hand out of his pocket, then put it back in.

"Don't let it worry you none," she said. "I had all kinds. It don't

132

make no difference to me. Ponies and racehorses and mules. They's all the same."

John Fletcher stood there with his hands in his pockets, looking down at her. He didn't say anything.

"Let's have supper," he said.

He went out into the kitchen and got the TV dinners out of the oven. He wanted to put them on regular plates, but was afraid he would make a mess of it if he tried. So he brought them in to the table in their aluminum trays, with a plate underneath.

"*TV* dinners?" said Nettie, looking at them.

"Yes," said John Fletcher, smiling with his eyebrow up. "I'm not much of a cook."

"The meat's all right," said Nettie, "but the vegetables taste like shit. I'd as soon eat the box it come in as those green peas there."

"The steaks are good, I hear," said John Fletcher.

"I already had me a steak," she said. She held up her hand, the thumb and forefinger two inches apart. "That thick," she said. "With onions and french fries."

"Well," said John Fletcher. "I hear they're very good."

"Get me some more of that wine," she said. "Maybe a couple more shots of that and I'll get hungry again."

John Fletcher reached for her glass, but she held it away. "Just bring in the bottle," she said. "No need to keep running back and forth."

John Fletcher went out into the kitchen and got the bottle.

She had two more glasses quickly.

"Come on," she said. "We'll try your Salisbury steaks." She got up and went to the table. John Fletcher tried to put his glass down and get there in time to pull the chair out for her. He spilled more wine on the couch, and when he got to her and tried to help, she was already sitting down. She heaved up the chair, getting closer to the table, and put one of the legs down on his foot.

"You got to move fast to keep up with me," she said. She slapped him on the leg again. "Maybe you ought to eat mine too," she said. "Put some meat on your bones. You ever tried taking any kind of tonic?"

John Fletcher was getting into his chair. He hit the table, and the bottle with the candle turned over. When he lit a match to look for it, it was lying in his plate.

"Now you got to take mine," said Nettie. "I done had me a steak tonight anyway." While John Fletcher got the bottle up and the candle relit, Nettie swapped plates with him.

"How about vitamins?" she said.

"What?" said John Fletcher.

"You ever take vitamins to try and make you gain some weight?"

"I'm bigger than my pa," he said.

"Jesus," said Nettie, "your pa ain't hardly five feet tall."

"But it's in the family," he said.

"Lee Jay is going to be a big man," said Nettie.

"Lee Jay is weak in the head," said John Fletcher.

"Well," said Nettie, "I just wondered. It don't make no difference to me. Big or little. I seen all kinds. You ever tried Hadacol?"

"Pa tried it," he said. "We had to take it away from him."

"It's good stuff," she said.

"Pa quit eating," said John Fletcher. "He was drinking four bottles a day. Staggering around the house telling everybody how good he felt and trying to get Ma in the bedroom with him. We couldn't afford it. He never did put on no weight."

"You ought to try it sometimes," she said. "Or some vitamins. Just to see."

"Well," said John Fletcher.

He began eating his Salisbury steak in silence.

"Give me some more of that wine," said Nettie. "It sort of grows on you. It don't feel like my mouth is turning inside out no more." She held out her glass to him. He poured it full.

While he ate, she sipped the wine and looked around the room. "It ain't much of a place you got here," she said. "The pictures is nice." She raised her glass toward the Rex Harrison picture.

"Yes," said John Fletcher. "I got them at the picture show."

"I can't never remember," she said, nodding toward the Rex Harrison picture, "what's his name?"

John Fletcher looked around at the poster. "Rex Harrison," he said.

"He looks kind of fruity," she said, sipping the wine. "All right in the face, you know, but . . . something . . . fruity is what it is. Like he's got lace on his drawers." She emptied her glass and put it down on the table. "Myself," she said, "John Wayne . . . that's my type. Big Boy Williams . . . he's cute too."

John Fletcher didn't say anything.

She picked up the bottle and poured herself another glass of wine. "Want some more?" she said, looking at John Fletcher. Before he could answer, she poured the rest of the bottle into his glass. "That's all she wrote," she said. She drained her glass and slapped it down onto the table. John Fletcher caught the candle before it toppled over again.

"You go on eating," she said, standing up. "Got to put some meat on your bones. I'm going to get more comfortable."

She walked over to the couch, kicking off her shoes as she went. Then she peeled off her dress, pulling it over her head and dropping it on one of the end tables. She had on black underwear. Across the front of the panties was written in red, "Friday." It was Tuesday. With her back to John Fletcher, she unfastened her brassiere and dropped it on her dress; then she massaged her breasts, kneading them together and pushing them up from underneath. "That feels good," she said, looking back at him.

She took off the panties. Flexed her knees and made a downward motion with her arms; then she was stepping out of them. John Fletcher couldn't follow the motion. Just suddenly she didn't have them on.

He sat at the table watching her with his mouth sprung open, the fork poised in midair, trembling, the peas falling off into his lap.

After she had got her clothes off, Nettie gave an angular pirouette-like spin—she had a baton twirler's grace, had been one in high school—and collapsed backward onto the couch, her legs spread wide apart and sticking out stiff in front of her, her arms raised and hugging the back of her neck.

"You about ready to commence?" she said. Her head was thrown back, and she looked at him under lowered lids.

John Fletcher lowered his fork slowly, not looking where he was putting it. It dropped off the plate and into his lap. He rose slowly from the table, his right hand in his pocket, his left adjusting his tie. He spoke with a croak. "Maybe . . ." He cleared his throat. "Maybe I ought to clear away the dishes," he said.

"Not now, John Fletcher," she said. With her knees locked stiff, she raised and lowered her legs, drumming on the floor with her heels.

John Fletcher took a step, kicking the table and overturning the candle. He lit a match.

"Whyn't you turn on the lights?" said Nettie.

"The pink is shitty looking," he said.

"What?" she said.

"It's a shitty-looking pink," he said. "The walls."

The match went out, burning his fingers. "Jesus," he said. He lit another and set the candle upright on the table again.

"The candle is better," he said.

"Come over here, pony boy," she said.

He walked over with his hand in his pocket.

"Sit down," she said, slapping the sofa.

John Fletcher stood looking down at her. "Why . . ." He cleared his throat. "Why . . ."

She looked down at herself. "Do it every day," she said. "Shave all over. ALL over." She rubbed her hands up her legs and over her belly. "Started with a fella I used to go with once. He said he was paying to see it all, and he was, by God, going to *see* it. He done it himself with a *straight* razor. That was one hell of a sensation, I can tell you. I was afraid I'd twitch the wrong way and he'd put me out of business. But it come out all right. He never even nicked me."

She locked her fingers together and pushed them away, cracking her knuckles. "He had a nice touch," she said.

"When it started to grow back, it scratched so much I had to keep up the shaving. I figure it's a good idea anyway—kind of a conversation piece."

She laughed. "How about that?" she said. "Conversation *piece* . . . Get it?"

John Fletcher rocked on his heels and giggled.

"Anyways," she said, "it keeps down the crabs."

"It certainly does," he said.

She raised her hand and tried to unzip his fly. He looked up at the landscape painting. When she touched him, he flinched his hips backwards, pulling away from her.

"Hadn't we ought to go in the bedroom?" he said.

"You're the doctor," she said.

She stood up, running her hands up her body, massaging her breasts and holding them with her hands cupped under them. "That feels so good," she said. She twisted from side to side, rubbing them against him.

John Fletcher stood with his hands in his coat pockets, jumping his eyes up and down from her face to her breasts and back again. "It certainly does," he said.

They went into the bedroom. It was lit by a bare sixty-watt bulb hanging from a long cord in the middle of the room. The blue walls were better than the pink or the green, but still depressing. The bed was a massive walnut one—a lathe turner's dream come true, with posts that looked like strings of shiny black croquet balls. Festoons of smaller turnings had been worked into every available space. A bulbous tour de force. It filled two-thirds of the room. A matching wardrobe of the same massive design stood on one side. Something about its proportions was reminiscent of a 1940 Wurlitzer jukebox, though not so gaudy, of course. The two pieces of furniture accounted for most of the available floor space. Jammed between the bed and the wall there was an upended orange crate that served as a bedside table. On it was an autographed picture of Rex Harrison. *"Best Wishes,"* it said. There was also another chocolate-brown Stuckey's ashtray.

"You know that fruity guy?" Nettie said, pointing to the picture.

"Not really," said John Fletcher.

"How'd you get the picture?" she said. "He wrote on it for you."

"Just sent him a letter and asked him for it," he said.

She leaned over and looked at it closely. "I wonder if John Wayne would send you a picture if you asked him?"

"Yes," said John Fletcher. "They all do."

She stood up, spread-eagled her arms, and fell backward onto the bed. "Let's commence," she said.

John Fletcher turned the picture face down on the table, gently. Then he went over and turned out the light.

"Hey," she said. "You can't see."

"There's enough light from the other room," he said, coming over to the bed. He stood looking down at her. "You're a beautiful woman, Nettie," he said.

She worked her right leg between his and moved it in and out. "You're all right yourself, pony boy," she said.

She sat up on the edge of the bed and unzipped his fly. Then she undid his belt and peeled down his pants and underpants.

"That's as pretty as ever a one I did see," she said, holding him in both her hands. One hand underneath, one on top, stroking him.

". . . thank you," he said.

He cleared his throat. "I thought . . . ," he said, ". . . I was afraid . . ."

She looked up at his face. "What?" she said.

". . . you seen all kinds," he said. ". . . It's . . . little . . . ain't it?"

She looked back down at him. "It's pretty," she said. "It don't go by the yard."

"I thought . . ."

She looked up at his face, then back down. "Don't worry, John Fletcher," she said. "I'd lot rather be tickled to death than choked."

John Fletcher didn't say anything. She went on stroking, sitting on the bed while he stood over her, his hands in his coat pockets, looking across at the wall over her head. With a slow, steady motion he began sinking at the knees, thrusting his hips forward and biting his lower lip. He reached down quickly, grabbing her hands with both of his.

"No," he said, holding her tight.

"Well," she said, looking down at him. "I *said* let's commence."

He looked down at her, opening his eyes. She was sitting with one hand cupped in her lap, the other poised, fingers spread, holding it away.

"Is it over?" he said, licking his lips.

"It's only just started, John Fletcher," she said, looking up at him. "Where's the bathroom?"

"There," he said, pointing.

She got up and walked over to it, still holding her hand cupped.

138

As she went by the door to the living room, she flipped on the light. He heard the water running, then the toilet flushing.

While she was gone, he wiped himself off with a handkerchief and pulled his pants and underpants back up.

She looked at him when she came out of the bathroom. "You ain't had enough?" she said.

"You said we'd only just started."

"Why'd you cover up?" she said.

"It bothers me," he said, not looking at her.

"I know," she said. "You'll get used to it. It's better bare assed."

He looked at her.

"It's pretty as a picture," she said. "Believe me. I know. They don't come no prettier."

She walked over to him. "I'll help," she said, reaching for his fly again.

"I'll do it," he said, catching her hand and holding it.

He began by taking off his coat, getting a coat hanger out of the wardrobe, and hanging it up. He took off his tie and began to unbutton his shirt.

"Why don't you go on back in the other room?" he said.

"I don't bother you, do I?" she said.

"You bother the shit out of me," he said. "Go on back in there, and I'll be along in a minute." He had to go to the bathroom and was afraid she would follow him. He couldn't make water with other people standing around. At the picture show he had to watch the rest room and go when nobody was in there, or go in right behind somebody else and hope he wouldn't use the booth.

"Second time is better," she said, going out of the room.

He went to the bathroom, then came back into the bedroom and undressed down to his underpants and socks. He didn't want to go barefoot, but had nothing else to wear.

Then he went back into the bathroom again and got a towel, wrapping it around his waist to cover up his shorts. When he went back into the living room, he found her dancing around to the transistor music. She had put her high-heel red shoes on, but nothing else. He went to the couch and sat down, watching her.

"I bet you cheated," she said, dancing over to him on the couch.

She twitched the towel away, revealing him in his Jockey shorts. John Fletcher sat with his arms resting beside him on the couch, hands gripping the edge.

She danced away from him.

"Nice music," she said. "Where's it at?"

"I thought you'd like it," he said. "Under the couch."

"I like to dance," she said.

"You certainly are a beautiful dancer," he said.

Her dancing was like a provocative calisthenics exercise. As long as she kept her arms and legs in close, it went okay. But she kept flinging them out and striking angular poses, like a cheerleader practicing cheers. She had gotten the wine down a little too fast.

John Fletcher sat watching her. After a while he crossed his legs. Once he drummed with his fingers on the cushion.

"Take your socks off," she said, dancing by him.

"I've got ugly feet," he said.

"They look funny," she said. "Not your feet . . . the socks."

John Fletcher tried to stick his feet under the couch.

She danced over beside the Marilyn Monroe poster and imitated the pose, mashing her breasts together with her arms.

"Sometimes people say I look like her," she said.

"Yes," said John Fletcher, shifting his eyes back and forth from the poster to Nettie. "Better," he said.

"Except for the black hair," she said.

"I like black hair better," he said.

The music changed. A slow tune. "Sentimental Journey." Nettie moved around more gracefully. Not kicking so much.

"How about some coffee?" said John Fletcher.

"Where's it at?" she said, stopping. She weaved a little standing there in the middle of the floor.

"I'll get it," he said.

"Woman's place is in the kitchen," she said.

"Some women," he said.

"Where's it at?" she said.

"It's on the stove," he said.

She went out to the kitchen and turned on the burner; then she came out and danced a fast song and two slow ones until it was ready. She poured it in the kitchen and brought the cups into the living room, sloshing coffee into the saucers.

"Let's sit at the table," he said.

He lit the candle and turned out the end-table lamp. This time he helped her into the chair. Then he sat there across from her, looking at her naked in the candlelight. He wanted to get down and look at her under the table too.

"My table. My house," he said.

"What?" she said.

"Nothing," he said.

"Let's dance," she said. The music was all slow now.

"I don't dance very well," he said.

"I'll teach you," she said.

They tried it once or twice around the floor. She stopped and kicked off her shoes. "Here," she said, holding him at arm's length. "Watch my feet." She did the step for him. Then they tried it together again. "Count," she said. "One-two-three-four . . . one-two-three-four." They moved around the floor. When the music stopped he stepped back from her.

"You'll catch on," she said. "you got rhythm."

"I have?" he said.

"You got natural rhythm," she said.

They tried two more slow dances. "Try counting to yourself," she said.

He stepped on her foot. "I'm sorry," he said.

"Don't apologize," she said. "Keep counting."

He stepped on her foot again. "Let's sit down for a while," he said.

They went to the couch. For a while they just sat there side by side not talking. Listening to the music. At eleven o'clock the music program went off and the news came on. Then the weather.

"Ninety-eight in Savannah today," said the weatherman. "Humidity eighty-nine percent."

"Ninety-eight degrees," said John Fletcher. "That's hot."

"I'd have died if I'd known it was that hot," said Nettie. " 'Course, I slept most of the day."

"Yes," said John Fletcher.

141

"It ain't the heat anyway," said Nettie. "It's the humidity gets you down."

"Ninety-eight is pretty hot," said John Fletcher.

"Yes," she said.

"Being in the picture show, I can't tell much about how it is outside," said John Fletcher. "It's always cool in the picture show."

"That's the nice part about working in the picture show," she said. "It's always air-conditioned."

"Sometimes it breaks down," said John Fletcher. "Not very often."

"That must be pretty bad when it does," she said.

"It certainly is," he said.

"It must be bad when you come out at night," she said. "That would make you feel it all the more."

"It certainly does," said John Fletcher.

After the weather report, the farm-and-home news came on. "Cotton is one hundred and sixty-three dollars the bale," said the announcer.

"Did he say a hundred and *sixteen* dollars?" said Nettie.

"Sixty-three," said John Fletcher.

"It sounded like sixteen to me," she said.

"I think it was sixty-three," he said. "I could have been mistaken."

"That's still low," she said.

"Maybe it was *two* hundred," he said.

"That's too high," she said. "Cotton wouldn't be going for no two hundred dollars."

"I thought it was a hundred," he said.

After the farm-and-market news, the obituary program of the day came on.

Organ music swelled in the background, playing "Rock of Ages," then the announcer's voice came on. "On the Other Side . . . ," he said. "Time, ladies and gentlemen, to pause for a moment in the hustle and bustle of weary workaday, and give a thought to those who have left us for a better place . . ."—the music swelled behind him, then died away—". . . on the Other Side. This memorial program is brought to you by Fenway Brothers Mortuary. On the square in Kose. Your grief is in good hands at Fenway Brothers Mortuary." The music swelled again and died away.

"It's creepy-sounding," said Nettie.

"The music is pretty, though," said John Fletcher. "Sometimes they play 'Softly as in a Morning Sunrise.' "

"What?" she said.

"The song," he said, " 'Softly as in a Morning Sunrise.' "

"He sounds happy about the Other Side," she said.

"He's got a good voice, though," said John Fletcher.

"Let's get something else," she said.

"Just a minute," said John Fletcher. "Softly as in a Morning Sunrise" would have made his cup run over. The song did turn up pretty frequently on the program.

The music continued softly behind the announcer's voice. "Mrs. Roscoe Powers passed away this morning at ten-forty-seven," he said, "after a lingering illness. She was in her eighty-ninth year, and had been bedridden since nineteen-forty-nine, in the loving care of her devoted daughter, Miss Glendanna Powers of four-twenty-three Swamp Street in Kose. The body is at rest for viewing at Fenway Brothers Mortuary in Kose. On the square. Graveside services will be held tomorrow at eleven o'clock at Dorchester Memorial Gardens."

"Get something else," said Nettie. "That's creepy-sounding."

"Maybe they'll play 'Softly as in a Morning Sunrise,' " he said.

". . . eight sons and three daughters, twenty-six grandchildren, and seven great-grandchildren . . . ," said the announcer.

"Where's it at, John Fletcher?" said Nettie. "Come on and get something else." She was bending over and reaching under the couch. John Fletcher got down and took out the transistor. She took it away from him, tuning it herself. Bill Haley and "Rock Around the Clock" came on.

"That's more like it," she said.

She got up and began dancing again by herself. "Watch this step," she said. She glided away, keeping her legs close together and wagging her behind at him. John Fletcher watched her going away.

She picked up the coffee cups and wiggled out into the kitchen. "Nigger work is what I'm best at," she said, dancing back in.

He didn't say anything.

The music changed to a slow one. "Blood will tell," she said, lighting a cigarette from the candle on the table, then sitting down backward in the tubular steel-and-formica chair, facing him.

"Don't talk about it," he said.

143

"Everybody knows anyway," she said. "Why not?"

"Don't keep doing it," he said.

"I don't keep doing it," she said. "I just said it once."

She inhaled a long drag from the cigarette and tapped the ashes onto the floor. John Fletcher handed her the Stuckey's ashtray.

"You don't need to keep talking about being a nigger," he said.

She took another drag on the cigarette. "You the one's keeping on," she said. "Anyway, I am."

"You're light as I am," he said.

She flipped the ashes off her cigarette, not looking at him, "Shit, John Fletcher," she said.

"You could pass anywheres," he said.

She looked at the burning tip of the cigarette. "Maggie was a sixteenth," she said. "That makes me a thirty-second." She looked at him. "Everybody knows that."

"Everybody in McAfee County," he said. "You're going to be a nigger long as you stay in McAfee County. You could pass anywheres else." He was watching the cigarette smoke. "Anywheres," he said.

"Well?" she said. "What am I going to do that would make it stop?" She drew her hair back over her shoulder by moving her hand beside her neck. The light of the candle behind her made it more black and shiny-looking. Thick. "It's not me that needs to keep it going."

"And it doesn't hurt the business none, does it?" he said.

She looked at him for a long time, tapping her cigarette. "I always did hate a smartass," she said.

"Well," he said, "why don't you move out of McAfee County? Go down to Jacksonville, or Savannah, if it bothers you?"

"It don't bother *me* any," she said. "*You* the one seems to be bringing it up and wanting to talk about it."

"But *that* bothers you, don't it?" he said. "What about Brunswick, maybe? They got a navy base in Brunswick."

"You trying to get me some work lined up, John Fletcher?" she said. "Or you trying to get me straightened out? What the hell are you trying to do for me?"

"I was just thinking," said John Fletcher.

"I don't need no more business," she said. "I'm starting to walk spraddle-legged from the business I got now. Being a white nigger has got its advantages. It kind of helps keep everything under control. You know?"

"It ain't much of a life," he said.

"What ain't?" she said. "It's a hell of a life, buddy. If I was just a plain little white twat, with my looks I'd have been knocked up and married off ten years ago. I wouldn't have had no chance. By now I'd have me a house full of kids. Streaks on my belly from swelling up with them, and my tiddies sucked down so I'd be dumping them in my lap every time I sat down." She hugged her breasts, looking down at them. "No thank you," she said, putting out her cigarette, "I'm doing just fine."

"You'd make more money in a big town."

"I got to hire me an accountant to figure my income taxes now," she said. "If I went to Jacksonville, I'd be clapped up and out of business inside of six months. Don't do me no favors. And quit worrying what it's going to be like the day after tomorrow. You got *this* whole night ahead of you."

"But wouldn't it be better without all this nigger talk?"

"That's part of it," she said. "Besides, nobody don't bring it up but rarely, John Fletcher."

"I couldn't think what it would be like," he said.

"It ain't your problem," she said. "So why don't you just put it out of your mind?"

"But I just can't think what it would be like," he said.

Neither one of them said anything for a while. She kept looking at him, but he looked away.

"What the hell is it, John Fletcher?" she said. "You figure you got it coming for what you're going to pay for this here night of love?"

He didn't say anything.

"It ain't that much *to* being a nigger," she said. "Not if you don't look like one."

"But don't you worry none?" he said. "Think what you could have been."

"I could have been ugly," she said. "Now *there's* something to make you sweat."

145

He didn't answer.

"How much you figure on giving me, anyway?" she said.

"Forget about it," he said in a low voice, still not looking at her. "Just forget about I ever asked you."

"You going to lay another five on the twenty you was figuring on to make it all worth my while?" she said. "Or maybe you was going to start to fall in love with me to pay it off. Or propose to go and marry me until you leave and join the navy next week? Maybe it was going to be something really serious like that. How much was it going to be worth to you to hear me tell that story about my nigger grandmammy?" She counted off on her fingers. "My great, great, *great,* nigger grandmammy, Coretta?" She looked at him over the back of the chair, resting her chin on her arms. "Coretta was Colonel Fanshawe's nigger slave," she said. "For poontang in particular."

John Fletcher wasn't looking at her. He was looking at the pictures behind her.

"*Pure* nigger," she said.

He flicked his eyes at her, then away.

"It was December of 'sixty-four," she said. "Sherman was just about to come down and take Fort Moultrie." She stopped and looked at him. "Are you listening?" she said.

He looked at her.

"I ain't going to tell this but one time," she said. "Is it okay so far? That's the way you heard it, ain't it?"

He didn't say anything.

"It was December of 'sixty-four," she said, going on, "Colonel Fanshawe took Bascombe in—that was his youngest son, Bascombe—to let him blow his cherry on Coretta like the other three Fanshawe boys done before they went away to the war. Bascombe was fourteen years old," she said. She took a drag on her cigarette and put it out in the Stuckey ashtray. "She got took with his child."

"All right," said John Fletcher. He looked at her, then he looked away. "All *right,*" he said.

"But you ain't never heard *me* tell it," she said. "You're paying for it, ain't you?"

He didn't say anything.

"It was December of 'sixty-four. . . . I said that," she said. "Then

Fort Moultrie got took the next day by the Yankees, because the Colonel forgot they could come from behind where he couldn't aim his guns. So he had to surrender the fort. Then he took Bascombe into the magazine and blowed his brains out for him. Just before he blowed out his own brains." She paused. Them Fanshawes was a stupid bunch of farts," she said. "Too stupid to live, if you ask me. I hate to claim kin with a stupid bunch of farts like that."

"All *right*," said John Fletcher. He looked back at her again.

"You wanted it," she said. "What was it you was going to do for me to make it up? Something I wouldn't never forget? Was you going to pay me or thrill me, John Fletcher?"

"Excuse me," he said. His voice was low and courteous, the way he would ask her if there was something he could do for her. He stood up and leaned over toward her. Then his hand swept in a wide motion, coming around hard so that Nettie's head flicked under the impact of the blow. After he slapped her, her head didn't seem to have moved. She sat there staring at him over the back of the chair.

"Shit on your story, Nettie," he said. "I already heard it from everybody *but* you anyways."

"God damn," she said, lifting her hand to her cheek, touching it gently with the fingers. "God damn, you got a heavy hand, John Fletcher."

"Well," he said, not looking at her, "I'll give you five dollars extra." He lit a cigarette. "I'll give you five dollars extra, and I'll marry you to boot." He blew a big mouthful of smoke in her direction. "And if you try to tell me that goddamn story"—he blew another mouthful of smoke in her direction—"I'm going to beat your ass with a hairbrush and wash your mouth out with Octagon soap."

She looked at John Fletcher. "Let's get back in the bed," she said. "We was doing all right before all this ever come up."

John Fletcher looked at her. "Sit down," he said. "We'll get back in the bed directly. I ain't finished smoking my cigarette yet."

"Jesus Christ," said Nettie. "You're a crazy fucker, John Fletcher."

John Fletcher looked at her. She was feeling her cheek with the tips of her fingers.

"Don't call me that," he said.

147

"Well, you are," she said.

"I don't mean 'crazy,' " he said. "You can call me that. Only don't say 'fucker.' It don't sound right. You ain't got the face to say 'fucker.' "

"What the hell you think I am, John Fletcher? The Rose of Tralee or something? I been saying 'fucker' all my life."

"Well, just don't say it tonight where I can hear it," he said. "You ain't got the face for it. I'm paying you not to say it."

They looked at each other across the back of the chair for a while.

"And don't say 'shit' no more, either," he said. "I'm paying you not to say that too."

"You just got to hear me tell it, ain't you?" she said.

John Fletcher didn't say anything. ". . . Sometime," he said.

"You got any more of that wine?" she said. "I need me a drink."

"No," he said.

"Well, I can't just sit here not saying 'fucker,' " she said. "We got to *do* something."

He didn't answer.

"Come on," she said. "Let's dance." She stood up, reaching over and taking his hands to pull him up.

They danced a couple of slow ones. Then a fast one came on, and they had to go sit on the couch. While he was stooping to sit down, she stripped his shorts off down to his knees.

"Damn!" he said, standing up. "It sticks you, don't it?" He rubbed his backside where the coarse material on the couch had scratched him. Then he sat down, turning to the side slightly and raising his leg to cover himself.

"It's more fun, ain't it?" she said.

"Not yet," he said.

His shorts were still down around his ankles. She bent down, and he let her strip them off. She started to strip off his socks too.

"My feet're ugly," he said, holding her hand.

"But it looks funny," she said, "with just nothing but the socks."

"I could get another color," he said.

She looked at him without saying anything. Still bent over. He let go her hands, and she stripped them off. Then she got up onto the couch beside him and pulled him down on top of her. He tucked his feet down between the cushion and the arm of the couch so they wouldn't show.

"Second time is better," he said after a while.

"Yes," she said.

For a while they didn't say anything. Just lay there holding on and listening to the radio under the couch.

"You going in next week?" she said.

"What?" he said.

"The navy," she said. "You going in next week?"

"Thursday," he said.

"You'll like it," she said. "Navy boys has lots of fun."

"Poontang," he said.

"What?" she said.

"Poontang," he said. "I just had me some poontang."

She didn't say anything.

"I like that word," he said. "Pooooon—taaang."

"That's what you had, John Fletcher," she said. "Like the story says. It's true. I got to tell it to you sometime," she said. "Really tell you."

"Sometime," said John Fletcher. "Maybe I shouldn't have said that," he said.

She didn't say anything.

At two o'clock they had another cup of coffee. Then John Fletcher went and got the envelope, with her card and the check and the passes in it.

"What's this?" she said.

"It's for you," he said.

She opened the envelope and took out the card. The check and the passes fell out in her lap. She picked up the passes.

"Passes to the picture show?" she said.

"Extra," he said.

She looked at the check. "What's this?" she said.

"Your check," said John Fletcher.

"My check?" she said.

"Yes," he said.

"Where's the money?" she said.

149

"That's it," he said. "I made you a check."

"I don't want no check, buddy," she said. "Cash money. That's what I want."

John Fletcher looked at her. "I ain't got no cash money," he said.

"My business is always cash money," she said, holding out her palm and cutting across it with the edge of her other hand. "Right on the line," she said.

"I don't like that cash money," he said. "Not for this."

"Funny," she said. "I seem to of heard that before." She held out her hand, palm up. "Twenty-five dollars. Lay it right there."

"John Henry said twenty," he said.

"You said five extra," she said. "That's what the check says anyway." She held the check up for him to see.

"I was *giving* you that," he said. "Extra."

"I need the cash," she said.

"I just ain't got it," he said.

"You better have it," she said.

"The check is good," he said.

"Ain't they all?" she said.

"Well," he said, "what're we going to do? I ain't got it. I just ain't got it."

She looked at him a minute. She stood with her weight on one hip, her right hand extended palm up, her left holding her right elbow, bracing under her breasts. Then she turned and went to the couch, getting her things. He watched her as she got dressed.

"I'm going to get me some security," she said. "Not that I don't trust you, John Fletcher." She looked at him for a long minute. "Maybe one of your balls," she said. "Or that pretty little talleywacker of yours."

John Fletcher stood in the center of the room, one foot lapped over the other, covering it. His hands were clapsed in front, hanging down to cover himself there.

She turned on her heel and went to the couch. Getting down on her hands and knees, she reached under and pulled out the transistor radio. The farm-and-market man was back on. ". . . here's good news for hog growers . . . ," he said. She cut it off.

"This'll do for part of it," she said.

She looked around the room. "Jesus God, John Fletcher," she said. She looked at him. "I'm going to need me a bushel basket. Ain't you got nothing *little* that's worth something?" She looked at him for another long minute. "I mean besides your talleywacker," she said. She strode past him into the bedroom. John Fletcher stood there not moving, holding himself.

When she came back out of the bedroom, she had the cufflinks and tie pin in her hand. Also the black Swank wallet. She was holding the wallet open. "Five dollars," she said. "You're right. You ain't got that kind of money. Shit, John Fletcher, you ain't got no money at all." She took out the five and put it into the front of her dress. "For my tip," she said.

While she had been in the bedroom, John Fletcher had gotten his shorts and socks and put them on. He was standing by the couch.

"Turn on the light," she said.

He switched on the bourbon-bottle end-table lamp.

She put the things down on the card table and looked at them— totaling them up. "It ain't enough," she said.

"It cost more than twenty dollars," he said.

"Twenty-five," she said.

"You got the five," he said.

"I thought that was my tip," she said.

He didn't say anything.

"Anyway," she said, "it ain't worth it to me."

She looked at the things for a while. Then she looked at John Fletcher. She turned and went back into the bedroom. When she came out she had his coat.

John Fletcher took a step toward her. "Not the coat," he said.

She held out her hand to stop him. "You'll get it back when you pay me," she said. "It's just for security. Believe me, I'd rather have the money—even if it was real."

"I'll pay you in the morning," he said.

"You'll get your stuff back in the morning," she said.

She put the things in the pockets of the coat, then slung it over her shoulder and started out the door.

151

"Wait," said John Fletcher.

She stopped and looked at him. "That's all," she said. "You ain't all of a sudden found you some money, have you?"

"Take the card," he said. He picked it up off the table and handed it to her.

She looked at him from the doorway. "Save it for Valentine's," she said.

He held the card out, looking at her. "It's for you," he said.

"I don't want it," she said.

He slipped the passes out of the envelope and held them out to her. "Take these anyways," he said.

She looked at him.

"Give them to John Henry if you don't want to use them," he said.

She stood at the door while he came over and gave them to her. After she took them and put them into the pocket of the coat, she started out the door.

"Maybe I'll see you again," he said.

"I'd better see you in the morning," she said.

"Yes," he said. "Maybe when I come home from the navy."

She looked at him, holding back the screen. "Maybe," she said. "If you save up your money. Ain't all poontang cheap."

"I'll see you in the morning," he said.

"Yes," she said. "You'd better . . ."

Then he thought about the other present he had gotten for her. "Wait," he said.

"What?" she said.

"What would you say about a chocolate-covered cherry?" he said.

She looked at him hard for a minute. "Good night . . . white boy," she said.

She went out the door, letting the screen slam shut behind her.

Six days later he himself walked out of the door to catch the bus for Jacksonville and the navy.

The first move was to the south, but all those that came after were to the west. The remainder of his short life consisted of a series of removes, each more Hesperian than the last.

Great Lakes Naval Training Station and Chicago . . . San Francisco . . . San Diego . . . Tijuana . . . Honolulu . . . Guam . . . At each stopping place he found someone—some girl, each more exotic than the last—who would dally with him at a sailor's price.

A mulatto whore in a red-headed wig in Chicago. In San Francisco a girl who claimed distant Kiowa ancestry, and wore a headband to prove it. A Nisei waitress in San Diego, who kept a naked Samurai sword across the foot of her bed, and made him beat her with the flat of the blade before she would have intercourse with him. A *mestiza* that he bought out of a Tijuana bar (she slept with him one time, and gave him his first dose of clap—he felt a kind of gentle affection for her on account of it). In Honolulu a Chinese girl with a speech impediment. And on Guam a gentle, sarong-wearing Micronesian, who seemed to come to him always fresh from the sea, wearing a hibiscus in her hair.

He missed most of the fine points. But he had the sense that the tendency was the right one. Westering. The Pacific. It was the place he had always wanted to be—in atavistic flight from civilization, like a color-blind Gauguin, without brush or canvas.

Through the whole journey he carried the recollection of Nettie Oatley's honey-yellow eye. Flitting in the darkness of his mind like a spectral firefly, leading him on, to strand and beach him under the high, flaking ceiling of the ward of a navy hospital, set on a green-and-purple island in the middle of the Great South Sea.

As he was lying on the bed in the ward, Nettie's eye would rise behind his retina. A gigantic golden circle—green-flecked, with a center velvet black—like the mouth of a tunnel of love, into which he glided on a float shaped like a swan. Through the yellow gate and into the velvet darkness. The light going away as he drifted through . . . gray . . . gray . . .

. . . the bubble turned slowly, quivering, compressing and elongating as it rose . . . turning gray in the pale green-gray liquid . . . a thick, steady movement . . .

"Seamanwillistonseamanwillistonseamanwilliston . . ." The voice went dying away.

. . . he cartwheeled slowly . . . holding to the bubble . . .

Lewis Grizzard

Good Men of God

BROTHER DAVE GARDNER, the southern philosopher, used to talk about how his mother had wanted him to be a man of God.

"My mother used to say, 'Son, you could make a million dollars preaching,' " he would begin. "I'd say, 'Yeah, Mama, but what the hell would I spend it on?' "

It's not easy being a preacher, especially these days. Preachers have to work harder than ever before keeping their flocks in line what with temptations at a new all-time high. I suppose the really big-time preachers, like Billy Graham and Oral Roberts and Jerry Falwell, have it made, though. Every time I pick up a newspaper there's a story about one of those heavyweight television preachers making a trip to Russia, or speaking out on international issues, or having a vision that tells him to go out and raise a few million bucks.

I always wonder when those guys find time to work on their sermons. When do they visit the sick and marry people and preach funerals?

Who mows the grass around their churches, and if one of their followers has a problem, like he lost his job and his wife split and his trailer burned all in the same week, when do those preachers have time to go talk to the poor soul?

I'm old-fashioned when it comes to preachers. I grew up in a small Methodist congregation, and I got used to preachers who were always there when you needed them, who mowed the grass around the church, and who even knocked down the dirt daubers' nests in the windows of the sanctuary so the dirt daubers wouldn't bother the

154

worshippers while the preacher was trying to run the devil out of town on Sunday mornings. Every time I see Billy Graham on Meet the Press or catch Oral Roberts or Jerry Falwell on the tube, I always wonder if they have ever knocked down any dirt daubers' nests. Every time I see any of those high-powered evangelists, I also wonder whatever happened to Brother Roy Dodd Hembree, who tried but never quite made it over the hump into the land of evangelical milk and honey.

Brother Roy Dodd came to town every summer when I was a kid with his traveling tent revival and his two daughters, Nora and Cora. Nora was the better looking of the two, but Cora had more sense. Nora would do just about anything, including get bad drunk and then tell her daddy what local bird dog had bought her the beer. Brother Roy Dodd would then alert the sheriff's office in whatever county he happened to be preaching in at the time and demand the heathen buying Nora beer be locked up for the duration of his revival as a means of protecting his daughters.

Neither Nora nor Cora needed much protection, if the truth be known. Nora could cuss her way out of most any tight spot, and Cora had a black belt in switchblade.

Brother Roy Dodd's tent revival was the highlight of our summer, not only because of the opportunities Nora and Cora afforded, but also because Brother Roy Dodd put on a show that was in thrills and sheer excitement second only to the geek who bit the heads off live chickens at the county fair each fall.

They said Brother Roy Dodd was from over in Alabama and he used to be a Triple-A country singer until he got messed up with a woman one night in a beer joint where he was singing. The woman did a lot of winking and lip-pooching at Brother Roy Dodd during his act, and later, she told him her husband had gone to Shreveport to pick up a load of chickens and wouldn't be home until Saturday morning and there was still an hour or so left in Thursday.

Brother Roy Dodd, they said, knew there was trouble when, as he and the woman were in the midst of celebrating Friday night, he detected a poultry-like odor about the room. That was just before he heard two gunshots. Brother Roy Dodd caught one in each hip and it was shortly after the shooting, he found the Lord.

155

When he had recovered from his injuries, Brother Roy Dodd bought a tent and an old school bus and set out to spread the Word and his interpretation of it with a Bible he borrowed from his hospital room.

One night in Palatka, Florida, Brother Roy Dodd converted fourteen, including a young woman who had done some winking and lip-poaching of her own during the service.

After the service, Brother Roy Dodd confirmed the fact his winking and lip-poaching convert had no husband nor any connection with the business of transporting chickens, and asked the young woman if she would like to leave Palatka behind her. She consented and they said Brother Roy Dodd married himself to her, standing right there in the sawdust.

Her name was Dora. Hence, Nora and Cora. Dora learned to play piano and accompany Brother Roy Dodd when he sang the hymn of invitation each night, "Just As I Am (Without One Plea)," but Nora and Cora strayed early. Nora was smoking when she was nine, drinking when she was eleven, and she ran off one night with a sawmill hand from Boaz, Alabama, when she was thirteen, but came back three weeks later, with his truck and the $50 he gave her to leave.

Cora was a couple of years younger than Nora and they said she had taken after her daddy as far as music went, but she had a wild side, too, and learned how to knife fight the year she spent in reform school when she was fourteen. Her crime was lifting the wallet out of a deputy sheriff's trousers, the pair he shouldn't have taken off in the back seat of his cruiser out behind the tent one night during a revival near Swainsboro, Georgia.

My older cousin took me to see Brother Roy Dodd the first time. I was nine. My cousin was sixteen and he had a car. Everybody else came to find the Lord. My cousin came to find Nora and Cora, which he did. I said I could find a ride home, and the next day, he told me how Nora had taken drunk later that night and how Cora had tried to cut a man for looking at her wrong.

"I never heard such cussing as Nora did," my cousin said.

"You ought to have heard her daddy," I said.

I had never heard anybody speak in tongues before I heard Brother

Roy Dodd. He was up in front of everybody and he was rolling forth out of Galatians, when, suddenly, he was caught in the spirit.

His eyes rolled back in his head and his voice boomed out through the tent:

"ALIDEEDOO! ALUDEEDOO! BOOLEYBOOLEYBOOLEY-BOO!"

"Praise God, he's in the spirit!" said a woman behind me.

"Praise God, he is!" said her husband.

"Don't reckon Brother Roy Dodd's sick, do you?" asked another man, obviously a first-timer.

Brother Roy Dodd tongue-spoke for a good six or eight minutes before the spirit finally left him and he went back to talking so you could understand what he was saying.

Brother Roy Dodd explained that the "tongue" was a gift only a blessed few received. I asked the Lord to forgive me, but I was deeply hopeful at that moment I would never be so blessed. I was afraid I might get in the spirit and never get out.

A couple of years later, there was some more excitement at Brother Roy Dodd's revival. In the middle of one of Brother Roy Dodd's sermons, a man stood up in the back and shouted, "Brother Roy Dodd! Have you ever taken up the serpent?"

Brother Roy Dodd said he hadn't.

"Would you take up the serpent to prove your faith?" asked the man.

"Never been asked to," answered Brother Roy Dodd.

"Well, I'm asking you now!" bellowed the man, who rushed toward the pulpit with a wrinkled brown sack in his hand. He dumped the contents of the sack at Brother Roy Dodd's feet and the crowd gasped. Out of the sack came a cottonmouth moccasin of some size. The snake did not appear to be overjoyed with the fact it was currently involved in a religious experience.

I knew all about taking up the serpent. It had been in the papers. There was a sect that believed a certain passage of the Bible beseeched a man to hold a snake to prove his faith. The papers had a story about a man who had been bitten recently by a timber rattler during services over at a church in Talbot County. The faithless scoundrel nearly died.

157

Brother Roy Dodd wasted little time in dealing with the snake. He picked up a metal folding chair in front of the piano, the one his wife Dora had vacated immediately upon seeing the snake, and beat hell and guts out of it.

When the snake was no longer moving, Brother Roy Dodd picked it up and held it before the stunned crowd.

"Shame I didn't have a chance to save this bellycrawling sinner before the Lord called him home," said Brother Roy Dodd.

The crowds began falling off for Brother Roy Dodd as the years passed. He added a healing segment to his performance to try to pick things up.

Miss Inez Pickett, a stout woman in her late fifties, came to see Brother Roy Dodd one night, complaining of what women used to call "the old mess," some sort of kidney disorder that was usually only whispered about.

Brother Roy Dodd, dressed in a sequin jacket he'd held on to since his singing days, asked Miss Inez where it hurt.

"My back," said Miss Inez.

Brother Roy Dodd put his hands firmly on Miss Inez's back and shook her kidneys with great force as he prayed.

"Did you feel that, Sister Inez?" asked Brother Roy Dodd.

"Lord Godamighty, I think I did!" shouted Miss Inez.

"You're healed!" said Brother Roy Dodd.

Miss Inez, plagued by her infirmity for many years, bounded about the platform in the manner of a much younger woman and made a number of joyful noises. I was afraid she was going to break into tongue.

Instead, she fell off the platform in her excitement, and you could hear the bone snap in her leg.

"Somebody call an ambulance!" the first one to her said.

"No need to do that," said somebody else. "Just get Brother Roy Dodd to give her another healing."

"Don't do no broke bones," said Brother Roy Dodd. "Just vital organs."

I was sixteen the summer Brother Roy Dodd didn't come back anymore. We heard all sorts of things. Nora and Cora left him for good, they said. Dora, his wife, got sick and couldn't play piano anymore. There was even something about a sheriff down in Mississippi someplace finding some white liquor on Brother Roy Dodd's bus.

That was a long summer, that summer Brother Roy Dodd didn't come back. We just sort of sat around and waited for fall and the fair and the geek who bit the heads off live chickens.

William Price Fox

Doug Broome, Hamburger King

OUT UNDER THE red and green and the yellow fast-food neon that circles Columbia, like Mexican ball fringe, Doug Broome was always famous. As an eight-year-old curb hop, he carried a pair of pliers for turning down the edges of license plates on the non-tipping cars; he was already planning ahead. He grew up during the Depression in the kerosene-lit bottom one block from the cotton mill and two from the State Penitentiary. When he was nine, his father went out for a loaf of bread and, in storybook fashion, returned eighteen years later. Doug left school in the fourth grade, worked his way up from curb boy at the Pig Trail Inn out on the Broad River Road, to Baker's on Main Street, and finally to his own restaurants all over town.

There was a "Doug's" on Lady Street and, while I was still in junior high, he hired me on the sandwich board and the big grill. He taught me how to stay on the duckboards to keep from getting shin splints, how to make an omelet, and a hundred things behind the counter that made life easier. I copied his freewheeling moves with the spatula and the French knife, his chopping technique on onions, and his big takeaway when he sliced a grilled cheese or buttered toast. He also introduced a lot of us to the ten-hour day, the twelve-hour split shift, and the killer twenty-four hour rollover. Somehow he thought we all had his energy.

Doug Broome had energy, incredible energy. It may be the kind you see in skinny kids playing tag in a rainstorm or the stuff that comes with Holy Roller madness. He had black curly hair, bright blue eyes, wore outrageous clothes, and every year had the first straw-

160

berry Cadillac convertible in Columbia. When he was young he won the jitterbug contests all over town, taking shots at everything Gene Kelly was doing in the movies. He was wild with clothes. With cars. With women. Some of his checks may still be bouncing. To investors coming to town on business with him, Doug was a mystery, a threat. His pink-piped matching shirt and slacks and his lightning ways with money scared them off. To them, a bounced check or a bankruptcy judgment or a stack of subpoenas was like the neck bell and the tin plate of the leper, but in Doug's empire this was only his way of doing business. And Doug had an empire. He became the father he never had for his family, his help, and his friends. He worked them, loved them, punished them. Sometimes he would sit down and list the problems he was having with them. Someone was getting married before they were divorced, or divorced without benefit of attorney. Some couple would leave for a Stone Mountain honeymoon with the back seat stacked to the window level with Doug's beer and the trunk loaded down with Virginia hams and cigarettes. Someone was always running off with a friend's wife or husband, getting drunk, wrecking the wrong car, and getting locked up. And a few of the more spectacular cases managed to do everything at once.

Doug would just grin and say, "We're just one great big old family out here, mashing out hamburgers and making friends." When they were in jail, Doug bailed them out. When drunk, sobered them up, and when in trouble or sick, he gave them his lawyer and his doctor. He never took them off the payroll. They stole a little, but Doug with some sixth sense knew about how much and made them work longer hours. It was a good relationship, and when the unions came around to organize, Doug's people would just laugh and say they'd already been organized.

One day he told me, "Billy, these chain operations are ruining the hamburger. Ruining it. Most of them come from up north to begin with, so what in the hell they know about cooking? Any fool right off the street will tell you the minute you freeze hamburger you ain't got nothing. God Almighty, you slide one of those three-ouncers out of a bun and throw it across the room and it *will sail.* I ain't lying, that's how thin that thing is." He was eating his own Doug Broome Doubleburger. "Now you take this half-pound baby.

161

I don't care what you think you could do to it, there ain't no way in the world you can make it any better. No way. I use the finest ground meat there is. The finest lettuce, the finest tomatoes, and onions, and Billy, I fry this piece of meat in the finest grease money can buy. These chains are getting their meat up out of Mexico. Ain't no telling what's in it. Hell, I read that in a government magazine."

He went on about how he had gunned down the "Big Boy" franchise when it rolled into South Carolina. "Everybody in town knows I've always called my hamburger, 'Big Boy.' You used to serve them. Am I right or am I wrong?" He didn't wait for an answer. "Anyhow, they'd already steamrolled across everything west of the goddamn Mississippi. And here they come heading across Tennessee. Then across Alabama. Then across Georgia. But when they hit that South Carolina line, I said 'Whoa now! You ain't franchising no Big Boy in here because I am already the Big Boy. Gentlemen, you and me are going to the courts.' And that's what we did. They brought in a wheelbarrow of money and eight or nine Harvard Jew lawyers, and all I had going for me was my good name. And Billy, we beat them to death. I mean to death. They had to pay me sixty thousand dollars, all the court costs, and everything." He paused and sipped his coffee. "Well, you know I never like to kick a man when he's down, and those boys had all that money tied up in promos and 'Big Boy' neon, so I say 'Okay, y'all give me another ten thousand dollars and you can have the franchise, and I'll change my "Big Boy" to "Big Joy." ' "

I knew a few of the facts. "Come on, Doug."

And then he raised his hand to Heaven.

"Boy, why would I tell a lie about something like that?"

Part of the story was true. Outside on North Main the old "Big Boy" read "Big Joy." But the eight or nine Harvard lawyers turned out to be one old retainer out of Charlotte. The sixty thousand dollars was right, but it went the other way; Doug had been the infringer and had to pay them. The ten thousand dollars never existed. Doug was like that. Like all great storytellers, he was a consummate liar. A straight tale would be transformed into a richer, wilder mixture, and the final version, while sometimes spellbinding and always logical, would have absolutely nothing to do with the truth.

But I remember one crazy night on Harden Street. We were in

162

the kitchen. It was July. It was hot. Oral Roberts was in town. He was still lean and hungry and doing Pentecostal tent shows. "No! I'm not going to heal you! Jesus is! Jesus Christ is going to heal you! So I want you to place both hands on your television set. And I want you to pray along with me. And if you ain't got a television set, place your hands on your radio. And if you ain't got a radio, any electrical appliance will do."

At the air-conditioned eight-thousand-seat tent, it had been standing-room-only, and every soaring soul had descended on Doug's for hamburgers, barbecues, steak sandwiches, fries, and onion rings. Doug and I were on the big grill, the broilers, the Fryolaters. Lonnie was on the fountain. Betty Jean, under a foot-high, silver-tinted bee-hive, was on the counter and the cash register. The parking lot was jammed and another hundred cars were cruising in an Apache circle looking for a slot. In the kitchen the grease was so thick we had to salt down the duckboards to keep from slipping. The heat was a hundred and twenty degrees and rising. The grill was full. The broilers were full. There was no more room. There was no more time. We had lost track of what was going out and what was coming in. Horns were blowing. Lights were flashing. The curb girls and Betty Jean were pounding on the swinging doors, screaming for hamburgers, barbecues, steak sandwiches, anything. And then suddenly there was another problem. A bigger problem. The revivalists were tipping with religious tracts and pewter coins stamped with scriptural quotations.

The girls were furious. "One of them gave me a goddamn apple! Look! Look at it!"

And what did Doug Broome do? I'll tell you what he did. He stripped off his apron and pulled Betty Jean out from behind the counter. Then he triggered "The Honeydripper" on the juke. No one could believe what Doug was doing. He was dancing and Betty Jean was doing red-hot little solo kicks on his breaks. When the song ended, he announced that everyone was getting a twenty-five dollar bonus for working the Pentecostals, who had scriptural support for their stand on no-tipping. Then Doug flipped on the public address system and sang out over the cars and the neon and the night, "Ladies and gentlemen and boys and girls, I'd like to take this opportunity to remind you that you are now eating at one of the most famous drive-ins in the great Southeast. Our specialties are hamburgers, barbecues, and our famous steak sandwich, which is served with lettuce and to- mato, carrot curls, pickle chips, and a side of fries, all for the price of one-dollar-and-forty-nine-cents. And when you get home tonight and tell your friends about our fine food and fast service, please don't forget to mention that we have been internationally recognized by none other than Mister Duncan Hines himself. . . . . I thank you." Then tying on his apron and angling his cap, he came back to the grill and with some newer, faster, wilder speed I'd never seen, he caught the crest and broke it.

Doug had style, but it wasn't until years later that I realized what a profound effect it had on me. I was on a New York talk show hustling a novel. The host had led me down the garden path in the warm- up, promising we'd discuss pole beans and the price of cotton. But when the camera light came on, his voice dropped into low and mean- ingful. We discussed the Mythic South, the Gothic South, Faulkner's South, and the relevance of the agrarian metaphor. I was a complete disaster. All I wanted was out. And then he asked how I would define style. It was a high pitch right across the letters, and I dug in and took a full cut. I told him about one day during a lunch rush at Doug's on Harden Street. There had been a dozen customers on the horseshoe counter and a man came in and ordered a cheese om- elet. I'd never made one before, but I'd watched Doug do it. I chopped the cheese, broke three eggs into a shake can, added milk, and hung it on the mixer. Then I poured it out on the big grill. I'd used too much milk and it shot out to the four corners getting ready to burn there in twenty seconds. I almost panicked. Then I remembered Doug's long, smooth moves with the spatulas and pulled them out of the rack like Smith and Wesson .44s. I began rounding it up.

As I worked, I flexed my elbows and dipped my knees and did a little two-beat rhythm behind my teeth. I kept singing, kept moving, and just at the critical moment I folded it over, tucked it in, and slid it onto the plate. Then with parsley bouquets on the ends, and toast points down the sides, I served it with one of Doug's long flour- ishes and stepped back.

The man forked off an end cut. He chewed it slowly and closed his eyes in concentration. Then he laid his fork down, and with both hands on the counter, he looked me in the eye. "Young man," he said, "that's the finest omelet I've ever put in my mouth."

I wound up telling the stunned interviewer that *that* was style, and all you can do is point at it when you see it winging by and maybe listen for the ricochet. I don't think he understood, but I knew I did. I knew that style wasn't an exclusive property in the aristocracy of the arts. A jockey, a shortstop, a used-car salesman, or even a mechanic grinding valves can have it, and the feather-trimmed hookers working the curbs along Gervais and Millwood are not without it. But Doug Broome not only had it, he knew he had it, and he staged it with wild clothes and great music, and he backlighted it with red and yellow and purple flashing neon.

Well, Doug's gone now, and with him goes his high-pitched voice on the p.a. and the nights and the music and the great curb girls out on Harden Street who got us all in trouble. He's gone and with him go those irreplaceable primary parts of Columbia that shimmered out there under the cartoon-colored neon. There will be no buildings or interstate cut-offs named for him, nor will there be a chandeliered Doug Broome Room at The Summit Club. But some nights out on North Main or Harden or Rosewood, when the moon's right and the neon's right, and a juke box is thumping out some sixties jump or Fats Domino is up on "Blueberry Hill," it will be impossible not to see him sliding doubleburgers and Sunday beers in milkshake cups down the counter. And if you're as lucky as a lot of us who knew him, you'll probably see him pinch the curb girl at the pick-up window and give her that big smile and say, "Baby Doll, remember there's no such thing as a small Coke."

165

Harry Crews

Tuesday Night with Cody, Jimbo, and a Fish of Some Proportion

CODY CAME INTO the bar sometime before midnight with a big brown paper sack in one hand and an open can of Pearl in the other, shouting that he'd just caught a bass, a big one.

"Damn thing must go twelve, fourteen pounds," he called down the bar, waving the sack and signaling the bartender for another Pearl. Then: "Hell, give everybody another drink. I feel good . . . gooooood!" He threw back his head and howled the last word like a dog cutting a hot trail.

While Mac was putting up another round, Jimbo, a tall, big-jawed boy about Cody's age, said: "Git it outen the sack then and let's all have a look."

Cody set his new Pearl down on the bar and reached into the sack.

" 'Fore you even bring it out, though," said Jimbo, "I got two one-dollar bills says whatever you got in there don't weigh ten pound." He looked around at the other five or six guys sitting with him and winked broadly, showing his blunt, widely spaced teeth. "Probably ain't even a bass."

Cody stopped with his hand in the sack. "Don't try to ruin my fun, Jimbo."

"I ain't tryin' to ruin nothing. You want my two dollars or not? Ain't nobody else gone take it. Know you probably got a speck in there, or maybe a catfish."

Cody still hadn't taken his hand out of the sack. "You tryin' to ruin my fun?"

"One thing I noticed," said Jimbo. "Ever' time you git drunk, your fish git heavier. I just thought to make myself two dollars."

Cody wasn't drunk, but he was drinking pretty good for a Tuesday night. If I'd been inclined to do it, though, I would've offered the bet myself, because that paper sack didn't look like it had twelve pounds of fish in it. But I hadn't known these boys long, and it wouldn't do to act pushy. Besides, as short a time as I'd been around them, I knew it was a very private thing that was going on between Cody and Jimbo. They were good friends, had been for years, and out of a great respect and mutual admiration they often locked up toe to toe and beat each other severely about the head and shoulders.

The first night I'd started drinking in the bar, Jimbo had shown Cody his knife in an argument that started over whether they were going to watch Loretta Lynn on the television or listen to Johnny Rodriguez on the jukebox. Nobody'd been cut, but Cody did manage to loosen Jimbo's earlobe with a shot in the side of the head with a half-empty beer pitcher. It did not surprise me at all to see them two nights later drinking together. They were laughing and playing a Grit version of the dozens with each other. The only sign of their TV-jukebox thrash was a nasty clot of blood on Jimbo's ear.

"There's mine, sumbitch, if you even *got* two dollars," said Cody.

When Jimbo got his money on the bar, Cody whipped his big-mouth bass out of the sack. There was a discreet silence along the row of stools. Cody glanced from the silent faces to his fish and back again.

Jimbo said: "That fish has lost weight."

As if on signal, the stools scraped back and everybody headed for the little room in back where Mac kept a scale he used for weighing barbecue and roast beef. Cody threw the fish on the scale, and the needle swung and held at nine-and-a-half pounds.

"It's something wrong with that scale," said Cody.

"Mac, is it something wrong with that scale?" asked Jimbo.

Mac, a great bartender: "I don't *think* it's anything wrong with that scale, but I ain't ready to say one way or the other if it's right or if it's wrong."

"You owe me two dollars, boy," said Jimbo.

"Wait a minute," said Cody, chewing for all he was worth. "How many is it here thinks this scale is right?"

Before it was all out of his mouth—because we could see what was coming—everybody had headed back to the bar, including Mac. We sat down and sipped the round Cody had bought and listened to them shouting over the scale in the little room behind us.

I sat there drinking a vodka and feeling good, feeling the way a man does when he knows he's home. A month earlier I'd moved off Lake Swan, where I'd lived for five years. The move meant I had to give up Lonnie's Tavern in Putnam Hall and find a new place to sit and drink while thinking over my little ball of wax. So I searched out Mac's place the way other men might search out the right wife or the right church. No blasphemy intended, but I learned a long time ago that for many of us *where* we drink is more important than *what* we drink, more important even than *if* we drink, because a bar that's right is a place you can go and sit for hours in the friendly supportive dark, sipping warm Coke and eating endless bags of fried hogskins, greasing and regreasing your stomach after some mild outrage in the same bar the night before.

Such a bar should never be crowded. If a bar's crowded, you know immediately it's no good because there are never enough people who know a good bar from a bad bar to cause a crowd. A crowded bar always pours a lot of things like Tequila Sunrises and Black Russians, drinks that have nothing to do with the pleasures of whiskey.

Not too long ago, I was drinking whiskey with Madison Jones in Alabama and a boy at the table ordered a Bloody Mary. When it came, Madison watched the thing for a moment and said: "What's in one of them, anyhow?"

The boy said: "Well, it's a little tomato juice and a little Worcestershire sauce and some salt and just a touch or two of Tabasco and. . . ."

"You put a little hamburger in that you'd have a whole meal, wouldn't you?" Madison said.

Just so. Whiskey with food is fine, but putting whiskey and food in more or less equal amounts in the same glass is uncivilized. And just as uncivilized is a bar that has things in it that are too new. Formica or chrome won't do unless it has been dinged so many times and encrusted so deeply with the leavings of countless nights that it is unrecognizable. Say it's sentimental or romantic or silly, but I'm convinced nothing new will work with whiskey because whiskey is never new. It's old and it likes old things.

Once when I was a boy, my uncle and I drove to the county line to have a drink. I'd never been to the place where he took us, a plain place with uncovered wooden floors and heavy wooden tables with benches instead of chairs. We bought a bottle and sat down with it. Being young and inexperienced in such matters, I proceeded to tell my uncle that he ought to try going to a bar I'd been to several times on the other side of the county because it was closer to home. What I hadn't stopped to consider was that while it was closer, it was also filled full of glass and plastic and other shiny things.

My uncle set it all straight by snorting through his nose and saying: "I was over there about two years ago the first time. Last time, too. I'd as soon drink my whiskey in a drugstore."

Cody had finally paid Jimbo the two dollars, which Jimbo spent on several of Mac's pickled eggs, half of which Cody ate himself while Jimbo shouted to the rest of the bar to watch *by dammit* what Cody was doing. Watching them was a whole lot better than watching TV, because even though they were playing, it was play with blood in it. They were deadly earnest and by now fairly deadly drunk.

Shortly after midnight they began to discuss the merits of their pickup trucks. Jimbo pretty much wanted to limit the conversation to the last two pulls they'd had, because he had won them both. But Cody kept pointing to the record of total pulls printed on tablet paper hanging from a nail behind the bar. The tablet paper clearly showed that out of twenty-two pulls, Cody had won fifteen of them.

"You ain't got the reflexes of my granny," Cody said. "An' that poor ole lady's been dead four years."

That apparently was enough to do it. They bet ten dollars and headed for the parking lot. The rest of us, including Mac, followed them outside, where they backed their pickups tailgate to tailgate. The parking lot was an empty field about three acres big with an

169

oak tree in the center of it. We stood under the oak tree smoking and drinking while Cody and Jimbo fastened the two trucks together with logging chains. Some of the men laid off small bets on one or the other of the trucks.

One of the men went over to drop a white handkerchief for the start. Cody and Jimbo were both in the cabs of their trucks, engines whining, peaked out. They watched the white handkerchief in their rearview mirrors, and when the handkerchief dropped, they popped their clutches and the trucks fishtailed and disappeared in rooster tails of dust that rose two stories high.

Unlike horse pulling, there are no rules in pickup pulling. Somebody has to ask, often *beg,* for it to stop. He has to scream out of the window that he's been *beat!* And also scream whatever else the other guy might want him to.

Cody still had his mind on the fish. He was dragging Jimbo around and around the field at what looked to be about twenty miles an hour, scattering us from under the oak tree like a covey of quail, as he leaned out of the window with the bloated fish by the tail and screamed: "How big's the goddamn fish, Jimbo?"

Jimbo was spinning for all he was worth, but he could find no traction, none at all. He finally—when it looked like he was about to be thrown over—stuck his white face out of the cab window. "Beat!" he croaked. "Beat! I been beat! *Beeeaatt.*"

Every time Jimbo shouted he was beaten Cody seemed to haul him around the field a little faster, and from Cody's raging face came the maniacal demand: "How big? How big's my goddamn fish?"

Jimbo was totally out of it now. He fought the wheel, trying to keep it right as Cody seemed to find a little more speed.

Finally: "Ten! Ten!" shouted Jimbo, almost losing his truck in a tight turn.

"How big?"

"Twelve!"

"How big?"

Now Jimbo made it a question, a hysterical question: "Fourteen? Is it fourteen, Cody? Fourteen?"

Cody lightened up, and they came to a stop in the swirling dust. He got out of his truck swinging his fish like a bell. He'd stopped

170

chewing his teeth, and his eyes had gone suddenly sane. He walked back to Jimbo's truck and said: "Yep, I think fourteen'll do her."

Jimbo came bellowing out of the truck, and they would've probably locked up right there if we hadn't got between them. Jimbo was yelling that Cody had weighted his truck, put weight on it, and by God he'd find it.

Cody, his face flushed and his mouth beginning to chew again, said: "It's virgin. My truck's virgin, Jimbo. Don't say nothing about my truck."

"Weighted!"

"Virgin!"

It was a standoff, and God knows what would've happened if Cody, like a lot of other men before him, hadn't let victory overload his tongue. He suddenly blurted: "My pickup can pull your logger. Bring that logging truck down here and this little old GMC'll cut the nuts off it." He reached over and patted the rear fender of his truck the way men in an earlier time patted the withers of their best horse.

Jimbo calmed right down. His voice was sweet as a baby's after a warm bottle. "Pull my logger?"

Cody did a little shuffle in the dust. "This little old GMC *wants* that logger."

"My logger's settin' dead on ready."

"Git it."

Jimbo turned on his heel, got in his truck, and spun out of the lot. We stood watching him leave. The truck he was going for had once been used to haul logs to the pulpwood mill. Jimbo had converted it to take watermelons to Cordele, Georgia. Both Cody and Jimbo worked with their daddies on two of the biggest watermelon farms in North Florida, the watermelon capital of the world. Years of tossing thirty-pound melons up to a man on a high-sided truck from first light to first dusk had given them bodies so keyed up, coiled, and ready to strike that if they weren't actually heaving melons, they literally did not know what to do, how to act. The problem resolved itself in random violence full of joy and love masquerading as anger. Nobody ever said it, but everybody knew it. It was this knowledge that gave the senseless, meaningless, childish moments late at night a certain and very real dignity.

171

We had time to go back into the bar and have a drink and eat bloody roast beef sandwiches on rye with a little mustard. Mustard is allowed in a good bar, but there is never any mayonnaise. Mayonnaise won't do. And it cannot be explained. Either you know right off that mayonnaise doesn't belong in a bar or you can never know. The absence of mayonnaise in a good bar is a part of the natural order of things, like a rock falling *down* when you turn it loose instead of falling sideways.

We heard the logging truck and got outside while Jimbo was still backing up to Cody's pickup, smiling and whistling something that was not a song.

"Wanta go for twenty?" said Jimbo. "That way I'll get my ten back and you'll only be down ten yourself."

"Make it light on yourself," said Cody.

They got in their trucks, and the handkerchief was dropped. Cody popped the clutch on his pickup, and when he hit the end of the chain, he came to a dead and sudden stop as though he'd been chained to the oak tree in the center of the lot. Jimbo looked at him through the rear window and then moved off slowly with little more trouble than he might have had if he'd been pulling away from the curb. Cody's truck was spinning and whining, but Jimbo, now and then showing his quietly vicious smile in the rear window, wound out across the field without even breaking traction. When he took second, he didn't even grind the gears, and by the time he went through the first tight turn—slinging the pickup through an arc of about seventy-five feet—he must have been doing twenty-five or thirty. In the middle of the arc, Cody stuck his head out and screamed: "Whoa! Wwwwhhhoooaaa!"

But Jimbo didn't slow down, and he didn't look back anymore. He dragged Cody all over the lot, and when he tired of that, he dragged him across the highway, hitting the median as he went, blowing one of Cody's front tires. Cody gave up trying to control his pickup and leaned out of the window instead, confessing everything he could think of to confess: that he was beaten, that his fish was a runt, that *he* was a runt, and that his pickup was, too. Jimbo finally got enough of whatever he was after and brought Cody back across the highway and stopped under the oak tree. When they got out of their trucks, they were both soaked with sweat and very sober. Cody still carried his fish by the tail as he came to lean on the fender of the logging truck with Jimbo.

"That was a ride," said Cody.

"It's not just the sort of thing a man'd want to do ever' night."

Cody seemed to see the fish in his hand for the first time. He half-turned and laid it on the hood of the logging truck. And that's where he left it as the two of them—without ever taking the chains off their trucks parked there under the oak tree—went back into the bar.

Marion Montgomery

I Got a Gal

IT WAS NEARLY eight o'clock and the August sun was already
hot behind the chinaberry tree when he got water in the A-model
and called Sara to come on and get in. She didn't answer. He stood
in the shade leaning on the spare tire waiting a minute. Then he
went over to where he could look in the window. He couldn't see
in the dim room at first.

"It's time we was going," he said. A fly cleaned its hind legs on
the window sill, pointing its rear at him.

"I know it."

"Well, you'd better hurry up," he said. He could make out the
back of her head a little. Sitting in front of the mirror brushing that
long wavy hair again.

"You can just wait, Jim Patterson," she said, "because I'm not
a-going till I get myself ready."

The fly he was watching crawled out of the edge of shade to
where another one was dozing on the bleached pine window sill,
and then both went whirling out into the sunlight. A year ago he
would have already been in town by this time, but that was before
they had to have the car. That was when they drove Tilly and his
daddy's buggy the ten miles. But that wasn't for long after they got
married.

He walked over and threw the empty bucket down beside the well
curbing and wiped his hands on an old rag. First of all, he had slept
late. That was what Sara said they could do once they got a car.
They wouldn't have to get such an early start with the automobile.
So he slept late, almost to six-fifteen. The car would be the ruination

of him yet. If he slept till six-fifteen on Saturday, no telling what time it would be Sunday. And then Monday . . .

At six-thirty, after he finally roused Sara, he had gone out to see about the car. He tossed a rolled-up burlap bag in the back seat and picked up the water bucket. The radiator leaked and you had to put in water every five miles—or after half an hour when it was just resting under the chinaberry tree. But when he got the radiator filled he noticed that the left rear tire was flat. He had had to fix a flat on the way home last Saturday, and now there was one even before they got started. Old Man Lebius had let the car sit up under his shed till the tires near rotted off before he sold it to Sam Benson. And then he, Jim, had let Sara and that crooked mule dealer sell it to him for a hundred and twenty-five dollars. But Sara had to have a car. Arguments hadn't been worth a toot in a whistle factory to Sara. He finally gave in and bought it.

He finally bought that five dollar jar of cream too, and that ought to have been enough. Sara had seen it in the Sunday funny papers one week, and had hounded him for the next two till he let her send off for it. She kept the clipping stuck in the edge of the bureau mirror where she could see it the first thing in the morning and the last thing before she blew out the lamp at night just in case she might forget to mention it. He argued about that cream. She was only seventeen. When she got her first baby they would get bigger.

"I seen too many yearlings come in," he said. "You don't need no New York cream. All you need is a youngun to nuss."

"It ain't New York, it's Paris." She pointed out the name too, *La Contour for Mademoiselle.* "That's French. Sudy Lou's husband said it was. He's been to France. He ought to know."

"Sudy Lou's husband be damned," he said. "It says New York right on the paper here. That's where you send the money, ain't it?"

That's where he sent the money. After she cried and pouted and burned the biscuits and undercooked the blackeyed peas. She left the clipping stuck in the mirror frame with its French words and New York address and what looked to Jim like a big radio tower in the background and a lot of black-headed women pushing balloons ahead of them. The cream came all right, a piddling little old jar of white stuff about the size of a Vicks salve. And Sara kept burning the biscuits. She like to have worn out the tape measure the first two weeks too, and kept talking about how the cream was working. But he couldn't see a bit of difference in the world. Still couldn't.

He got the patching on the innertube that was already so patched it looked like somebody had shot it with number nine bird shot. He got the boot worked back into place. But the water had leaked out of the radiator and he had to fill it again. When Tilly stuck her head over the lot gate and brayed at him, he picked up a clod of dirt and threw it hard as he could. It shattered against the barn and sprayed dirt all over the mule.

Then he stomped into the house. Sara was still at the mirror. Used to he'd have had his breakfast over with and done, and she hadn't even got the coffee made. So by the time they got the coffee made and the biscuits done, there wasn't anything to do but fill the radiator again before they left. Sara said he ought to have waited anyhow.

So there it was nearly eight o'clock, and they hadn't started yet. He hung the rag he'd been wiping his hands with back on the nail at the well curb.

"Sara," he yelled again. "Sara, if you're going with me you'd better git on out here. I have to fill this damn croakersack of a radiator again, I'm going to walk."

The front screen door banged and Sara came down the steps. No wonder she was late. Dressed up in her Sunday dress, big green and red flowers on it, and that hat and everything. It looked like ever since he got the automobile she spent most of her time either getting ready to go to town on Saturday or talking about getting ready. She didn't even fix his breakfast till she got her hair all primped up like a nigger on the 29th of May and put some of the cream on. No blessed wonder it took him so long to get to the field.

"I'm coming," Sara said. She climbed up in the front seat and Jim set the water bucket in the back. He was about to get in when Tilly brayed at him again. He reached down and got another clod of dirt and threw it over the car at the mule. A scattering of it managed to get on Sara's dress and she began brushing it off like it was something worse than dirt.

He slammed the door and stepped on the starter. He turned the key in the switch two or three times and tried again. There was a puny groan once from the motor, and then it didn't do any good to step on the starter anymore. Jim sat there a minute, clutching the wheel in both hands.

"What's the matter now?" asked Sara.

"The matter is that I ought never let you talk me into getting this damn heap of junk, that's what the matter is." He got out and slammed the door behind him. Tilly was back at the lot gate with her head over watching when Jim got the bridle off the peg. But Tilly wanted to play. She kicked up her heels and ran around and around the lot. He finally hemmed her up in a corner and got a rope around her neck, but she wouldn't take the bit. Stubborn as Sara sometimes. He twisted her nose sharply and slipped the piece of steel between her teeth. Then he yanked her ears through the halter and led her into the barn. All that time Sara just sat there in the car watching, clasping her hands and unclasping them. When Jim came out of the barn with Tilly, she had on her plow harness. He scraped his shoes on a clump of bermuda grass.

He didn't say a word to Sara. When he got Tilly around in front of the A-model, he hitched the traces around the bumper. Then he got on the running board so he could guide the car with one hand and hold the plow lines with the other.

"All right now, git up!"

Tilly just stood there, looking back over her shoulder at Jim and then at the automobile. "Git up, goddamn it!" She moved forward till she took up the slack. Then she looked back at him again.

"I wish you wouldn't cuss so, Jim," Sara said softly, looking down at her hands. "Mama says it don't sound right. I never heard Sudy Lou's husband cuss a-tall, and he was in the Army."

Jim went around in front of Tilly and grabbed her halter with both hands. She strained a little and the car began moving.

"Two mistakes an old fool like me ought never make," he said between his teeth at Tilly. "One is marry a little old gal that's too young and full of mama and going. Other is to buy a fool automobile."

Tilly pulled half-heartedly at the unfamiliar burden. He slapped her on the side with the plow lines and hollered at her again. He could see Sara sitting up there holding on to the door for dear life though the car was only going at a creep. The second time he slapped Tilly she got the devil in her tail and started hard as she could go. They got to the little rise and over it before he could get her stopped. The mule and the car were well on their way to the bottom of the hill with the A-model gaining when Jim managed to get in and step on the brakes. Tilly jerked up tight in her harness and just stood there panting and trembling.

"I ought never to have sold my buggy to the mule stealer."

Sara was white and scared, but she was quiet for a change. Jim left her holding the brake on with both feet while he got out and scotched a rock under the front wheel. Then he unhitched Tilly and led her to the barn. When he got back to the car, he moved the rock, gave the car a little shove, and jumped in. He pushed the clutch in, wrestled the gears into second from neutral, and let the wheels turn the motor. The first time it didn't catch. He leaned forward. They were nearly at the bottom of the hill when he tried again, and this time the motor caught and sputtered and started.

When they got out to the highway and things seemed to be going all right, Sara loosened up. "Maybe we ought to get another one," she said.

Jim was still hunched over the wheel gritting his teeth when the black Chevrolet came whizzing up alongside, slowed down, and the driver started honking his horn at them. He didn't even look. Sudy Lou's husband. He'd done the same thing when he had that little old Ford and Jim and Sara rode to town in the buggy. The black car shot on ahead so they could see its jewelled mud flaps and exhaust. All that show and all that Sunday talk at Sara's mama's house was what got her started harping on trading the buggy in the first place. Nothing would do but Jim must see about getting an automobile. It took two weeks for the fancy cream. She wore him down in a month about the car. She like to have drove him crazy till he couldn't stand it any more and spoke to Sam Benson. Sam wanted Tilly, but Jim wouldn't trade her. They finally traded for the A-model, and Jim shelled out a hundred and twenty-five dollars for it, twenty-five of it credit for the buggy. But that hadn't satisfied Sara for long.

"If we was to just get us a little better one, Jim," she said, "we wouldn't have all this trouble like this. You wouldn't have to fill the radiator and fix the tires and all. It would be a lot better."

"The next trade I make," Jim said, "is going to be for my buggy. It's already ten o'clock. If we'd been driving Tilly, we'd already be there and out of this sun. Next trade is going to be for my buggy again."

Sara pouted then for awhile, but Jim didn't care. He had made up his mind, no matter if she did pout and wheedle.

They were three and a half miles from home when the car choked, ran another few yards gasping. It sounded like the gas tank was empty. He managed to get the car off the road on the shoulder before it stopped rolling. Then he got out. He cut off a piece of pop-gun elder beside the road and stuck it down in the tank. It came out damp. He smelled it. It was gas. He raised the hood and poked around at the spark plugs. He couldn't find anything wrong. Only thing it could be, he decided, was the fuel line choked up.

"Maybe if we'd just get us a better one," Sara said, "we wouldn't keep having this trouble." She said it like it was a new idea she'd just thought of. The sun was really coming down on Jim's neck now. He got in and stepped on the starter again.

"Maybe we ought to stop and see Sam Benson on the way in," Sara said. "Sudy Lou's husband says . . ."

Jim reached in the back seat and got the rolled-up burlap bag. He unrolled it slowly, watching Sara coldly as her red pout changed to white. She put her hand over her mouth when he pulled the .38 Special out of the sack. Then he walked around to the raised hood and fired four shots into the motor, pausing a second after each. Sara sat there with her lip trembling, watching wide-eyed and silent. He clicked the cylinder out in his palm and blew the smoke from the barrel, looking at Sara through the windshield. Then he wrapped the gun up in the burlap and stuck it under his arm. He held a steady pace toward town, not looking back and not seeing Sara burst into tears. When he was nearly out of sight, she pulled off her shoes and headed for home.

Jim stopped off at Walt Jenkins' place before he got to town. He found Walt out at the barn and sold him what was left of the car for ten dollars. Then he tramped on to town, the burlap bag under his arm. When he got to the Happy House Restaurant he went in and drank two beers. By that time he was feeling a little better and on the way out he bought two pints of blackberry wine. What was left of the ten dollars he stuffed in a hip pocket. He stopped off in the men's room and drank a quarter of one of the pints and wrapped the bottles in the burlap bag with the gun.

Down the street he bought a ticket to the jungle movie and watched a black-headed woman push her balloons all over the screen. He wondered if she used French cream. He asked the lady next to him and she got up and moved. Then he started talking to a fellow in front of him and the people got to shushing him. When the black-headed woman's fellow commenced swinging on long vines, he began to feel sick. He got up and went to the men's room and washed his face. That made him feel a little better and he drank another quarter.

But he didn't go back and watch the rest of the picture show. He walked around the courthouse square looking for Sudy Lou's husband and the black Chevrolet. He couldn't find them. After awhile he thought about the mule trader and got mad again. He tried to stop a fellow and tell him about it, but the man laughed and said he had to go. Jim stood looking after him a long minute. Then he struck out for Sam Benson's buy-and-trade mule barn. Sam hadn't sold the buggy when he got there and that sure was good. He traded for it, giving Sam five dollars down. Then he worked at the buggy top till he got it collapsed and tied. Sam loaned him a mule till Sunday, and it was dusk when he got her hitched to the buggy and started home.

Every time a car passed him on the big road, he stood up and waved his hat and shouted. Then he would take another pull at the blackberry wine. When the buggy swung in the side yard, the moon was up and he was singing.

Ducks in the pond and geese in the ocean
Hi ho diddle um day

He stopped under the chinaberry tree and put the borrowed mule in the barn lot. Tilly wanted to play again, but he hemmed her up in a stall and got the bit in her mouth.

Devil's in a woman if she takes the notion
Hi ho diddle um day

He brought her out into the moonlight and hitched her to the buggy. Around and around the house then, singing and shouting at the moon and the car lights down on the highway every once in awhile. By the bottom of the second pint he could hardly get the old girl unharnessed. He patted her on the neck, telling her what a good mule she was. So happy he could cry. He stood there with his arm around Tilly's neck crying for a long time. He drained the empty bottle once more and threw it out across the cotton field, watching it flash in the moonlight. Then he started toward the house to find the French cream, singing again.

I got a gal on Sourwood Mountain
Hi ho diddle um day
She won't come and I won't come git her
Hi ho diddle um day.

Sara pretended she was asleep as long as he would let her.

Ferrol Sams

from Run with the Horsemen

A T PERIODIC BUT infrequent intervals the boy was given a dime
and sent to get his hair cut after school. This involved a two
block walk to the courthouse square. He had to go past Babcock's
barn, a long, low, cavernous structure emptied for years of any
livestock. Then came the two story wooden Lodge Hall, always empty
and always reputed to be filled with skeletons and coffins, its upper
windows blankly staring like dark, dead eyes. He went all the way
to the corner where he encountered the paved sidewalk and turned
right through the entrance to Babcock's bank. This was a yellow brick
building with its door in the corner. It was vacant, busted, so they
said, in final defeat by the rival Marsengill clan. Comp was wont to
mutter darkly that the Babcocks had taken mortagages on dead mules
and in addition had ruint Dr. Landers. The father and grandfather,
Babcock loyalists through years of political warfare, were never heard
to comment. The grandmother was never heard to comment either.
She just rocked, dipped snuff, smiled, and put all her money in a
fruit jar in the bottom of her closet.

From here he walked the rest of the block beneath the tin sheds
to the two story brick building on the other corner. Here was Mr.
Isaac Harte's barbershop. On the wall outside was fixed a red and
white striped cylinder which revolved endlessly, looking like a huge
candy cane being augered constantly from nowhere to nowhere. This
was a great fascination to the boy and never ceased to puzzle him.

He hated to get his hair cut, but he loved to go to the barbershop.
Mr Isaac Harte had a long cigarette holder, a taciturn attitude toward
life in general, and a stern intolerance of small boys. Everything he

used in his shop made one either itch or sneeze. Wiggling was forbidden. Since he always had clippers or wickedly slim scissors in his hand and would mutter threats of cutting one's ears off, it was most important to sit motionless on the board stretched across the arms of the barber chair. It was interesting to consider that he was the father of Tater Harte, who kept blowing his fingers off playing with dynamite caps. He also had five other children. He raised them all and fed them well by cutting hair for ten and fifteen cents and shaving men for a dime. He took frequent fishing and drinking breaks, usually on Mondays, and had the best vegetable garden in town. The only words he ever addressed to the boy were, "Sit still or I'll cut your ears off," and "Hey, Lord," the latter uttered on the expiratory phase of a deep sigh. With grownups, however, he was quite sociable, although always serious. The information exchanged between him and the adults in his shop was varied and fascinating and made the ordeal of the haircut worthwhile.

Particularly interesting was Mr. Lum Thornton. In warm weather Mr. Lum Thornton always sat in a wooden chair leaned against the light pole on the sidewalk outside Mr. Isaac Harte's barbershop. In cold weather he sat inside the shop, but he didn't come to town as much in the winter. He lived at the Poor Farm. The Poor Farm was located two miles from town near the convict camp and consisted of a row of five houses. They had no foundation planting or flower beds but just sat there on rock pillars by the side of the dirt road, each in the middle of a bare dirt yard.

Whenever the county commissioners were petitioned to help a pauper, they investigated the case, and, if the person qualified, he or she was moved into one of the stark little cottages to measure out a drab and pitiful life. The inmates were fed the same fare provided for the chain gang, cheap, ribsticking victuals consisting mostly of dried peas, fat meat, and lots of syrup.

This was a very convenient arrangement. The church people had no difficulty knowing where to take boxes at Christmas, Easter, and revival time. The non-church-goers who had clothes to discard in those prewelfare days could do so virtuously and charitably without being afraid they were donating them to someone who secretly had a radio or a daughter with a Cadillac. So abject was the poverty involved, so patently miserable the people, so profoundly horrible the conditions that it was a perfect example of the life to avoid. Even the most indifferent children were round-eyed with awe when they drove by and saw the row of houses with dulled, motionless people sitting on the porches. They had the fires of capitalistic ambition ignited forever within them. Thus were recruited the slaves to the Protestant work ethic.

It was humiliating, degrading, and shameful to have to go to the Poor Farm, and any child in the county would rather die than have a relative of his wind up there. This contributed to making Mr. Lum Thornton as fascinating and puzzling as the revolving barber pole. The boy never tired of watching him. He gave no sign of feeling either humiliated, degraded, or ashamed about being an inmate of the Poor Farm. In fact he gave the impression that he felt he was just as good as anybody else and a sight better than most. He had definite opinions about everybody in town and a total lack of inhibition about voicing his opinions. In addition to this, he laughed a lot. He was the only one who could get a smile out of Mr. Isaac Harte.

One afternoon the boy hunched immobile beneath the cloth apron, fearful for the integrity of his ears, looking at the piles of varicolored hair on the floor. The owner of the building pushed down the brass latch of the front door with his thumb and stuck his head in. "Just want to remind you that the rent is due tomorrow," he said. With this he closed the door and retired to his law office in the other half of the building.

Mr. Isaac Harte put another Camel into his cigarette holder and said, "Hey, Lord, hold still or I'll cut your ears off. I ain't never failed to pay the rent yet."

With this, Mr. Lum Thornton raised the lid to the small stove, spit tobacco juice audibly on the hot coals, and said, "Hell, Isaac, don't pay no attention to that pissant. He'd still be the letter carrier if his wife wadn't rich as six inches up a bull's ass."

Mr. Isaac Harte smiled, took a long draw through his cigarette holder, and said, "I expect you're right, Lum."

Once Mr. Lum Thornton took note directly of the boy. "What grade you in, boy? The sixth? Well, I know you're scared you goan be a runt all your life, but you ain't. All yo family grows up to have big dicks and be mean as hell." He paused and added judiciously, "They bad to git drunk, though, and shoot theyselves." While the boy's cheeks flamed hot, Mr. Isaac Harte said, "Hey, Lord, hold still or I'll cut your ears off." The boy saw in the mirror that he was smiling.

One spring day Mr. Lum Thornton was rared back in his chair on the sidewalk, leaning against the light pole. His shirt sleeves were rolled halfway up his forearms and his collar unbuttoned at the neck. He had such thick, vibrant body hair that the boy was reminded in amazement of an animal pelt. Mr. Isaac Harte, temporarily out of customers since he had finished shearing the boy's neck and scalp to its summertime scantiness, leaned laconically against the doorjamb with his cigarette holder clamped between his teeth. Up the sidewalk, regally erect and self-assured, on her way to call on Mrs. Babcock, swept the venerable and proud Miss Hess Meriwether. Pausing to acknowledge the nodding heads and respectfully murmured greetings of the group, her eyes fixed on the contented figure seated at the edge of the sidewalk. "My word, Lum," she said, "are you that hairy all over?"

The chair never budged. The eyes of the pauper met the eyes of the aristocrat. "Miss Hess," he drawled, "hit's a damn sight wuss'n that in spots."

As the rebuked lady bustled hurriedly across the street, Mr. Isaac Harte smiled.

Once Mr. Sam Percy was waiting his turn on a Saturday morning for a haircut and shave. He was making detailed anatomical comments about each and every female who walked down the street or across the courthouse square. Finally one young girl hove into view, and Mr. Sam was silent. Mr. Lum Thornton loudly remarked, "Now there's a fine one. That's as big a pair of tits as you'll find in the county, and her ass looks like two coons fighting in a croker sack."

"Dammit, Lum," complained Mr. Sam Percy, "watch your mouth. That's my daughter."

Mr. Isaac Harte flipped his brush around the neck of the current customer, creating a cloud of talcum powder. "Sam," he said softly, "ever one of them girls was somebody's daughter."

Then he smiled.

One Sunday Mr. Lum Thornton was sitting on the porch of his house at the Poor Farm with Old Man Tom Pearce, who shared the house with him. These men were equally poor, there being no degree of poverty below the absolute; they were equally ancient; and they were identically garbed. Yet one was called "old man," a Southern title used behind a person's back which denoted condescension, familiarity, and just a soupcon of mild contempt, while the other was accorded the courtesy title of "mister." The boy never figured out the difference in this situation, but he conformed.

The men waited on this Sunday afternoon for the chance call of a relative or a carload of Royal Ambassadors, gangling adolescent Baptist boys bent on Christian charity under the tutelage of their knowing elders. Old Man Tom Pearce fell to bemoaning his fate. "Oh, the pity of it all!" he wailed. "To think that I've worked as hard as I have all my life, made as good a living as I have, and now here I am in my old age reduced to living on the Poor Farm with nothing to comfort me but the prospect of a pauper's grave. Oh, it's terrible! Oh, it's tragic! To have prospered like I have and to wind up a pauper!"

As he warmed to his subject, repetition inflaming him, Old Man Tom Pearce began keening like a Jew at the Wailing Wall. Finally, just as the Royal Ambassadors rolled up, Mr. Lum Thornton growled at him, "Aw shut up, Tom. I've knowed you for seventy years, and you ain't never been nothing but a pauper."

"That's a damn lie!" shrieked Old Man Tom Pearce.

He launched himself in arm-swinging fury upon the other old man, knocking him in surprise out of his chair. Locked in combat, they rolled across the porch and finally tumbled four feet to the ground. Still fighting, they wallowed in the yard before the startled boys until finally Old Man Tom Pearce got Mr. Lum Thornton's thumb in his mouth. He clamped down with a bite that would have shamed a possum and delighted an alligator. Mr. Lum began yelling, "Get him off, get him off, get him off!" precipitating the onlookers into the delighted activity of forceful peacemakers. They finally managed to prize Old Man Tom Pearce's jaws open and extract Mr. Lum Thornton's mangled thumb, but it was a job.

Old Man Tom Pearce never forgave his former housemate and

had to be moved for peace and safety to another cottage at the Poor Farm. Mr. Lum Thornton had to have a lot of attention from Dr. Witherspoon. When he finally made it back to the barbershop, some of the shock the event had created in town had worn off, but he was still an object of curiosity. It takes some kind of courage to appear in public for the first time after being whipped by an octogenarian. His hand was still swollen to twice its size, swathed in bandages, and carried tenderly in a sling. Mr. Lum rolled his eyes sheepishly at Mr. Isaac Harte and gruffly spoke his first word, "Hell, Isaac, I wouldn'ta thought the old buzzard had a tooth in his head."

Mr. Isaac Harte took a deep breath, sighed deeply, and smiled. "Hey, Lord. Hell, Lum, I woulda thought you woulda been right," he said. "Come on in."

When Mr. Lum Thornton died, Mr. Isaac Harte stayed fishing for ten days. When he came back, his eyes were red and puffed, and his hand trembled when he held his cigarette holder. The boy went for a haircut, and the whole time he was in the shop he never saw a smile. He felt empty. Later he persuaded his parents to let him walk all the way across town, three blocks farther, to the other barbershop. This one was run by Mr. Arthur Masters, an immaculate, softspoken bachelor. The boy opened the door to the new place timidly and slid inconspicuously into a seat which held a fattened, two-year-old copy of *Collier's Magazine*. He pretended to read while he diffidently studied the strange surroundings. The door opened, and Mr. Boss Chapman walked in. Fascinated, the boy looked at the short, pudgy, erect figure with a head too big for the body, hat cocked on one side, two inches of battered cigar stuck in the folds of his face approximately where a mouth should be. A gold ring with a huge yellow set blazed on one finger.

" 'Y golly, Arthur, you remember that old blind Nigra I was telling you about? The one that's made me so much cotton and that I think so much of? Old Uncle Will? Well, I sent him to a specialist, and, 'y golly, he's got a cadillac in both eyes and it's gonna cost me near a thousand dollars, 'y golly, to have em took out."

Mr. Arthur Masters inserted a Lucky Strike cigarette into a long holder. He grinned broadly. "Tell us about it, Boss," he said.

The boy gazed at his magazine and contentedly waited his turn.

Roy Blount, Jr.

Heterosexism and Dancing

What's so special about these Georgians—they don't wear queer clothes, they don't wear masks, they're not hermaphrodites.
—ALICE ROOSEVELT LONGWORTH

IN NASHVILLE JUST before he died I visited Allen Tate, the distinguished Southern poet and critic, whose notions included *tension* (the truth is established by bias, counterposing, suspension), "the fallacy of communication" (if you think you have signified anything by just opening your mouth and *disclosing,* you have another think coming), and the trashiness of modern Northern-industrial-dominated life. Notions such as these, with which I was imbued by the Vanderbilt English Department in the early sixties, when I should have been doing more to help desegregate luncheonettes, have meant a lot to my sensibility, such as it is.

Tate's poetry, Edmund Wilson observed, is "stony, nodulous and tight." To love much of it, you have to be receptive to an attitude of "Thank God I've kept my sense of loss." Some of it, however, is great country music:

> Far off a precise whistle is escheat
> To the dark.

And some of it great sportswriting:

> The going years, caught in an accurate glow,
> Reverse like balls englished upon green baize.

Anybody who can english a ball on a page, my hat is off to. And there curled on a narrow bed Tate was in the flesh, almost weightless, half-blind, nearly eighty, emphysemic and rigged up so he could push a lever and take bottled oxygen, as he needed it, directly into his nose through a tube.

He still had that great strange node of a head I had seen in photographs, and it was fine to see him carrying right on in vigorous conversation as though he was paying no mind to how little corporeality he had left. I asked him whether he had found himself stereotyped, down through the years, as a white Southerner. He said he sure had. Even in Paris in the twenties in Gertrude Stein's *salon*.

He remembered giving a lecture once in New York and pointing out that literary historians were like the old lady in the Faulkner story "A Rose for Miss Emily"—they were sleeping with their loved one's corpse. "And this symposium was *scandalized*. They said that kind of thing went on only in the South! Well, that same week in the paper there was a story about a woman in New York who had been sleeping with her dead lover."

Tate—who wrote a great poem about a lynching—shook his head over "Northern propaganda" which tried to make out that the darker side of the human condition was manifest only in Dixie. I was thinking amen almost wholeheartedly to that, when Tate went on to say he didn't respect W. H. Auden much as a poet because he was homosexual. "Now they're demanding their *rights!*" he cried. "The next thing you know *whores* will be demanding rights!"

Tate added that the trouble with homosexual poetry is, there are no women in it. There may be a sense in which that is so. And maybe the trouble with whores, although I believe they already have rights, is there is not enough woman in them. And let me just mention that I like plenty of women in my writing, as many as three or four in one sentence. I'll tell you something I'd like to get into poetry: the back of a woman's neck.

> The way you hold your head up,
> Dear, keeps me afloat.
> The smooth back of your neck there
> Gives me a lump in my throat.

189

That's just personal, and probably sexist. But I'm not going to lie and say, "What I like about a woman is the way she shoots her cuffs," or "What I like about a *person* is the back of her neck."

Still, I had to wonder why, if Tate could accommodate the notion of women sleeping with dead men, he couldn't accommodate the notion of live men sleeping with each other. And wouldn't you think a poet could disapprove of something without coming out against rights? Why is it that whenever people start demanding rights, *anywhere in the free world,* a clear plurality of my people gets so pissed off? Why is it that when I visit a distinguished poet of my people, he has to devote some of his last breath to assailing a minority? "That is the kind of distinguished poet," I can hear crisp Northern voices snapping, "your people would have."

"I don't *understand* homosexuals," Tate exclaimed. "How do people *get* that way?" This damn thing of people being homosexual just stuck in his craw. It looked like he never would get over it. *He didn't want there to be people he didn't understand.* And when he said understand, he *meant* understand.

In the background, from somewhere else in Tate's house, I kept hearing something incongruous. What it was, I realized as I left, was Tate's two young children, in the next room, plinking out on a piano the *Close Encounters* intergalactic communication music:

Ba-*bah* bahh, bah *baaaaaahm*
Ba-*bah* bahh, bah *baaaaaahm.*

I'll say this. If any outer-space people ever descended unto Tate and asked about homosexuality on earth, I know he gave them an honest answer. He didn't say, "Oh, I can give you the psychology on that." He said he was *mystified.*

I lay no claims, myself, to an understanding of anybody's sexuality except, of course, the President's, but I am tempted to envy those homosexuals who write. I don't like the idea, from either end, of what would appear to be implied when some gay men are said to be "good with their fists"; and I don't especially want to have to cut my hair short and grow it on my chest, either. But the *license.*

One form of freedom is being able to say *anything* in a certain tone of voice. Here, in *The Village Voice,* is Arthur Bell, sympathetically, on "the life of the gay outlaw":

"What they look for is Mother with a big penis to share the dream."

If you can get away with an image like that, you can get away with anything. Hippogriffs, flies with fawns' eyes, stones that have long telephone conversations. It's almost as good as being South American. What if you could be a Cracker with that kind of literary abandon? "What they want is Mammy with a big sweet-potato pie to (sort of) share the dream." "What they want is a mammary with a big fishing pole to share the bream." If I wrote something like that, people would think I was putting the Cracker outlaw down.

I'm not dumb. I know it is firmly established that we all have some gaiety deep down inside. Listen here: we all have a *bunch* of things down inside. I asked a psychiatrist friend of mine once whether it was true, as I had heard, that you can't hypnotize a person to do anything the person doesn't really want to do. "That is true," he said. "But everybody wants to do everything." For all I know, a caveman would couple with whatever he could get a good grip on. ("Since You Lost Your Love Handles / I Feel You Slipping Away.") I can sit here and deny until I am blue in the face that I have any gaiety to speak of, and everybody will just say, "Uh-huh, that's the tipoff. He's got a *lot.*" But a great many people get away with denying that they have any redneck in them. (You think a caveman didn't have any of that?) And—how can I put this?—there are writers who parade an innocence which I think it would not be unfair to call an at least partly homocentric lack of common sense.

Gore Vidal can say in a national magazine that when supposedly straight guys go together for days at a time, they of course roll out the other side of their bisexuality. In fact, when supposedly straight guys go off to hunting lodges together for days at a time, they by and large drink beer, shoot at inoffensive animals, and talk about pussy. Nobody would print it if I wanted to announce that when Eastern intellectuals go off to symposia together for days at a time,

191

they of course cook chitlins, dip snuff, and tell jokes like, "Did you hear the one about a black person's idea of a holiday weekend?"

"No, what is a black person's idea of a holiday weekend?"

"Forty hours of fucking and eight hours of changing tires."

Vidal is a great critic, but he is at his worst, if not *anybody's* worst, at sexual fantasy (a Breckenridge who is both Myra and Myron, and either way an asshole) and identification. He writes in the *New York Review of Books* that he can't understand why a wife should be at pains to keep her husband's ardor up over the years. "As far as I know no one in tribal lore has ever asked the simple question: Why bother? Why not move on?" Which is the equivalent, for appreciation of common human tribulation and entanglement, of "Why hasn't anyone suggested that they eat cake?" No wonder Vidal has never written a country song.

Arthur Bell can not only confer credence upon a quest for mutual revery with a well-hung mom, he can also write about how he tried to stop an inferably homophobic movie—*Cruising*—from being made in New York. Who would buy two thousand words from me about how I tried to obstruct the filming of *Roots*? I wouldn't feel *entitled* to obstruct the filming of *Roots,* although it sure did present my people in a stupid light. I would be among the last to deny that my people deserve intelligent opprobrium, and my objection to *Roots* is not that it is at least as likely to inspire a misguided individual to murder redneck people as *Cruising* is to inspire one to murder gay people. My objection to *Roots* is that slavery is too important to be turned into schlock. And, incidentally, that the supposedly sympathetic white characters in *Roots* are as false as most of the unsympathetic ones are.

Now, I am not opposed to any form of liberation. I can't afford to be. If I were to say, "Well, I think this Scots Lib has gone too far," people's reaction would be: "Because you're Southern." (Either that or "Yeah, you're right, let's you and me go roll a Scot.") And I would not only be giving a boost to Scots Lib but setting back Cracker Lib. A Cracker Libber will just be counterproductive if he takes to the streets with signs that say PINEY WOODS PRIDE. In order not to have what several of President Carter's pronouncements have been said to have—"a boomerang effect"—we would have to go into the streets carrying signs that say CRACKERS FOR RIGHTS FOR EVERYBODY ELSE.

So it may just be reverse ethnicism on my part, but I am inclined to favor every rights movement going. Years before it was fashionable, I sent my shirts to a bisexual laundress and they didn't feel funny when they came back. I have been around gay couples who seemed a lot better matched than I have been with several women.

But the demonstrations of Gay Pride that I have seen looked to me like the work of FBI provocateurs. In Black Pride marches, you didn't have people walking by dressed as Hattie McDaniel, Butterfly McQueen, and the Zebra Killer. Back in the sixties, I went to a Gay Lib parade in Greenwich Village. A hairy-legged man in tight short-shorts went by carrying a sign that said I AM YOUR WORST FEAR AND YOUR BEST FANTASY. Well, he lied. He wasn't either one of them. And if he had been, he would have let me down by being so out-and-out about it. Nor was he doing much of a job, it seemed to me, of exorcising himself, if that was what he had in mind. He should have been carrying a sign that said I AM JUST ABOUT WHAT YOU EXPECTED IN A PARADE LIKE THIS: THE TYPE OF PERSON WHO GOES AROUND WITH HAIRY LEGS AND SHORT-SHORTS AND THINKS HE IS YOUR WORST FEAR AND YOUR BEST FANTASY.

In this parade there were men in harem pants and frilly dresses with signs commenting on the Vietnam War: GAY FEMMES SAY OUT NOW. What nation's army (I know, I know what they say about Frederick the Great's) is ever going to withdraw from anywhere at the behest of a man in harem pants?

In this procession, women in blue jeans strode along like artificial cowboys in town for trouble on Saturday night, with signs saying I'M PROUD OF BEING A DYKE and WE ARE LESBIANS AND WE ARE ALL BEAUTIFUL.

Men in high-heel shoes went by singing, "When the gays . . . go flaming in . . ." HOMOSEXUAL LOVE IS BEAUTIFUL said a sign carried by a heavily muscled bald man in earrings, walking with a small sandy man in a brown suit.

The last, and I thought most eloquent, person in the parade was a man whose only statement was to ride a bicycle with a white kitten

193

in the basket. He pumped slowly, so as to keep the same pace as the walkers, but held the basket so level that the kitten slept. The parade disappeared up the street toward Sheridan Square, and the man next to me sighed. "See," he said, "that's where it's all leading."

Ten years later, in October '79, I read that fifty thousand homosexuals had gathered on the Mall below the Washington Monument to hear speakers denounce the "heterosexism" of mainstream Americans.

Nobody wants to *espouse* an ism any more, everybody just wants to find one for everybody else. Wants to accuse everybody else of a largely unconscious but institutionalized ism which is responsible for what is wrong, and which has been fettering the accusing party's consciousness until recently.

But all right, heterosexism it is—and just as I was getting it down pretty good.

No wonder the President doesn't have much panache. If an American white Southern straight Gentile man under sixty who grew up eating animals were ever to cut loose, in clear view of the nation, and do something that made him feel real good deep down, he would incur about forty-eight isms. Jimmy ran on all the things he wasn't. He wasn't a racist, an elitist, a sexist, a Washingtonian, a dimwit, a liar, a lawyer, a warmonger, a peacenik, a big spender, a Republican, an authoritarian, an idealogue, a paranoid, or a crook. He had found one last creditable ism: isn'tism. People in Georgia had said of him, "Well, there's not a whole lot *to* him." Jimmy turned that into a forte.

And he may have expected people to love him for it. Not just accept his bent toward extreme neutrality, but love him *for* it. That's where I think people who jump from being ashamed of their political, racial, or sexual orientation, on the one hand, to being ebullient about it, on the other, get carried away. A person's orientation doesn't make his or her shit bad; not in America. *But it doesn't make it good either.* I admired a black woman I saw once on the subway. She was wearing a button that said BEING BLACK OR PUERTO RICAN ISN'T ENOUGH.

Senator Sam Ervin Jr. was a fine figure of Southern White Pride until he started enjoying himself a little too much on TV. (Then he even started doing commercials. I swear, if Diogenes were alive today, he'd be doing lantern commercials.) When he was in his prime, Senator Ervin asked a member of the Nixon administration, a Mr. Sneed, how that administration could justify its having "impounded" funds that the Congress had allocated for social programs.

MR. SNEED: "Well, as I say, when we get down to, as I mention in my formal statement, situations in which all of the statutory justifications for impounding were stripped away and we have simply a question of whether there is any constitutional power of the President to impound and Congress has said you must spend, it is our contention that he may refuse to spend and that the collision in that case between the Congress and the President is a political question that is not justifiable."

SENATOR ERVIN: "I am reminded of the story of the deacon who desired to preach. The deacon went to the board of deacons and wanted to know why they fired him, and he asked the chairman, 'Don't I argufy?' He said, 'Yes, you argufy, yes.' He said, 'Don't I sputify?' The chairman said, 'Yes, you sure do sputify.' He said, 'What's the trouble with my preaching?' The chairman said, 'You don't show wherein.' "

Allen Tate would tell you that poetry has to show wherein. So does politics. The way to show pride is to show something other people will grant you reason to be proud of.

The Arthur Bell piece that had the image of beschlonged maternity is mostly about finding a typical middle-American gay person in Dayton, Ohio. When Bell finds him they have this colloquy:

> I mention that the trend in New York is macho.
> "That's okay with me," he says. "I've got tons of Levi's and denim and checkered shirts."
> Does he consider himself masculine?
> "Yes."
> Does he consider himself feminine?
> He hesitates. "I can see myself enjoying things both ways. I

195

enjoy the contrast. It's so beautiful to be a strong, virile, handsome
kind of man who talks in a sensitive, romantic way and subscribes
to cooking and needlepoint."

Bell finds such talk, and Dayton in general (where "even the bellboys
are giving"), a breath of fresh air. If a heterosexual person were to
talk about himself, herself, or any other person in terms such as those,
everyone within earshot would be hooting and gasping for air.

By the way, *Levi's are work-clothes.* And I wouldn't be surprised if
a greater percentage of people appreciated them for their function
in Dayton than in Manhattan. When you get to loving your sensibility
you stop being sensible, especially in the context of Dayton and especially if your sensibility is at the service of your sexuality and especially
if your sensibility doesn't seem to incorporate the *vaguest notion* of
what the inertia you are working against is like.

Growing up in the South, I got to where I couldn't stand people
who were satisfied to think of themselves as dignified or sweet, who
were proud of their mores, who had little ways that they thought
were the most precious things in the world. I grew up wishing I
could plant about half the adults I knew in the middle of Harlem at
midnight naked. It wouldn't be fair, but it would be a step toward
making them Americans.

"We are not all that civilized a people" was my feeling, growing up
in the South. *"We are outlandish!"* Today, having moved North and
traveled West, I would add: *"So is the rest of America."*

I am for gay public figures who work with that. Allen Ginsberg
has. "America I am putting my queer shoulder to the wheel." Nothing
shamefaced there, and nothing cultish.

You should have heard my internal voice that night when I visited
Studio 54. *"Git the hell out of this place,* boy! Right now!"

I had, myself, long reviled the very notion of this place, where
costumed residents of Queens, some of them nearly naked, stood
outside pleading to be allowed in to view Halston and Liza Minnelli
at play. I wouldn't know Halston from a sack of sand, but I knew I
didn't want to view anybody who designed clothes. I had admired
Liza Minnelli in *Cabaret,* but having seen her on television talking

about how she was really just a regular kinda kooky person at heart,
I knew I didn't want to view her in person. Furthermore, I had read
something about goings-on at Studio 54 that included the name Lala
de la Lamour.

Now, I have no earthly idea, to this day, who Lala de la Lamour
is. She may be eleven or sixty-three, or a man, for all I know. But
it is just my luck that I would go into Studio 54 and she'd be there
and she'd be like Mrs. Watts in *Wise Blood:* "Her grin was as curved
and sharp as the blade of a sickle. It was plain that she was so well-
adjusted that she didn't have to think any more. Her eyes took everything in whole, like quicksand," and I'd become infatuated with her—
it wouldn't be anywhere *near* characteristic of me, I am just saying
"What if"—and I'd go off to Antibes with her and run out of money
inside of two days and become drunken and boring and she would
treat me like shit and I would moon around for a while and overhear
Halston murmuring, "Lala, *honestly,* who *is* he?" and I'd act like I
was getting ready to hit Halston and that would really tear it and
tout le monde would be wondering how anybody could have ever
thought anybody from Georgia was chic, and I wouldn't have plane
fare back and I'd have to work as a gigolo and finally I would put
together a few hundred dollars hocking crazy old bony rich women's
gold cigarette lighters I'd stolen from their purses and I'd crawl back
to New York, take the bus up to Canaan, hitchhike the last few miles
north, walk around to the back of the house and look at the compost
heap, knock on the door, and my wife wouldn't have anything to
do with me; who could blame her? And the kids wouldn't, either.
And the dogs—not just Ned, who could be expected to side with
whichever of his loved ones controlled the living room couch, but
even *Peggy* would look at me sadly and decline to wag her tail. ("I
am I because my little dog knows me"—Gertrude Stein.) And the
cats, even. And the horse. And our friends the Swans, and Lee and
Jim down at the store, and Addie at the post office, and my softball
team.

And I'd drift back to Georgia and drink a lot without enjoying it,
and get a job at the *Journal* writing obits, and I'd walk into the composing room and I'd see Wilcy—who when I told him back in '68 I
was moving to New York looked at me as though I had said something

197

filthy—and he'd give me a look that was only too keen to be gloating
and he'd say:

"Um. Understand you um run off with a woman to France somewhere and left your wife and young ones and dogs and livestock
and um softball team."

". . ." I would nod.

"And then when you come groveling back, um, they wouldn't take
you in."

". . ." I wouldn't even have to nod.

"Um. Just curious—um what was that woman's *name?*"

And, spiritually dead, I would have to answer:

"Lala de la Lamour."

But I figured I had to go into Studio 54 once to prove I wasn't
afraid of it. (I think that's what Hamilton Jordan probably had in
mind. Hell, a person from the South ought not to be scared of deca-
dence.) And the first thing I saw hit me like the shrunken man in
the museum hits Hazel Motes in *Wise Blood,* the shrunken man about
whom Sabbath Hawks later thinks, "There was something in him of
everyone she had ever known, as if they had all been rolled into
one person and killed and shrunk and dried."

It was a strange smooth two-backed beast: two expressionless
bearded men of exactly the same stature hunching each other rhyth-
mically at slight removes. Discoing with each other to beat the band.
Both of them doing exactly the same thing. Two perfectly compensat-
ing dovetailed pistons, hyperkinetically yet nonchalantly canceling
each other out.

I had always adhered to the old Cracker *koan,* "What is the sense
of two men dancing?" But now I could see it: it was perfect, a closed
system, perpetual motion, like two United Daughters of the Confeder-
acy discussing history, or one movie critic writing about another one.
That it gave me the creeps was attributable, I guess, to heterosexism:
I didn't *want* to be turned on by that shit. It would make me doubt
my motives for either wearing or not wearing Levi's forever. But I
was fascinated.

The sound system was blaring "YMCA," by the Village People.
Now, there are many modes of androgyny for which I have enthusiasm:

the Tiresian, the Beerbohmian, the Billyjeanian, and others. The only
one I can't stand is that which puts together the most obnoxious of
both sexes: the flouncy-brutish. The Village People—dressed as Indian, Cowboy, Construction Worker, Policeman, etc.—are Barbiken
dolls who bump with no contact and grind with no grist. If the Beatles
or the Supremes or the Marx Brothers had ever dressed as the Supreme Court, the Supreme Court would have been enhanced; if the
Village People ever dressed as the Supreme Court the legal system
would be undermined. I had never been able to comprehend why
anybody would want to be both swishy and muscle-bound; but now
as I watched these two men dance to this brain-squelching music, I
could see. It was what Yeats thought he was safe in yearning for
because it would never happen: "two natures blent into a sphere,"
leaving no nature at all.

Now this may be some kind of tacky Georgia notion. I don't know.
But my understanding is that loneliness abides, neurosis builds, and
generation occurs in the ineluctable pockets of space between people,
between sexes, between ethnoses, between people and other people's
perception of them, between people and their own perception of
themselves, between the dancer and the dance.

For a gay person there might be a temptation to believe that those
lacunae disappear outside the closet. (And Jimmy may have thought
they would disappear outside Georgia.) Every liberationist group has
to get beyond the notion that pride of group will bridge all a person's
gaps, but blacks and women have had reason, pre-Lib, to realize the
pleasures and limitations of public wiggliness. Gay people, before
they got into Lib, were traditionally splendid at detachment, at *acerb*
roleplaying. In society, Lissome Movie-Stopping Me is not much of
a role.

Okay, here it is, heterosexist case study: *I don't think Broadway chorus
boys are a pretty sight, either.* Just *feverishly* grinning—worse than Jimmy
used to—for one thing. And moving themselves any way they want
to, twitching their hips the same way a girl would, if she had hardly
any hips. *Dancing* is when people with something besides dancing
in them dance. In Betty's Place, a restaurant in Dublin, Georgia, I
saw a stout middle-aged woman in pants really dance—though only
minimally; she was carrying a plate of catfish while she did it—to

Charley Pride singing "Kiss an Angel Good Morning" (". . . and love her like the devil when you get back home") on the jukebox. To enjoy watching people strut their stuff, you have to be able to want to get into their stuff, one way or another.

But these two men dancing in Studio 54 looked like all strut and no stuff. I don't think Oscar Wilde and Noël Coward would have danced together like that. Noël Coward played a character based on Mountbatten in the movie *In Which We Serve,* and Oscar Wilde was a big hit in mining camps. They could *cut across lines* and yet keep a working sense of their peculiarity. I have always felt that homosexuals, like Southerners, are chosen people; it is our part to be out of whack, to hold back, to be unamalgamated. "In this country, I don't think you would ever have the Nazis," Art Rooney, the owner of the Pittsburgh Steelers, told me once. "The Jews, the Irish, Syrians, Italians, blacks. They wouldn't let them. It's not like there was all one kind of people, that could be fooled at once."

On the day of the Inauguration, the Washington *Post* published a tedious celebratory piece by Reynolds Price, the Southern novelist, in which he said the idea that the Southerner was peculiar was spread by Northeastern journalists who had "understandably stultified themselves on a diet of Faulkner and Flannery O'Connor (writers whom some thoughtful Southerners see as sports to the region—homeless rhapsodists, fantasts, mesmerized haters)." That is a treasonous thing for a Southern writer to say. But that's the Carterian spirit for you.

In fact, Carter himself, in an interview with Harvey Shapiro in *The New York Times Book Review,* said that Faulkner, O'Conner, and other Southern grotesquists "have analyzed very carefully the buildup in the South of a special consciousness brought about by the self-condemnation resulting from slavery, the humiliation following the War Between the States and the hope, sometimes expressed timidly, for redemption. I think in many ways now that those former dark moods in the South of recrimination against self and others and alienation from the rest of the nation—I think they've been alleviated."

No, by heaven! That's Southern Chamber of Commerce Pride talking. Writers are *supposed* to be sports; and Southern writers have always had the advantage of being sports in a region of sports. *"The hope, sometimes expressed timidly, for redemption,"* is it? "Alleviated," is it? *Shit,* Jimmy.

Speaking of sports, the waiters at Studio 54 were striplings clad in basketball shorts, no shirts, only skins. The two-man dancing I saw was a little like basketball, but not enough. In basketball, one person is trying to outmove the other, get past him, take something away from him. No denying the homoerotic in basketball—here is Bill Russell on guarding Elgin Baylor: "We'd both take off and go up in the air together, with him wiggling around the way he always did. . . . We'd both laugh. . . . He had an instinctive awareness of the eccentricities of my game." But basketball has a point beyond sinuousness. "You know what I want them to be like?" asks Albert Murray, speaking of the new generation of blacks in *South to a Very Old Place.* "Our prizefighters. Our baseball players. Like our basketball players. You know what I mean?

"Then you'll see something. Then you'll see them riffing on history because they know history. Riffing on politics because they know politics. One of the main things that too many spokesmen seem to forget these days is the fact you really have to know a hell of a lot about the system in order to know whether you're operating within it or outside it. . . . The difference between riffing and shucking is knowing the goddam fundamentals. Man, when I see one of us up at Harvard or Yale I want to be able to feel like you used to feel seeing Sugar Ray in Madison Square Garden or Big Oscar there, or Willie Mays coming to bat in an All-Star game. You know what I mean?"

That's the way I feel reading Faulkner and Flannery O'Connor, and I sincerely want to work it out so that I can feel that way about the Carter administration. But I'll tell you what I am afraid happened. I am afraid Hamilton Jordan went in there to Studio 54 back before the election and saw them two scooters dancing. And it revealed to him how even rednecks could round themselves off.

Florence King

"Would Youall Be Good Enough to Excuse Me While I Have an Identity Crisis?"

NOVELISTS PREFER COMPLEX women for their protagonists, which is why the Southern woman has been the heroine of so many more novels than her Northern sister. The cult of Southern womanhood endowed her with at least five totally different images and asked her to be good enough to adopt all of them. She is required to be frigid, passionate, sweet, bitchy, and scatterbrained—all at the same time. Her problems spring from the fact that she succeeds.

Antebellum Southern civilization was built upon the white woman's untouchable image. In order to keep her footing on the pedestal men had erected for her, she had to be aloof, aristocratic, and haughty. These qualities have always been required of women in societies based upon vast, entailed estates, but they were especially necessary in the South. They enabled the white woman to maintain her sanity when she saw light-skinned slave children, who were the very spit of Old Massa, running around the plantation. By being sufficiently frosty and above it all, she was able to ignore and endure the evidence of intercaste sexuality that surrounded her.

When the disregard she cultivated was mixed with the inevitable disgust she felt, the result was often frigidity. Southern men have actually been known to drink a toast to women's sexual coldness. The best of these florid paeans has been recorded by Carl Carmer in *Stars Fell on Alabama:* "To Woman, lovely woman of the Southland, as pure and chaste as this sparkling water, as cold as this gleaming ice, we lift this cup, and we pledge our hearts and our lives to the protection of her virtue and chastity."

Southernese loses a great deal in translation. Here's what the toast really means: "To Woman, without whose purity and chastity we could never have justified slavery and segregation, without whose coldness we wouldn't have had the excuse we needed for messing around down in the slave cabins and getting plenty of poontang. We pledge our hearts and our lives to the protection of her virtue and chastity because they are the best political leverage we ever did see."

As male propaganda continued through the years, Southern women came to believe these fulsome testimonials to their purity and tried to find a middle road between their normal desires and their male-manufactured image. Anything can happen in a land where men drink toasts to frigidity, so the Southern woman often decided to enjoy sex as much as possible while remaining a virgin—a compromise that won her a reputation as a sadistic flirt.

More time passed, and other American women gained greater sexual freedom, so the Southern woman evolved another compromise. It was easy for her to do this sort of thing because she was the product of a region that had spent two centuries justifying itself to the rest of the country. After performing the kind of mental gymnastics it takes to prove that slavery is God's will, rationalizing mere sexual peccadilloes was child's play. She hit upon another modus vivendi, a much more swinging one this time, that would permit her to lose her virginity, enjoy a regular sex life, and yet soothe her male-induced guilt. She would throw away her hot pantalets, do as she pleased, and convince herself that her hymen was still intact.

She became a self-rejuvenating virgin.

To recycle her pearl beyond price, certain ground rules had to be established. First, premeditation was forbidden. The self-rejuvenating virgin never planned ahead, she was always "swept off her feet." If she could not make herself believe this, she engineered bizarre sexual encounters that were never quite the real thing, so that the next morning she could tell herself, "It didn't really happen because . . ."

1. I was drunk.

2. We didn't take all our clothes off.
3. We didn't do it in a bed.
4. He didn't put it all the way inside me.
5. He didn't come inside me.
6. I didn't come.
7. . . . Well, not really.

The self-rejuvenating virgin never bothered with contraceptives because that was premeditation. If her date wanted to use one, that was *his* business. They might drive past two dozen drugstores on their way to the woods, but she never said a word until the very last minute—at which point she shrieked: "Do you have something?" (He nearly always did.) Thanks to the self-rejuvenating virgin, the wallet of a Southern man in pre-pill days was likely to contain more condoms than money.

The woods, of course, was the only place a respectable self-rejuvenating virgin could go to earth. The very idea of making love in a bed threw her into conflict—it was too official, too premeditated, and too comfortable. She preferred to mortify her flesh in the woods, where she could count the chiggers and ticks as punishment.

When I was at Ole Miss in 1958, the boys were so used to self-rejuvenating virgins that they automatically headed for the woods even when a bed was available. Every car trunk contained both a blanket and the most Southern of all contraceptives, a bottle of warm Coca-Cola, because the self-rejuvenating virgin would walk over hot coals before she would ever buy a douche bag.

If her date failed to use a "precaution" and if the douche-that-refreshes did not work, the self-rejuvenating virgin could claim the best excuse in her rule book:

"It didn't really happen, because I'm pregnant."

This is the webby Southern mind at its best. Translation: "I let him do it to me and I enjoyed it, but now I'm being punished, which wipes out the pleasure and therefore the entire act."

Some self-rejuvenating virgins behaved themselves at home but went into a sexual frenzy on holiday trips. Their lovers were men they met in hotels and resorts. Thanks to this vacation psychology, they were able to go home and tell themselves: "It didn't really happen because . . ."

1. I'll never see him again.
2. I don't remember his name.
3. He never told me his name.
4. I didn't tell him my name.
5. It happened in New York.

The self-rejuvenating virgin might fondle a man's privates as he drove to the motel, but when he pulled up to room 102 she refused to go in.

"Let's just sit here a minute," she said, and the next minute was all over him. A steamy petting session ensued, but when they became excited to the point of adjourning to the paid-for room, she said, "Let's go somewhere!" Meaning, of course, the woods.

Sometimes she was drunk enough to enter the motel room, tear off her clothes, and fall backward onto the bed. She landed in the missionary position and promptly passed out—or pretended to. The next morning she awoke naked, next to a naked man, stared at him in horror, and then shook him awake: "Did anything happen? Tell me the truth."

Southern men always knew what to say.

"No, honcy, nothin' happened, I swear it didn't."

The self-rejuvenating virgin always had a ladylike orgasm, a pelvic legerdemain that she infused with fey girlishness. When she felt it coming on, she giggled—a feat that ought to be worth an Oscar or two—and when it hit she trembled prettily in the zephyr range. Afterward, she registered an awesome combination of astonishment and innocence: "Ohhh, what happened to me?"

The birth-control pill has all but wiped the self-rejuvenating virgin and her plea of crime passionnel from the face of the South. She must now own up to the fact that she is guilty of canoodling in the first degree.

I am glad she is passing into history, but I will miss her, because she made life, particularly dormitory life, most lively and interesting. The self-rejuvenating virgin I will never forget was a Mississippi girl who, without a doubt, had the most active sex life of any woman since Pauline Bonaparte—and, of course, convinced all of her lovers that she was a virgin. Her secret weapon was an alum-spiked red mouthwash that assured her of having pucker-power.

Readers of those moonlight-and-magnolia historical novels so popular in the Forties quickly became accustomed to certain words used to describe the patrician heroine. Somewhere around midbook she hauled off and melted, becoming: *languid, voluptuous, sinuous, sultry, abandoned,* and above all, *wanton.*

"Isn't that what you want? Wanton?" she breathed, her hot, *tremulous* lips moving against the hero's ear. *Suddenly,* she became *insatiable* and *demanding,* and, what's more, she started to *pulsate.*

The motivation for her startling change was usually a last-ditch attempt to drag a Southern gentleman from the arms of another female character called, invariably, "the insolent, sloe-eyed Zerline." Zerline was a slave—but always a high-yellow one—to whom the hero had turned for affection after Miss Lily had gone as stiff as a board on him for the four hundredth time. She went so stiff on her wedding night that he could have picked her up by her feet; she assumed this military posture every time he approached her bed, naturally driving him into the arms of Zerline.

Underneath the thesaurus style of plantation novelists lay a basic truth: Being "good in bed" is the Southern woman's specialty if not one of her most cherished arts. The novelists were also correct about her original motivation for taking up the sensual arts: competition. The nineteenth-century South Carolinian and enthusiastic diarist Mary Boykin Chesnut hints at this motivation in her angry comment: "Mrs. Stowe did not hit the sorest spots. She makes Legree a bachelor." Mary Chesnut stated bluntly that she hated slavery, but it was a selfish hatred. What really bothered her was not so much the misery of the slaves but the provocative ways of the slave women.

All Southerners are easily challenged, and pride is never far below the surface. When the plantation novelist's well-bred heroine made her inevitable decision to "fight back," she was simply being Southern. Gentlemen danced attendance on her, showered her with extravagant gallantries, and generally egged her along the road to narcissism and boundless conceit. The easy sensuality of slave women, for whom sex was life's only pleasure, became an ever-present challenge to the white woman, whose ego had been engorged by the code of chivalry.

A further puff for her ego—but really intended as a defense of slavery—was the Southern gentleman's boast that black men had to be kept in chains lest they make a beeline for the inordinately desirable Miss Lily, the mere sight of whom was enough to drive all males mad.

Being human, Miss Lily reveled in such compliments, whether direct or implied, and soon came to believe them. Once the twin gauntlets of the black woman's competition and the white man's press agentry had been flung down before her, she responded in predictable ways. Most Victorian women did not become wanton—that had to wait for a later day—but they did take up arms in the cause of sensual allure. The cult of the delectable belle was born. Her motto was: "Promise him anything." She may have delivered nothing except sidelong glances, but it is on such propaganda that images are built, and it is in the nature of Southerners to believe their own propaganda. When the passage of time brought greater sexual freedom to women, Miss Lily indeed became good in bed. Northern soldiers stationed in the many Army camps in the South licked their chops the moment they received their orders and said: "Oh, boy, Southern girls!"

Even when Miss Lily did not actually come across, she performed all the preliminaries with a fiery abandon that many Yankees, especially those with immigrant Catholic backgrounds, had never before encountered. Living in the myth-drenched South had made Lily a fine actress, and she had the Southern gift for playing to the galleries; she did more moaning, writhing, and scratching than Salvatore and Patrick had ever seen nice girls do. There was no doubt that Lily was nice, for in her nonsexual moments she danced the measured ballet of Southern life with exquisite propriety. She was a *hot lady,* a contradiction guaranteed to intrigue all men.

The Southern woman's sensuality is aided by her Anglo-Saxon heritage. Being Protestant, the Southern woman does not grow up under the shadow of Virgins, Madonnas, and saints. She might be a rock-ribbed fundamentalist, but old-time religion contains a great deal of sensuality, especially when the preachers let loose and everyone starts swaying and rolling. If the Southern woman is an Episcopalian, as many are, the battle of being good in bed is half-won by definition; Episcopalians, especially in the South, pride themselves on their sophistication. They also drink.

Healthy sexuality is easier to come by in rural areas. The Southern woman has an earthy streak that serves her well. If she belongs to the horsey set, loss of hang-ups is almost certain, because horsey people are constantly talking about mating.

Living in the South would make anyone sexy. The long-hot-summer tensions of Southern life create an aura of *waiting,* a perpetual alertness, and a sensation that something is about to happen. Such a mood turns people's minds to sex because it is the only form of release available. Quite often something does happen, and the ensuing excitement also stirs sex drives.

Finally, the Southern woman's sensual talents can be traced to her relationship with her father. Southern fathers behave very seductively around their daughters. Southerners in general tend to be physically affectionate, and in addition, the Southern father is obsessed with sexual differentiation. He wants his sons to be manly and his daughters to be womanly, with no shades of gray in between. Subconsciously he begins, early in her life, to ensure her proper development by training her to respond to men. His modus operandi includes a great deal of hugging, kissing, and lap-sitting, which launches a little girl onto the path of sexual response. She grows to like the way men smell, the feel of whiskers and hard muscles, and connects these things with the security of father's love. *Provided this love affair does not go too far,* the Southern daughter emerges from it as a very fortunate young woman. She is used to men, and she has also practiced her flirting on her father. Since she is the "apple of his eye," he always responds with elaborate fervor to her techniques, which instills supreme confidence in her and makes it virtually impossible for her to doubt her womanly charms. Used to a steady stream of male approbation and blandishments, she can hardly wait to get more of the same. The best way to get them is to be good in bed, and so she sees to it that she is.

Some Southern women love sex so much that they appear to be near-nymphomaniacs. Actually; they are not so passionate as they seem, for their attachment to bed sport is mainly an ego trip. Sex as ego-satisfaction is a pratfall that looms before all women in a man's world; much female sexuality is a substitution for success, money, and fame, a way to become a VIP without endangering one's femininity. The Southern woman is more susceptible to this psychological transference; she frequently throws herself into a virtual debauch simply because she has a human need to excel.

The Hollywood casting office has done its part in promoting the near-nymphomaniac to almost legendary heights, but she is a bona fide fixture of Southern life. I knew one, whose problems sprang from her father's Miss America complex.

She was his youngest child and only daughter. Overjoyed at her birth, he insisted upon giving her a name that, he felt, represented the sultry sensuality of the Southern woman at her tempting best. He called her Velvet, and she was baptized with this symbolic moniker in the poshest Episcopal church in town.

In case Velvet missed the point of Daddy's christening caper, he drummed it into her head that she was supposed to "grow up and become Miss America," "grow up and break men's hearts," "grow up and be a beautiful movie star."

What Velvet did was simply to grow up—in record time. As soon as she could walk, she put on her mother's high heels, smeared her mouth with filched lipstick, and sashayed down the street like a halfpint hooker, with Daddy behind her calling: "Hold on! Say I'm a little lady that behaves myself, say butter wouldn't melt in my mouth 'cause I'm so fine and sweet, say I'm just a little princess!"

He tried to ensure her fastidiousness by telling her the story of "The Princess and the Pea," but all Velvet got out of it was a fondness for lots of mattresses. From the age of fourteen, she oozed musk and wreaked havoc throughout a five-county area. Wives shot husbands, husbands shot wives, and private detectives made a fortune, all because Velvet devoted her every waking moment to living up to her name.

At no time in her nefarious growing years did Daddy speak of college, future careers, or constructive ambitions. The only time he mentioned Velvet's future was the day he made vague allusions to the fact that young ladies who become professional correspondents in divorce cases might hurt their Miss America chances.

Velvet did go to college, but only because it provided a happy hunting ground, and because Miss America contestants who are coeds are better representatives of the American dream than those who never go beyond high school. She became a dilettante, dabbling in writing, acting, sketching, and modern dance, and showing some talent for all of them. She especially liked art and drew very well. In one of her rare nonsexual moments she expressed a desire to go to art school in Chicago, but Daddy would not hear of it, and Velvet eventually forgot about her ambitions.

The urge to excel remained, however, and Velvet turned her energies to sex "showings" instead of art showings. She craved recognition and exposure; she wanted to be caught in the act, and, not unsurprisingly, she got her wish most of the time.

Like the good artist she was, Velvet was discovered by none other than Miss Lulugrace Tewksbury, Clerk of the State Senate, who barged into a young legislator's office and found Velvet and the statesman locked into a complicated cubist posture on his desk. Miss Tewk, as she was affectionately known throughout the state, took one look, screamed, and ran down the hall of the statehouse in such hysteria that she forgot about the lovely antebellum staircase at the end of it. She rolled like a ball down the entire flight and, thanks to the lovely thick carpeting, she arose unhurt, just like Vivien Leigh's stunt girl.

She was barely on her feet before she was telling everyone what she had seen, which was just what Velvet wanted.

The conflict between ice maiden and pulsating temptress often rages in the Southern woman's breast. The Miss America contestant is a case in point: She parades before crowds of strange men in a bathing suit and sings a torch song, but when she wins the crown, waves of guilt and confusion rush to the surface and cause her to make statements to the press like: "God is not dead, he's alive in my heart."

Movie bills of the Thirties and Forties left no doubt what the Southern woman was like.

She was Jezebelle.

"Drusilla was a clawing cat! A hot-tempered virago! Spoiled, self-centered, she always got her way!"

In the middle of this splash of words stood Drusilla herself, ready to burst a blood vessel. Here was your true Southern vixen, full of sound and fury, her mouth twisted in a red wound of rage, and a vase or a riding crop in her soft, dimpled hand. "No man had ever mastered her until. . . ."

Enter the hero on another movie bill.

"Trask Fontaine was all MAN! A ruthless riverboat gambler, Trask tamed his women the way he tamed his horses—with a firm hand, a curb bit, and if necessary a WHIP!"

In addition to being as cold as a witch's tit and pulsating with passion, the Southern woman is expected to behave in a manner that warrants commitment for observation. In Jezebelle novels and movies all she does is fight, fight, fight. The battle royal begins the moment Drusilla and Trask meet. She flays him with her crop, rakes him with her nails, hurls priceless objets d'art at his head (she always misses), and destroys the pianoforte with a crashing two-fisted discord.

Throughout her uninterrupted attacks of grand mal, Trask remains unmoved—even amused. He grins at her, "undresses her with his eyes," and says: "You look mighty pretty when you're mad."

It all ends with a spanking, or with a knock-down, drag-out struggle in which Drusilla suddenly relaxes and stills her pounding fists. Helplessly, her arms rise to encircle Trask's neck in a sinous embrace. The shrew is tamed.

A professional bitch does the Southern man proud. If she is skittish, high-strung, and easily upset, that means she is a thoroughbred with good blood as opposed to a sluggish peasant. Good blood became very important in a region where white men were busy mixing theirs with blacks, so the Southern woman was given the job of proving how aristocratic everybody was. Whenever she shied violently, showed the whites of her eyes, and laid her ears back, the South could feel superior to the egalitarian North.

For a woman who does not know whether to be hot or cold, temper tantrums are a convenient compromise. Men find it very easy to translate female rage into female *genital* rage. She indeed looks mighty pretty when she's mad; her cheeks flame, her eyes glitter, and she trembles uncontrollably. It looks like an orgasm; it even sounds like one. The Southern woman at last found a way to indicate her hot blood without doing anything unladylike. All she had to do was throw things, keep her riding crop at the ready, and foam at the mouth a little. She learned to use bitchiness for the same reason that she used glycerine and rose water—it made her feminine and lovely so that men would WANT her.

Any woman who gets mad becomes a Southern belle in the minds

211

of male witnesses. Angry feminists who have been the target of that famous diagnosis, "What she needs is a good screw," can thank the Jezebelle novelists and the cult of Southern womanhood.

"She was the only completely kind person I ever knew," sighed Rhett Butler of Melanie's death, and with that eulogy, the image of the Southern woman as a gentle, self-effacing comforter of the afflicted was assured.

The specter of unflagging virtue has haunted all women since time immemorial; the angel in the house simply will not leave, she hangs around like the last drunken guest who keeps saying: "Just one more cigarette."

The Southern woman's problem with the virtuous image has been intensified by constant articulation. One minute she is called a "lady-bug," the next minute a "heartbreaker," so it is not surprising that she behaves like Scarlett O'Hara for a month and then puts in a week as Sweet Melanie Wilkes.

The Melanie Syndrome is responsible for those trumpet blasts of self-effacement that Southern women emit and which sound to the Northern ear like an insufferably hypocritical game of Alphonse-Gaston. Saucy belles, who have the instincts and ethics of a cobra, break down from time to time and hunt themselves to earth with protestations such as:

"You dance so much better than I do! Why, I just have two left feet compared to you!"

"You'd look better in rags than I would in a Dior!"

"Oh, I wish I had your hair! Mine is just so ugly!" (It's strawberry blond and naturally curly.)

It sounds catty, but it isn't. It's just Melanie trying to get some fresh air after being walled up in the belle's psyche for the past two weeks.

The Melanie Syndrome is responsible for the Southern woman's fashion "look," which is somewhat less than chic. The compulsive need to *be* sweet is often translated into an attempt to *look* sweet that results in "busy" ensembles. A little more lace here, a few more tucks there, something "cute" pinned on the waist of a svelte dress, or even today, a flower garden of a hat.

The Melanie Syndrome is also responsible for the inordinate

amount of home sewing that goes on in the South, most of which is done by mothers of belles who want to make sure that Daughter looks just darlin' no matter what she does on those nights when she returns home with liquor on her breath and her pants in her pocketbook. The Southern mother is no more able than her daughter to cope with the intricacies of the cult of womanhood; she "would rather not know" what her daughter is up to because such knowledge might unearth some conflict of her own and cause her to have one of those Southern nervous breakdowns known as "going to pieces."

The Jewish mother snoops to keep her daughter in line; the Southern mother sews. Permissive because it is too disturbing to be otherwise, she tries to exert some control over her daughter by "running up" sweet-looking dresses for her in a spirit of genteel compromise: If the dress her daughter pulls up in the back seat of a car is made of dotted Swiss, then surely virtue cannot be far behind.

In addition to being cold, hot, bitchy, and sweet, the Southern woman is required to be something called "pert."

Pertness grew out of psychological and political necessity in the Old South. The slaveholder, secretly guilty and doubtful of his clout, needed to feel that the medieval fief he had created produced delirious joy in those who lived on it. It was only logical that he turned to his slaves and his women for reassurance on this score.

Blacks played the banjo for him and grinned or giggled whenever he caught their eye. His women did even better. They tinkled with insouciant gaiety and became saucy, piquant, lively, merry, sparkling, vivacious—in a word, "pert." The Southern woman did everything but lead a Virginia reel between labor pains; as secession and conflict loomed, her spirits rose higher and higher, keeping pace with her laughter. By the time Old Massa went off to war, he was certain that he could lick the Yankees in a month.

He lost, which meant that he needed pertness more than ever to bolster his fallen ego. It did not matter that his war had brought poverty and Reconstruction down on everyone's head; Miss Dixie could be happy no matter what. To prove it, she followed the first commandment of pertness: *Thou shalt have the time of your life.* She detonated into a flurry of excitement over the slightest thing, bubbled with ecstasy at every gathering, and ran up and down the floor in

213

her patched party dress, shrieking: " 'Deed I'm just havin' such a wonderful time I don't know what to do!' "

The second commandment of pertness is: *Thou shalt entertain.* People forget their troubles when they're being entertained, so the Southern woman learned the art of being onstage at all times, performing like Dr. Johnson's dancing dog no matter how she felt. She had to sing, play the piano, and tell clever stories with the expert timing of a stand-up comedian.

The third commandment of pertness is: *Thou shalt play dumb.* Men who have lost a war must feel superior to someone. Dumb women cannot tell clever stories, however, so dumbness had to be mixed with pertness to achieve a brew that suited Southern tastes. Since under no circumstances could Miss Dixie grow logy with stupidity, she chose an energetic form of dumbness that involved a lot of haphazard motion. She became scatterbrained, empty-headed, helpless, doe-eyed, forgetful, confused, and simpleminded. Men delighted in her arch panic, especially when she threw herself into their arms and screamed: "Oh, I just don't know what to do!"

Being pleasant and agreeable is one thing, but the Southern woman overdid it until pertness became an ingrained habit. She could not stop giggling, any more than she could lower her voice. She became an irretrievable victim of the Pert Plague, that hyperkinetic frenzy that still exists in the South.

Simulating convulsive mirth is an exhausting business. The Pert Plague has affected the Southern woman's habits and priorities to an inordinate degree. Our friend Dr. Jonathan Latham encountered one of its chief effects on his first visit to a Southern home.

Aware of the Southern woman's hospitality and her fondness for antiques and other "fine things," he assumed that she would be a superb housekeeper, the kind of whom it is said, "You could eat off her floors." But the moment he entered his hostess's house, he realized that it would take a strong man even to eat off her table. It was piled high with weeks' worth of undiscarded newspapers, an overflowing sewing basket, hair rollers, and a cluster of grape seeds.

In horror, he looked down at the exquisite Persian rug and saw thereon a clump of something that he associated with the sidewalks of Beacon Hill. Balls of dust lay everywhere, like gone-to-seed dandelions, and the unwashed windows were caked with grime. And what was his elegant hostess doing when Dr. Latham arrived? She was seated at her sticky groaning board polishing her silver, or, as she took pains to point out, her great-grandmother's silver. Latham watched in amazement as she dug down carefully into the elaborate curliques with a gauze-wrapped toothpick: the silver, shining to begin with, was the one thing in the house that didn't need cleaning.

Dr. Latham did not remain in the South long enough to learn about the Pert Plague: many Southern women are simply too tired to clean house. Their silver is kept spotless because it's *silver* and because this is one housekeeping task that can be done while sitting down.

The Pert Plague also takes its toll outside the home. An enormous amount of time is wasted in Southern offices by the otherwise capable and intelligent women who simply cannot calm down. If someone brings a woman a file, she will not say "Thank You," but: "Oh! You've rescued me from the horns of a dilemma! Whatever would I do without you!"

After such a metaphorical litany, a simple "You're welcome" would sound painfully inadequate if not downright rude. The proper Southern reply? "Oh, I'm more than happy to do it for you! It was no trouble whatsoever, 'deed it wasn't!"

Northerners living and working the South, impatient with these matins and lauds, often voice that well-known Yankee criticism: "Nothing ever gets done!" There is some truth in this because Southerners use up so much of their energy simply being nice that they have to take work home—which never gets done there, either, because they spend the evening being nice to their guests.

The Pert Plague is not only a spectacle for men; Southern women also pull out all the stops for each other. When two of them meet, whether they have been separated for years, weeks, or days, they immediately begin to shriek—literally. The decibel level has to be heard to be believed, but it goes something like this:

"Yeeeeeeeeeee! Oh! I'm just so thrilled to see you again!"

"Yeeeeeeeeee! It can't be you, it just can't be! I just don't believe it!"

At which point they fall into each other's arms.

The Pert Plague is responsible for the general confusion in which so many Southern women dwell, known as being "on the horns of a dilemma." They are so busy talking, flirting, and laughing that they create an aura of turmoil in which they lose things, drop things, and spend a great deal of time rooting in their handbags like pigs at a trough, wailing: "Oh, I've lost my ticket! . . . Oh, I can't find my baggage check! . . . Now where's my wallet? I had it just a minute ago, and now it's gone!"

Sometimes they even lose people. Prearranged meetings get snarled, itineraries are misread, someone misunderstands or never hears an instruction about time and place. . . . Soon it's all hopelessly snafued and everybody gets on the telephone to everybody else: "Have you seen Mary Lou? No, she's not here, I thought she was *there!*"

When the Southern woman's hyped-up nervous system is unleashed, it is not long before a simple misunderstanding becomes a federal case. Thanks to every Southerner's tendency to exaggeration, when nobody can find Mary Lou the verdict is:

"She's just vanished into thin air!"

When I was a little girl, we lost Mama somewhere on the boardwalk at Colonial Beach. Granny immediately set up an outcry and churned up the atmosphere with melodramatic allusions to foul play.

"She's disappeared! She was here just a minute ago, and now it's like she never was. It's like somebody snatched her up and took her off!"

Instead of staying put and waiting, Granny added to the confusion in true Southern style by organizing a search party and sending people hither and yon, with the result that my aunts kept finding each other and my father was nearly beaten up by the husband of a woman who looked like Mama—from the rear. (We finally found her crouched under a slimy pier like a troll in a fairy tale, desperately puffing away on a Lucky Strike because ladies do not smoke on boardwalks.)

The Pert Plague takes a heavy toll from Southern men, whose gallantry can be strained to the breaking point by Miss Dixie's spirited frenzies. In a letter to me, a Southern man had this to say about his former wife:

> She had that maddeningly imprecise quality of mind that made
> her sure no plane would dare leave without her no matter how

late she got to the airport. She thought it was "cute" to rush through the terminal, giving voice like a hound on the scent, and that I would be charmed by this evidence of her femininity and feel more masculine thereby. At first I was charmed—but then I started having chest pains.

Many Southern women subconsciously use the Pert Plague as revenge on men. When a woman approaches the ladies' room at an airport, some man will button-hole her and say: "I beg your pardon, ma'am, but my wife is in there someplace. Her name is Cindy Lee MacIvor. Would you be good enough to tell her to hurry up or else we're gonna miss our plane?"

When the messenger enters the rest room, she calls out merrily, "Cindy Lee MacIvor? Your husband's outside. He says for you to hurry," whereupon all the women shriek with laughter.

It was the Pert Plague that led many Americans to think that Martha Mitchell was insane when she first told her kidnapping story. From the beginning of the dull Nixon administration, Martha was a classic example of Southern vivacity, famous thanks to her spontaneity and her sometimes calculated wackiness. Compared to the dark-suited Nixon crowd, her colorful behavior made her seem more or less crazy by default.

To make matters worse, the kidnapping incident occurred during America's obsession with Zelda Fitzgerald. The analogy was too much for many people, who decided that Martha was just another one of those bananas belles. Later, of course, crazy Martha was redeemed in all her glory. Thanks to her, pertness was displayed at its best on the Mike Douglas TV show, when she told the entire Watergate saga, complete with hilarious imitations of the principals. Whatever else it has done, the Pert Plague has made the Southern woman a most delightful raconteuse.

Every great civilization has had its courtesans, witty women who reigned in salons and enchanted men with their conversational powers. The Southern woman's lively charm has made her the last of America's courtesans.

Lisa Alther

The Art of Dying Well

M Y FAMILY ALWAYS has been into death. My father, the Major,
used to insist on having an ice pick next to his placemat at
meals so that he could perform an emergency tracheotomy when
one of us strangled on a piece of meat. Even now, by running my
index fingers along my collarbones to the indentation where the bones
join, I can locate the optimal site for a tracheal puncture with the
same deftness as a junky a vein.

The Major wasn't always a virtuoso at disaster prediction, however.
When I was very young, he was all brisk efficiency, and made no
room whatsoever for the unscheduled or the unexpected. "Ridiculous!" he would bark at Mother as she sat composing drafts of her
epitaph. "Do you want to turn the children into a bunch of psychotics
like the rest of your crazy family?" Perhaps, like my southern mother,
you have to be the heiress to a conquered civilization to take your
own vulnerability seriously prior to actually experiencing it. At least
if you were born, as was the Major, in 1918 B.B. (Before the Bomb).

Whatever the reason, the Major's Cassandra complex developed
later in life. He was a carpetbagger by profession, brought to Hullsport, Tennessee, from Boston to run the chemical plant that is the
town's only industry. During the Korean War the plant, with its acres
of red brick buildings and forests of billowing smoke stacks, was converted from production of synthetic fabrics to munitions; there were
contracts from the federal government and top-secret contracts with
the laboratories at Oak Ridge. On summer evenings, the Major used
to take us kids out for cones of soft ice cream dipped in chocolate
glaze, and then to the firing range where the new shell models were

tested. Licking our dripping cones, we would watch proudly as the Major, tall and thin and elegant, listing forward on the balls of his feet, signaled the blasts with upraised arms, like an orchestra conductor cuing cymbal crashes.

Shortly after the conversion of the plant to munitions, the Major experienced his own personal conversion, and in a fashion that even an experienced aficionado of calamity like Mother could never have foreseen: He caught his platinum wedding band on a loose screw on a loaded truck bed at the factory and was dragged along until his ring finger popped out of its socket like a fried chicken wing being dismembered. Then his legs were run over by the rear wheels. There he lay, a fallen industrial cowboy, his boot caught in a stirrup, trampled by his own horse. Truckloads of hams and cakes and casseroles began arriving at the house from bereaved admirers/employees. All the downtown churches offered up hours of prayers for his recovery.

Ira was hurt, in the early days of our marriage, when I wouldn't wear my wedding band. He considered it symbolic of the tepidity of my response to him. Maybe he was right, but Ira had never seen a hand with only the bloody remains of a knuckle socket where the ring finger used to be. He merely assumed, until the day he ran me out of his house in Vermont with a rifle, that I was frigid. Well, he had to find some rational explanation for the failure of our union, because it was impossible for him to entertain the notion that he, Ira Braithwaite Bliss IV, might simply have picked a lemon from the tree of life.

When the Major emerged from his casts, a metamorphosis had occurred: He was no longer bold and brash. In fact, the first project he undertook was to renovate the basement family room into a bomb shelter as a surprise for Mother's birthday. *Her* reaction to the atmospheric nuclear tests going on all over the world then was to join a group in Hullsport called Mothers' Organization for Peace. MOP consisted of a dozen housewives, mostly wives of chemical plant executives who'd been exiled to Hullsport for a dreary year as grooming for high managerial posts in Boston. MOP meetings consisted of a handful of women with abrasive Yankee accents who sipped tea and twisted handkerchief corners and insisted bravely that Russian mothers *must* feel the same about strontium 90 in *their* babies' bones.

The Major, sneering at MOP, kept going with his bomb shelter. We kids were delighted. I took my girl friends down there to play house; and we confronted such ethical issues as whether or not to let old Mr. Thornberg next door share our shelter when the bomb dropped, or whether to slam the door in his miserly face, as he did to us on Halloween nights. Later we girls took Clem Cloyd and the acned boys from Magnolia Manor development down there to play Five Minutes in Heaven. While the others counted outside, the designated couple went into the chemical toilet enclosure to execute the painful grinding of braces that left us all with raw and bruised mouths . . . but in love. And in high school I brought dates down for serious sessions of heavy petting. In fact, I broke the heart of Joe Bob Sparks, star tailback of the Hullsport Pirates and body beautiful of Hullsport Regional High School, by forfeiting my maidenhead to Clem Cloyd one night on the altarlike wooden sleeping platform, double-locked behind the foot-thick steel door, while Mother and the Major slept on blissfully unaware upstairs.

Soon, no situation was too safe for the Major to be unable to locate its potential for tragedy. Death to him was not the inevitable companion of one's later years, the kindly warden who freed each soul from its earthly prison. Death to him was a sneak and a cheat who was ever vigilant to ambush the unwary, of whom the Major was determined not to be one. In contrast to Mother, who regarded Death as some kind of demon lover. The challenge, as she saw it, was to be ready for the assignation, so that you weren't distracted during consummation by unresolved earthly matters. The trick was in being both willing to die and able to at the same time. Dying properly was like achieving simultaneous orgasm.

Mother had many photographs, matted in eggshell white and framed in narrow black wood, on the fireplace mantle in her bedroom. As I was growing up, she would sit me on her lap and take down these yellowed cracked photos and tell me about the people in them, people who had already experienced, prepared for it or not, this ultimate fuck with Death. Her grandmother, Dixie Lee Hull, in a blouse with a high lace neck, who had cut her finger on a recipe card for spoon bread and had died of septicemia at age twenty-nine. Great-uncle Lester, a druggist in Sow Gap, who became addicted to cough syrup and one night threw himself under the southbound train to Chattanooga. Cousin Louella, who dove into a nest of water moccasins in an abandoned stone quarry at a family reunion in 1932. Another cousin who stuck his head out of a car window to read a historical marker about the Battle of Lookout Mountain and was sideswiped by a Mason-Dixon transport truck. It was always so unsatisfying to rage at her in a tantrum, as children do, "I *hate* you! I hope you *die!*" She'd reply calmly, "Don't worry, I will. And so will you."

At spots in our decor where lesser women would have settled for Audubon prints or college diplomas, Mother hung handsomely framed and matted rubbings of the tombstones of our forebears, done in dark chalk on fine rice paper. The Major always planned family vacations around business conferences so that expenses would be tax deductible and so that he wouldn't have to spend long stretches trapped with his family. Mother used to coordinate his meetings with trips for the rest of us to unvisited gravesites of remote relations. I spent most of my first seventeen summers weeding and edging and planting around obscure ancestral crypts. Mother considered these pilgrimages to burying plots around the nation as didactic exercises for us children, far superior to the overworked landmarks, like the Statue of Liberty, on the American Freedom Trail.

Apparently a trait like fascination with eschatology is hereditary. At any rate, it seems to run in *our* family. Mother's ancestors, however humble their circumstances (and most of them were in very humble circumstances, being dirt farmers and coal miners), invested a great deal of thought and money in their memorials to themselves. In any given cemetery, the most elaborately carved urns and weeping willows and hands pointing confidently to heaven invariably belong to my ancestors. Also the most catchy epitaphs: "Stop and look as you pass by./ As you are now, so once was I./ As I am now, so you will be./ Prepare to die and follow me." Mother considered that one, by a great-great-aunt named Hattie, the pinnacle of our family's achievement. Mother had dozens of trial epitaphs for herself, saved up in a small black loose-leaf notebook. The prime contender when I left

221

home for college in Boston was, "The way that is weary, dark and cold/ May lead to shelter within the fold./ Grieve not for me when I am gone./ The body's dark night: the soul's dawn."

When Mother wasn't working on her epitaph, she was rewriting her funeral ceremony. "Let's see—" she'd say to me as I sat on the floor beside her mahogany Chippendale desk dressing my doll in black crepe for a wake. "Do you think 'A Mighty Fortress Is Our God' should go before or after 'Deus Noster Refugium'?" I'd look up from my doll's funeral. "You won't forget, will you, dear?" she'd inquire sternly. "The agenda for my memorial service will be in my upper right-hand desk drawer."

Or she'd repolish her obituary and worry over whether or not the Knoxville *Sentinel* would accept it for publication. I have since come to understand her agony. When my classmates were taking frantic notes on penile lengths in first term Physiology 110 at Worthley College, I was diligently preparing the wording of my engagement announcement in the margin of my notebook: "Major and Mrs. Wesley Marshall Babcock IV of Hullsport, Tennessee, and Hickory, Virginia, take pleasure in announcing the engagement of their daughter Virginia Hull Babcock to Clemuel Cloyd. . . ." Years later, when the time finally came to dust off this draft and replace the name of Clemuel Cloyd with Ira Bliss, I discovered that the Boston *Globe* wouldn't print it, in spite of the fact that I'd read their damned paper dutifully every Sunday for the two years I'd been in college there. What could bring more posthumous humiliation than to have your obituary rejected by a paper like the Knoxville *Sentinel*?

Groggy with two in-flight martinis, Ginny huddled by the DC-7's emergency exit. When she'd picked up her ticket for this flight, she'd made a brave joke to the clerk about someone's wanting to hijack a plane bound between Stark's Bog, Vermont, and Hullsport, Tennessee. The clerk had replied without looking up, "Believe me, honey, no one in their right mind would want anything to do with those planes they send to Tennessee." To be aware of death was one thing, she mused; to accept it, another. All her life, awash with shame, she had secretly rejoiced over each plane crash as it was reported in the papers because it meant They'd missed her again.

She grabbed the plastic card from the nubby green seatback pocket and studied the operation of the plane's emergency exits, deployment procedures for the inflatable slide. It occurred to her that if use of the emergency exits was required, she'd be frozen by panic and trampled by all her frenzied fellow passengers as they tried to get past her and out the escape hatch. It also occurred to her that perhaps the reason every person in the plane didn't struggle to sit by an emergency exit, as she did, was that they knew something she didn't: that the likelihood of needing to clamber out the exit to safety was more than offset by the likelihood of the exit's flying open in midflight and sucking those near it into the troposphere.

But she knew that this pattern of blindly seeking out emergency exits was already too set in her to be thwarted with ease. Just as some people's eyes, due to early experience with The Breast, were irresistibly drawn to bosoms throughout their lives, so were hers riveted by neon signs saying EXIT. At the Saturday morning cowboy serials as a child, she had been required by the Major to sit right next to the exit sign in case the theater should catch fire. He told her about a Boston theater fire when he was young in which a crazed man had carved his way with a Bowie knife through the hysterical crowds to an exit. Ever since, she'd been unable to watch a movie or listen to a lecture or ride in a plane without the comforting glow of an exit sign next to her, like a nightlight in a small child's bedroom.

Nevertheless, on this particular flight, she first realized that the emergency exit, the escape lines coiled in the window casings, the yellow oxygen masks being playfully manipulated by the shapely stewardesses, were all totems designed to distract passengers from the fact that if the plane crashed, they'd all had it—splat! As eager as she was to deny the possibility of personal extinction while negotiating the hostile skies of United Air Lines, even Ginny was only faintly comforted by the presence of her seat cushion flotation device. She knew full well that the Blue Ridge Mountains of Virginia were below her should the engines falter and the plane flutter down like a winged bird. The sea was swelling some three hundred miles to the east. She tried to picture herself, stranded in a mountain crevice, afloat on her ritual seat cushion above a sea of gore and gasoline and in-flight martinis.

223

In the crush of the waiting room prior to boarding, Ginny had inspected with the intensity of the Ancient Mariner the visages of all her fellow passenger-victims: Were these the kind of people she'd want to be adrift with in a life raft? She could never decide how Fate worked it: Did planes stay aloft because of the absence of actively wicked people on board to be disposed of? Or was the opposite the case: Did planes falter and fall because of the absence of people sufficiently worthy to redeem the flight, people who had to be kept alive to perform crucial missions? Whichever was the case, Ginny had closely studied her companions in folly, looking for both damning and redeeming personality types and laying odds on a mid-air collision. With relief, she'd discovered three small babies.

Her fellow travelers had also scrutinized *her* upon boarding this winged silver coffin, Ginny reflected. In fact, one plump woman in a hideous Indian print caftan had studied her so closely that Ginny was sure the woman *knew* that she was the one who'd broken the macrobiotic recipe chain letter earlier that week. Which of the assembled Vermont housewives, they all must have wondered as they found their seats, would be the one to demand six thousand books of S & H Green Stamps and a parachute for a descent into a redemption center at a Paramus, New Jersey, shopping mall? Whose tote bag contained the bomb, nestled in a hollowed-out gift wheel of Vermont cheddar cheese, or submerged in a take-out container of spaghetti sauce? Ginny had often thought that she should carry such a bomb aboard her plane flights herself, because the likelihood of there being *two* bomb-toting psychopaths on the same flight was so infinitesimal as to be an impossibility. It was the mentality that fostered the arms race: Better to be done in by the bomb that she herself, in a last act of existential freedom, could detonate.

And, Ginny suspected, they were all—if they'd only admit it—inspecting each other with the care of housewives at a supermarket meat counter, as possible main courses should their craft be lost atop a remote peak in the Smokies.

But at least she still rode planes, Ginny reminded herself—unlike her mother, who in recent years had scarcely left the house at all for fear of being overtaken by disaster among strangers, insisting that it was vulgar to die among people one didn't know. How was her mother feeling about that now, as she lay in a hospital bed in Hullsport hemorrhaging like an overripe tomato? "A clotting disorder," their neighbor Mrs. Yancy had called it in her note suggesting that Ginny come down and keep her mother company while Mrs. Yancy went on a trip to the Holy Land. "Nothing serious," the note had assured her. Her mother knew she'd be out of the hospital soon and hadn't wanted to worry Ginny with the news. But if it wasn't serious, why was her mother in a place that she would necessarily hate, feeling as she did about strangers? And why had Mrs. Yancy asked Ginny to come down, knowing as she must that in recent years Ginny and her mother had been hitting it off like Moses and the Pharaoh?

Before giving up flying altogether, her mother had gone on business trips regularly with the Major. His condition on her going was that they take separate planes so that when one of them died during landing, the other would remain to carry on.

"Doesn't it just double the likelihood of one of your bags going to Des Moines?" Ginny had demanded of her mother one winter afternoon when she was in high school and was making her second trip to the airport, having taken the Major to catch *his* flight to New York that morning. They were in the Major's huge black Mercedes. Her mother had loved that car. Because it looked and drove like a hearse, Ginny suspected. Practice.

"Don't ask me. Ask your father," she replied, closing her eyes in anticipation of a head-on collision as Ginny negotiated a traffic circle. Any time her mother couldn't be bothered with having an opinion on something, she'd say, "Don't ask me. Ask your father." Ever since the Major had died, she must have been somewhat at a loss for words.

"I don't know why I go along with all this," she mused. "I wouldn't even *want* to 'carry on' if your father's plane crashed."

"You'd just throw yourself on his funeral pyre, like a suttee?" Ginny didn't enjoy being sarcastic to the woman who had rinsed her dirty diapers, but it seemed unjust that she should be saddled with these passive-dependent attitudes simply because this woman and she had lived in the same house for eighteen years. After all, what about free will?

"Yes, I think I would. I don't think it's such a bad custom at all."

225

"You don't," Ginny said flatly, more as a statement than as a question, since she knew her mother didn't. "Does it bother you that you don't?" Ginny asked this blandly to conceal how much it was bothering *her* that the custom appealed so enormously to her too.

"Bother me?" her mother asked with an intense frown, working an imaginary brake with her foot.

"*Please*, Mother, I'm a very safe driver," Ginny snapped. "Bother you. You know. Do you sometimes wish that there were things in life that seemed important to you other than your family?"

"I'm not really all that interested in life. I mean, it's okay, I guess. But I'm not hog wild about it."

"Well, why do you go on with it?" Ginny demanded irritably.

"Why not?"

"But if the only thing you're interested in is your great family reunion in the sky, why don't you get on with it? What keeps you hanging around here?"

Her mother looked at her thoughtfully for a while and then gave a careful and sincere answer: "It's character building. What does it matter what I might prefer?" As Ginny understood the lengthy explanation that ensued, her mother was saying that the human soul was like a green tomato that had to be ripened by the sun of earthly suffering before the gods would deign to pluck it for use at their cosmic clambake. It hadn't made sense to an impatient sixteen-year-old.

But that incident was why Ginny was so surprised several years later when her mother said, with great intensity, "Ginny, you must promise me that you will put me out of my misery if I'm ever sick and dying a lingering death."

Startled, Ginny had looked at her closely. She had crow's feet at the corners of her eyes and frown lines; and her neat cap of auburn hair was graying here and there. But she was agile and erect. With the insensitivity of the young to the concerns of their elders, Ginny laughed nervously and protested, "But *Mother!* Your hair is hardly even gray or anything. I'd say you've got a few years left!"

She gave Ginny a sharp look of betrayal and said sourly, "Believe me, after age thirty it's all downhill. Everything starts giving out and falling apart."

Her mother hadn't been hog wild about living eleven years ago. Ginny wondered how she was feeling about it now that her bluff was being called. But *was* it being called? "Not serious," Mrs. Yancy had said. And yet Ginny couldn't seem to prevent herself from leaping to all kinds of dire conclusions. Why was her mother in the hospital if it wasn't serious? How sick *was* she?

These questions, swarming through her head like fruit flies, temporarily distracted Ginny from the fact that she had survival problems of her own—both immediate, in that she was trapped aboard this airborne sarcophagus, and long-range with regard to the fact that she couldn't figure out what she wanted to be when she grew up. If indeed she did one day grow up, which was looking increasingly unlikely as she approached early middle age, with her twenty-seventh birthday recently behind her. The incidents in her life to date resembled the Stations of the Cross more than anything else. If this was adulthood, the only improvement she could detect in her situation was that now she could eat dessert without eating her vegetables.

Another problem was that the stewardesses were bullying the passengers that day. They kept parading past selling pennants and souvenirs, and requiring that everyone acknowledge their obvious talents with their lip brushes. Ginny finally concluded that the only way to get rid of them would be to throw up in the air-sickness bag and then try to find one of them to dispose of it.

And then there was the problem of the blond two-year-old in the next seat, imprisoned between her own mother and Ginny. The child kept popping up and down, unfastening and refastening her seat belt, lowering her seat-back tray and then replacing it, scattering the literature in the pocket all over the floor, putting the air-sickness bag over her head and then looking around for applause, removing her shoes and putting them back on the wrong feet, snapping the metal lid to the ashtray. It seemed a shame for all that energy to be going to waste, dissipating throughout the plane. Ginny suddenly understood the rationale behind child labor. Hooked up to a generator, this child's ceaseless contortions could have been fueling the plane.

She found herself unable not to watch the child, as irritating as all her relentless activities were. Ginny was experiencing the Phantom Limb Syndrome familiar to all recent amputees: She felt, unmistakably,

227

Wendy's presence next to her. When she looked over and discovered that this presence was merely an unfamiliar child of the same age, she was flooded with an overwhelming misery that caused her to shut her eyes tightly with pain. Wendy was in Vermont now with her father, the bastard Ira Bliss, living a life that excluded her wicked, adulterous mother.

Ginny reflected glumly that the racy view of her behavior credited her with much more sexual savoir-faire than she actually possessed. Although in principle she was promiscuous, feeling that the wealth should be shared, in practice she had always been morbidly monogamous, even before her marriage to Ira. In fact, until the appearance of Will Hawk that afternoon, nude in her swimming pool in Vermont, she had always been doglike in her devotion to one partner. Even with Hawk, her unfaithfulness to Ira was spiritual only, not physical—although Ira had found that impossible to believe the night he had discovered Ginny and Hawk in his family graveyard in poses that the unenlightened could only identify as postcoital.

Ginny tried to decide if her transports of fidelity were innate—an earthly translation of a transcendent intuition of oneness, a kind of sexual monotheism. Or whether she'd simply been brainwashed by a mother who would have liked nothing better than to throw herself on her husband's funeral pyre. Or whether it was unadulterated practicality, a question of knowing which side her bed was buttered on, her bod was bettered on—a very sensible refusal to bite the hand that feels her. In such a culture as this, perhaps the only prayer most women had was to find a patron and cling to him for all he was worth. People knew a man by the company he kept, but they generally knew a woman by the man who kept her. Or by the woman who kept her, in the case of Ginny and Edna.

At one point the child's mother, noticing Ginny's self-punishing absorption with the little girl, leaned forward and asked with a smile, "Do you have children?"

"Yes," Ginny replied with a pained smile. "One. Just this age."

"Oh, well!" the mother said briskly. "Then you'll want this." She took two index cards from her alligator pocketbook and began copying from one onto the other. When she finished, she reread what she'd written and handed it to Ginny with pride. It read: "Homemade Play

Doh: mix 2¼ cups flour with 1 cup salt; add 1 cup water mixed with 2 T vegetable oil; add food color to water before mixing."

"Neat," Ginny said, stuffing it quickly into the pocket of her patchwork peasant dress. "Thanks." She decided not to wreck this moment of sharing by mentioning that her child's father had kicked her out and that she might never see Wendy again, much less mix Play Doh for her.

"Be sure to use all the salt. Otherwise they eat it."

"I'll remember," Ginny assured her, wondering if Ira really could prevent her from ever seeing Wendy again, as he had vowed he would. In spite of her apparent moral turpitude, Ginny was still Wendy's natural mother. Didn't that count for something in the eyes of the law?

The child had ripped the arm off her doll and was hitting her mother over the head with it. It occurred to Ginny, as the plane's engines were cut and she grabbed the handle of the emergency door preparing to wrench it open, that someone should invent a God doll—wind Him up and He delivers us from evil. Mattel could make a fortune.

Rather than spiraling down into fiery death, the plane began its normal descent into the Crockett River valley. As it emerged from the fluffy white clouds, Ginny could see the Crockett, forking all along its length into hundreds of tiny capillarylike tributaries that interpenetrated the forested foothills and flashed silver in the sun. The treed bluffs on either side of the river were crimped like a pie crust of green Play Doh.

Soon Hullsport itself was beneath them, its defunct docks crumbling into the Crockett. They were low enough now so that the river, having had its moment of poetry from higher up, looked more like its old self—a dark muddy yellow frothed with chemical wastes from the Major's factory. The river valley containing the town was ringed by red clay foothills, which were gashed with deep red gullies from indiscriminate clearing for housing developments. From eight thousand feet Ginny's home town looked like a case of terminal acne.

Hullsport, Tennessee, the Model City, Pearl of the Crockett River valley, birthplace of such notables as Mrs. Melody Dawn Bledsoe, winner of the 1957 National Pillsbury Bake-Off, as a banner draped across Hull Street had reminded everyone ever since. Spawning ground of Joe Bob Sparks, All-South running back for the University of Northeastern Tennessee Renegades—and prince charming for a couple of years to Virginia Hull Babcock, Persimmon Plains Burly Tobacco Festival Queen of 1962. Ginny was prepared to acknowledge that time spent as Persimmon Plains Burly Tobacco Festival Queen sounded trivial in the face of personal and global extinction; but it was as tobacco queen that she had first understood why people were leaving their tobacco farms to crowd into Hullsport and work at the Major's munitions plant, why there were no longer clutches of farmers around the train station on Saturday mornings.

The plane was making its approach now to the pock-marked landing strip that Hullsport called its airport. Ginny could see the shadow of the plane passing over her childhood hermitage below—a huge white neo-Georgian thing with pillars and a portico across the front, a circular drive, a grove of towering magnolia trees out front which at that very moment would be laden with intoxicating cream-colored blossoms. It looked from a thousand feet up like the real thing—an authentic antebellum mansion. But it was a fraud. Her grandfather, apparently suffering the bends from a too-rapid ascent from the mines, had built it in 1921 on five hundred acres of farmland. It was copied from a plantation house in the delta near Memphis. The design clearly wasn't intended for the hills of east Tennessee. Hullsport had expanded to meet the house, which was now surrounded on three sides by housing developments. But behind the house stretched the farm—a tobacco and dairying operation run now by none other than Clem Cloyd, Ginny's first lover, whose father before him had run the farm for Ginny's grandfather and father. The Cloyds' small maroon-shingled house was diagonally across the five hundred acres from Ginny's house. And at the opposite end, in a cleared bowl ringed by wooded foothills, across the invisible Virginia state line, was the restored log cabin that Ginny's grandfather had withdrawn to toward the end of his life, in disgust with the progressive degradation of the Model City.

As she swooped down from the clouds to take the pulse of her ailing mother, Ginny felt a distinct kinship with the angel of death.

"I couldn't ask the boys to come," Mrs. Yancy's note had said. "They've got their own lives. Sons aren't like daughters." "Indeed," Ginny said to herself in imitation of Miss Head, her mentor at Worthley College, who used to warble the word with a pained grimace on similar occasions.

As they taxied up to the wind-socked cow shed that masqueraded as a terminal, Ginny was reminded of the many times she'd landed there in the past. Her mother had always been addicted to home movie-making and had choreographed the upbringing of Ginny and her brothers through the eyepiece of a camera, eternally poised to capture on Celluloid those golden moments—the first smile, the first step, the first tooth in, the first tooth out, the first day of school, the first dance, year after tedious year. Mother's Kinflicks, Ginny and her brothers had called them. A preview of the Kinflicks of Ginny's arrivals at and departures from this airport would have shown her descending or ascending the steps of neglected DC-7's in a dizzying succession of disguises—a black cardigan buttoned up the back and a too-tight straight skirt and Clem Cloyd's red silk Korean windbreaker when she left home for college in Boston; a smart tweed suit and horn-rim Ben Franklin glasses and a severe bun after a year at Worthley; wheat jeans and a black turtleneck and Goliath sandals after she became Eddie Holzer's lover and dropped out of Worthley; a red Stark's Bog Volunteer Fire Department Women's Auxiliary blazer after her marriage to Ira Bliss. In a restaurant after ordering, she always ended up hoping that the kitchen would be out of her original selection so that she could switch to what her neighbor had. That was the kind of person she was. Panhandlers asking for bus fare to visit dying mothers, bald saffron-robed Hare Krishna devotees with finger cymbals, Jesus freaks carrying signs reading "Come to the Rock and You Won't Have to Get Stoned Anymore"—all these people had invariably sought her out on the crowded Common when she had lived in Boston with Eddie. She had to admit that she was an easy lay, spiritually speaking. Apparently she looked lost and in need, anxious and dazed and vulnerable, a ready convert. And in this case, appearances weren't deceiving. It was quite true. Normally she was prepared to believe in anything. At least for a while.

Ginny remembered, upon each descent to this airport, spotting

her mother and the Major from the plane window—each time un-
changed, braced to see what form their protean daughter would have
assumed for *this* trip home. When Ginny thought of them, it was as
a unit, invincible and invulnerable, halves of a whole, silhouettes,
shape and bulk only, with features blurred. She decided it was a hold-
over from early infancy, when they probably hung over her crib and
doted, as parents tended to do before they really got to know their
offspring. But this trip home there was no one standing by the fence
to film her arrival—in a patchwork peasant dress and combat boots
and a frizzy Anglo-Afro hairdo, with a knapsack on her back and a
Peruvian llama wool poncho over the pack so that she looked like a
hunched crone, the thirteenth witch at Sleeping Beauty's christening.
Her mother was lying in a hospital bed; and the Major had "gone
beyond," as the undertaker with the waxen yellow hands had optimisti-
cally put it a year ago.

Apparently she was on her own now.

Ginny reflected that the last time she'd seen somebody off here
had been about a year and three months ago, when she'd brought
the Major out for a flight to Boston. It turned out to be the last
time she saw him alive. It was just at the end of her conciliatory
visit undertaken to display Ira and Wendy to her mother and the
Major. She had picked the Major up at his office late one afternoon
after working her way through gates and past guards by flashing his
identification at them like an FBI agent in a raid.

"Tell Ira that there are twenty-two bullets in the drawer by the
fireplace," he said casually as they drove toward the airport, just as
though he were informing her there were eggs and milk in the refriger-
ator to be used up.

Startled, having forgotten that this was the same man who had
given her a .38 special and a lifetime supply of bullets when she
left home for college, Ginny asked, "What for?"

"If anyone bothers you, don't hesitate to blast him one." Ginny
knew he meant it, too. Never mind if they *claimed* to be Bible salesmen
or trick-or-treaters or heart-fund volunteers. When in doubt, blast
them.

"You know something, Dad? You're getting as paranoid as *she* is."

"You call it paranoia, I call it reality."

"*I* think if you spend all your time dwelling on potential disasters, you attract them to yourself," Ginny snapped.

"You know," he said thoughtfully, "sending you to college in Boston was the worst investment I ever made. You used to be such an agreeable, respectful child."

Ginny shot him a look of outraged disbelief. She could recall nothing but conflict with him in the years preceding her departure.

"Well, *you're* the one who wanted me to go."

"*Me?* I assure you, Virginia, that I couldn't have cared less where you went to college. Or whether you went at all, for that matter." Ginny looked at him with astonishment. Was he lying, or had she lived part of her life fulfilling parental wishes that had existed only in her imagination? "I've *never* tried to influence the way you've lived your life."

Ginny gasped at him in fury and concentrated on the road, gripping the steering wheel so tightly that her knuckles turned white.

They rode in hostile silence for a while. Then he said gruffly, "If I don't see you again, Ginny, I want you to know that you've been a very satisfactory daughter, on the whole."

"Father, for *Christ's* sake!" Ginny shrieked, almost running head-on into a concrete abutment.

"Yes, but it's a distinct possibility when you fly as much as I have to. You don't seem to be aware of your own mortality."

Ginny glanced at him helplessly as he sat looking debonair in his three-piece pin-striped suit. "How could I *not* be? What else have I ever heard from you two all my life?"

By now they had reached the airport. Ginny parked the Jeep. "Come in and have a cup of coffee with me," the Major suggested as he hefted his bag out of the back. After checking in, he took Ginny's elbow and directed her to the gray metal flight insurance box in the waiting room, where he filled out a twenty-five-cent policy naming her beneficiary to $7,500 in the event of a fatal crash.

"Thanks," Ginny said absently, folding the policy and stuffing it in the pocket of her Women's Auxiliary blazer.

His hand still on her elbow, he directed her to the luncheonette. They sat at a small Formica table and ordered coffee. When the waitress brought it, they began the undeclared waiting game to see which of them would take the first sip, confirming for the other, like a canary in a coal mine, that the coffee wasn't poisoned, or the cream a host to ptomaine. It was a battle of nerves: Whose desire to drink still-warm coffee would first overcome his embarrassment at death in a public place?

Ginny lifted her cup and slurped, pretending to sip. The Major wasn't fooled. He shifted his lanky frame in the chair and stirred some cream into his coffee. To buy time, Ginny dumped a spoonful of sugar into her heavy white cup and asked, "What does Mother think about the house's being on the market?" Ginny knew what her mother thought, even though they hadn't talked about it: Her mother thought that the Major knew best—in all things.

"She agrees with me that the cabin is big enough for the two of us. We just rattle around in that white elephant. And it doesn't look as though you or the boys are going to want it."

In a diversionary maneuver, the Major removed a bottle from his suit jacket, unscrewed the lid, and took out two small white pills. These he popped into his mouth and downed with half a glass of water.

Watching him, Ginny unthinkingly took a sip of her coffee. Realizing too late what she'd done, she held the liquid in her mouth, trying to decide whether or not to return it unswallowed to the cup. Overcome finally by curiosity, she swallowed. As they both waited for her collapse, she asked, "What were those?"

"Coumadin," he answered blandly.

"Coumadin?"

"Coumadin."

"What *is* Coumadin?"

"An anticoagulant," he mumbled, averting his eyes.

"For your *heart?*" He nodded yes, glumly. "What's wrong with your heart?"

"Nothing. Just a little heart attack."

"*Heart* attack?" she shouted. "When?"

234

"Last month."

"Why wasn't I *told?*"

"It was nothing. I was just working too hard. I was in bed less than a week." He took a big drink of his coffee. A look of annoyance crossed his face because it was cool by now.

Ginny felt a great upsurge of anxiety. Sweat broke out on her forehead. She had difficulty breathing. So—the coffee was poisoned after all, and she was to meet her long-expected end here on the linoleum floor of this airport luncheonette. Her mother had always warned her to wear her best underwear when leaving the house, since one never knew when one might end up in the emergency room. But had Ginny listened? Of course not. And now here she was facing Eternity with safety pins holding up her bra straps.

"What's wrong?" the Major asked uneasily.

"Nothing," she replied bravely. And soon her symptoms abated, and her seizure assumed the proportions of a normal bout of separation anxiety, a malady she was intimately acquainted with. The house up for sale and the Major on the brink of a heart attack. Yes, those were valid grounds for a seizure.

"How long will you be gone?" she asked faintly.

"Two weeks," he replied with a wide smile. He went on business trips to Boston like a sailor going on shore leave after months of deprivation on the high seas.

"Business?"

"Mostly. I don't know if I told you—we're thinking of moving to Boston."

Scandalized, Ginny looked at him quickly. "How could you? This is our *home.*"

"Not mine it isn't. I've always hated this town. You know that. I intended to stay here just a year, as part of my training for a job in Boston. But then I met your mother, who couldn't bear the thought of leaving Hullsport. Though God only knows why."

"But how could you just torfeit thirty-five years of memories?" Ginny wailed, knowing the incredible difficulty she experienced in letting go of anything out of her past, however objectionable.

"Easily. Very easily," he said with a laugh. He threw down the rest of his coffee, stood up, kissed Ginny on the forehead, and raced for his plane, like the candidate for cardiac arrest that he was. Though how a heart of stone could be subject to malfunctions escaped Ginny at the time.

Two and a half months later he was dead, of a heart attack.

Franklin Ashley

"Listen, Buddy, We Don't Throw Gutter Balls Here"

THE BEST I EVER rolled, or shot, or whatever you call it was 100. Bowling was never a serious thing. It was less than a sport and barely a game, something played by drunks with one free arm, by matrons with empty afternoons, by college kids without enough money for a real night out. It was a game televised when football wasn't on. Its sound was as musical as the rhythm of an Akron assembly line.

I had never bowled at all except as a babysitting chore in Easley, S.C. I had used it as a diversion for my six-year-old brother-in-law, who liked hitting *things* and biting *me*. Not even the limited physical exertion of bowling attracted a non-athlete like me.

Then one day in March of 1978 I stepped up to the line in the practice round of the $100,000 Bowling Proprietors Association of America (BPAA) U.S. Open in Greensboro, N.C., a legal illegal entry. The lights and the cameras flashed at my back. My teal-blue Adidas shirt was heavy with sweat. Nothing to it, I thought, as I prepared to throw a few balls. The first one shivered down the gutter and made a sound like it had struck a large empty drum. "Hey!" came a voice from the next lane. A slim figure in a magenta shirt glided over to me. In an archetypal New Jersey accent, he explained the problem. "Listen, buddy, this is the U.S. Open. We don't throw *gutter balls* here."

I thanked him and tried to get the proper approach. I also tried to look slim and magenta-loving. I swung my arm, the ball sailed down the lane . . . and into the gutter again. *Whooma. Whooma.* Loud laughter behind me. I was in big trouble.

"Hold it," came a New York voice. "Keep your thumb toward your body."

I turned and saw one of bowling's slickest second-line stars, Johnny Petraglia, slipping on rose-tinted glasses as he approached me. Petraglia's hair shone like spun mahogany and his body consisted of more frame than flesh, nearly touching six feet but weighing less than 150 pounds.

A Staten Islander in his 30s, Petraglia's first recorded earnings as a pro, $300, came in 1965, and these days he was a $40,000-a-year man with his own Brunswick signature ball. Mustached and heavy-lidded, he magnetized the autograph-seeking children of Greensboro. Like most of the pros in this practice round, he had started on Lane 40 and worked his way to my end, trying out each lane. But I had stayed on Lane One the whole time to stay out of the way.

"Keep your thumb inside," Petraglia repeated. I nodded and slung the ball again. Five pins fell.

A noncommital "Yeah," from Petraglia, who then said, "Mind if I throw a couple?" The pins went up like Nagasaki. When Johnny finished, he whispered, "Who are *you*, anyhow?" I said I was doing a story for SPORT and mumbled that my average was only 100, but not always.

John shook his head, his complexion glowing blue-white in the fluorescent light. "Man, why did they send somebody like you?" Then he stepped off the lane before I could tell him more. Only three lanes away was Mark Roth, who had won a smidgen less than $100,000 the year before. Bowling's other superstar, Earl Anthony, who had topped the $100,000 total twice, was not at this tournament. But many of the second-line stars were here, the men who annually average between $20- and $30,000 in winnings on the Professional Bowlers Association tour.

By various Byzantine convolutions the BPAA had slipped me into this tournament. The 239 other entrants were either regulars on the pro tour or had pummeled and slammed their way through BPAA state tournaments to qualify for this $100,000 competition. Embarrassed at my performance, I grabbed my ball and eased out the side door. I wanted a beer real bad.

The bowlers stayed at the Rodeway Inn. Once inside, I could have been in Des Moines or Seattle or Salinas or Dallas. The same tan rugs, the same Formica tabletops, the same scrambled eggs, the same red candles in fishnet holders in the bar, the same Emmylou Harris songs.

And beer. Tables of beer, pitchers of beer, wet circles of beer, signs for beer.

"Pass me by, if you're only passin' through," the song began as another quarter fell in the crack of silence. I saw myself in the mirror. Me and 50 of the bowlers who were staying here. All following the PBA rules that require that they be beardless, their hair above the collar. There were no women customers or groupies in the Rodeway Bar. Only sad men on a Sunday night. Bowling, I decide, is not the kind of sport that's made for fighting or loving. The appeal is the chance to win money and the outside hope of an hour on ABC-TV. There is no grassy playing field, no fresh air, no balletic leaping, no graceful pirouetting, no one-on-one physical confrontation. The bowler's gallery—though standing-room-only during tournament play—looks like a Little League bleacher, and the players wear only half a uniform, a bowling shirt and street pants.

I looked at the men around me, and the air turned heavy. "Hey, bartender," I called, "gimme a Bud."

Then I heard it. A mumble about "some guy down here screwing up the tournament." Two boys in Ban-Lon shirts were growling and grumbling.

"No, No, No," Blue Ban-Lon barked to Green Ban-Lon. "SPORT magazine, not *Sports Illustrated.* They sent him to do a George Plimpton kind of act. You know, bowl with the pros?"

"Yeah, but Plimpton never played in the real thing," Green said. "It was all exhibitions. Not the *real* thing.

Blue took a swig from his glass. "Looks like they could of at least sent the real Plimpton. Instead, we got a *phony* Plimpton trying to do the *real* thing."

"It's gonna throw everybody's game off," Green said. "I'll bet he doesn't even know what double-jumping is."

He was right about that. Double-jumping was sure to cause me further embarrassment. In pro bowling, a pair of lanes must be open on each side of your own pair of lanes before you can make your

239

approach. But there is no clue in the system that tells you it is your turn. The day before, I had asked Dick Battista, a lefty with a heart transplant, about double-jumping.

Battista, a red-faced native of Astoria in Queens, N.Y., and a former Johnny Carson propman, is constantly hustling the fact that he is the only 50-year-old athlete in the world with a 19-year-old heart inside him.

"Dick," I had asked, "how do you know when it's time to bowl?"

"Hey!" Battista yelled. "I got nothing to lose in talking to you. I got a heart could go out on me any minute. Make a hell of a story. You know what I mean? But listen, if you feel like it's your time to bowl, you step up there and *bowl!* Don't take any crap off anybody. Just bowl."

Still uncertain, I asked, "What if they . . . ah . . . say it's *their* turn?"

Battista's red face purpled. "Look! It *ain't* their turn! You know what I'm sayin'? When you decide it's your turn to bowl, you bowl. You know what I mean?"

I didn't understand, but now in the Rodeway Bar I was shaken loose from memory by Blue Ban-Lon's next line: "If I find that guy— it's gonna be him and me. Him and me! What's he look like? Hunh? Anybody seen him?" He looked around the room. "Let's find him!" The Ban-Lon brothers rose.

I was able to make it to the elevator because just outside the men's room they mistook the fatty reporter from the Charlotte *Observer* for me. As the doors hissed shut I heard someone say, "Damn! This ain't the guy."

In my room among the clutter of empty aluminum cans and candy-bar wrappers, I looked at the tournament roster. There were three squads which would rotate throughout the tournament. I would be bowling with squad "C," along with Don Johnson, George Pappas and Mark Roth, all with averages well above 200. I could see the paper shake in my hand as I sought out my "partners." The first name I spotted was 'Jay Tartaglia' from 'Port Chester, N.Y.' Maybe he would tell me whether or not I should leave in the indigo night. I could slink back to my home in Columbia, change my phone number and get a mailbox downtown.

I found Tartaglia in his room not 20 paces from mine. He had black hair and a fat nose and was in his mid-20s. He looked like one of those guys in *Saturday Night Fever* who yells, "Hey, Tony! You ain't mad, are you?" Jay could not have weighted over 150 pounds. His roommate, Todd Strebel, also in our squad, was even smaller, about 5-9, 125 pounds. In 1977, Strebel had won $5,375 on the pro tour. Tartaglia was not even listed in the program.

I explained my problem to the pair, suggesting I was a somewhat better writer than bowler. But I still thought that with a few tips, I might be able to glom enough bowling technique to avoid complete humiliation.

"How much did you say you bowl?" Strebel asked incredulously.

"A hundred. A hundred, but not always."

"No kidding?" Strebel said.

"No kidding."

Tartaglia smiled, his heavy eyebrows jerking up. "Hey, Hey, I got it. Maybe you could tell everybody you were in an accident. A car accident. And . . . and it damaged your—" He pointed at me.

"Your brain!" Strebel added. "You had brain damage."

Tartaglia fell back on the bed laughing. "Yeah, people'll feel sorry for you and sorta help you."

When I asked for quick pointers, Strebel snorted, "Everybody hits the pockets here. There ain't any tricks. You gotta come in here knowing how to do it. *Then* you work on shading your game."

"You'll probably set a world's record," Tartaglia said. "The farthest in the red of anybody."

I felt my heart vibrating. To be in the "red" meant the bowler was under 200 pins per game. A pro's score is computed on a card and projected on an overhead screen. If he's really cooking the score will be in black, but if he is rolling a mere 187, he would receive 13 big, fat RED numerals. Tartaglia speculated that I would probably end up with 850 to 900 in the red and I would be remembered *forever* for it—a sort of "Wrong-Way Corrigan" of bowling.

I thanked both of them for their merciless candor and went back to my room to practice my approach. It was quite peculiar. I took five steps forward, then stopped dead like a spooked racehorse. I then let the ball go from a stationary position. From there the ball could easily spin into its natural path—the gutter.

I felt the cool surface of my ball, a black 16-pounder. It had been given to me by Dan Toma, the owner of Star Lanes bowling center in Columbia. Despite my 225-pound size, I had been more comfortable with a ten-pounder. But Toma insisted I take the 16-pound cannonball, the maximum weight allowed. It was a little like rolling an Oldsmobile, but I finally had become proficient enough to avoid splitting my thumb as I released the ball.

I went over my approach again and again without improvement, finally stumbling over to the bed. I lay down with my ball on the next pillow. Maybe *looking* at it could do something.

The phone call came near 2:30 A.M. as I lay there fully-clothed and semi-conscious.

"Frank," the voice whispered, "This is John. John Petraglia. Me and some of the boys wanna come down and talk to you."

I dumped the ball onto the rug and in less than two minutes heard the knock. I wished I had had some heat to wrap in a towel, maybe a Walther PPK.

"The boys" soon settled in my room. Slumping into a black vinyl chair was Everett Schofield, district manager of Brunswick, a 50ish man carrying a drink in his right hand. The tallest of the five visitors was the orange-haired Dave Davis, like Petraglia a veteran left-hander who regularly wins some $40,000 a year on the tour. Standing next to Davis was Petraglia, who was staring at his feet.

Pacing the room, his eyes all pupils and fire, was George Pappas, the chairman of the tournament committee. Pappas, known as the "Mouth of the South" and one of the few top players to come out of Dixie, has earned slightly more than Petraglia and Davis over the last three years.

Sitting on the arm of another chair was Leroy Harrelson, the P.R. man representing Brunswick. Harrelson had cottony gray hair, a pink face and looked like he'd just been cleaned and pressed.

"Guess you know why we're here," Petraglia croaked.

I waited.

"I'll take it," Pappas cut in. He tried to smile. "The point is, Frank, everybody saw you bowl today."

"Yeah," I said. "I'm not too much of a bowler—"

"Yeah," Davis said, "that's why we're here."

242

Pappas held up his hand. "Look, we represent—we just met with 30 or 40 guys downstairs and everybody says it. If you bowl—we're walking out. We're not gonna have a tournament."

The P.R. man waved his fingers and said, "Franklin is listening."

Then Pappas' mouth twitched. "Frank, you just can't do it. With you up there it's a damn farce."

Everett burped and shouted, "Franh!" slurring the "k" into an "h." "Goddamnit, Franh, I cain't let you bowl. I just cain't let you goddamn bowl."

"He's got a right to bowl," Petraglia said.

"I cain't let him do it, and that's that," Everett said.

Pappas scowled. "Everett, he's gotta right to bowl. The BPAA put him in. They're the ones at fault."

"Franklin understands this, fellows," the P.R. man said.

"I cain't let him goddamn bowl," Everett said.

"Everett, lemme handle it!" Pappas yelled.

Davis said, "He's got a right to bowl."

Petraglia squatted down by the bed. "Look! Look Frank, we think bowling deserves a story. . . . But if you step in there, it cheapens the whole thing."

"Franklin hears you," P.R. announced. "He hears you."

"I almost punched out one of those bowlers downstairs, Franh!" Everett screamed. "Giving me some crap about you. None of his business. He's just a damn bowler. I'm not gonna take anything off him—"

"Hold it, Everett," Pappas snapped, then said to me: "The point is, you wouldn't compete against Arnold Palmer in the Masters or Staubach in the Super Bowl."

"That isn't my story. I might, though, if I got the chance."

Finally P.R. stood up. "Fellows, Franklin is a southern gentleman. He teaches at the University of South Carolina. He's a *gentleman.*"

"Frank," Petraglia said, "bowling needs the story." His voice was gentle. "We want it. But a lot of the guys spent time, money, blood and a lot more to get here."

"Yeah," Davis said. "They're on the line for money."

"And they're afraid," Petraglia went on, "that you could affect their game if you stayed in."

243

"Frank," Pappas said, "I've never seen the bowlers so united about one thing: *You* not bowling."

I was furious and exuberant. I sat back on the bed and said, "I'm really pissed off that you guys came down here to my room at 2:30 in the morning like genteel wizards of the KKK and put the heat on. But—" I tried to look noble—"but I don't wanna hurt the tournament and cause everybody to walk out so—" I gave them a couple of seconds—"you can count me out." To be honest, I was relieved.

Everett, who had been practically catatonic, jerked up and said, "You're a great American, Franh. A damn great American."

When the group shuffled out the door, Petraglia turned and shook my hand. "I want you to know," he said softly, "this is one of the most embarrassing moments of my life—and thanks."

I nodded and shut the door. They were right, of course. Bowling is a very serious business to professionals. What I had never seen before were the faces of those who gave so much of their lives to bowling, to the 40 one-inch strips of pine and maple, the cacophonous harmony of falling pins, the lonely nights on the road with the watered beer and country music. I understood some of their rage, their frustration at the exposure and wealth that flows to players of football, basketball, baseball, golf, tennis *et al.*

Half on the edge of sleep I yanked my memory back to yesterday morning's practice session. Larry Lichstein was in the backroom examining bowling balls to make certain they conformed to PBA standards of weight and material. An aging bowler with a head as shiney as his ball stepped up to the table.

Lichstein weighed his ball and said, "You got too much side weight with this one."

The bowler frowned and retrieved his ball. "Aw, Larry, I don't care. I probably won't cash anyway." He ambled out of the room.

Larry turned to me and raised an eyebrow. "That's a hell of an attitude, isn't it? But you can't blame him." He rubbed his hands together. "There are only about 50 of these guys who are worth a damn and only two of them make big money." He picked up a new sphere. "It's a downer for bowlers, you know. The Chicago Cubs pay Dave Kingman $225,000 to bat .220. Roth, our best player, only made a hundred grand last year. Hell, Kingman couldn't carry Roth's bowling bag."

During practice that week Roth rarely failed to strike. He regularly fell into what is called "dead stroke," a sense of knowing that every ball he rolled would scatter ten pins. His concentration, timing and execution were precise, as could be expected from the 1977 PBA Bowler of the Year. Despite Roth's skills, though, the fact remained that few people outside the sport know him. That reminded me of something else Larry Lichstein had said about the current status of bowling: "Face it, Frank. There's champagne, there's liquor and there's beer. We're beer. And that may be all we'll ever be."

Now fully awake, I raised up on one elbow, glad to be out of the tournament. The bowlers were competing as they should, I thought. And now—I would go downstairs. If the bar was still open, I knew the drink that I wanted.

Larry King

The Best Little Whorehouse in Texas

IT WAS AS NICE a little whorehouse as you ever saw. It sat in a green Texas glade, white-shuttered and tidy, surrounded by leafy oak trees and a few slim renegade pines and the kind of pure, clean air the menthol-cigarette people advertise.

If you had country values in you and happened to stumble upon it, likely you would nod approval and think, *Yes, yes, these folks keep their barn painted and their fences up, and probably they'd do to ride the river with.* There was a small vegetable garden and a watermelon patch, neither lacking care. A good stand of corn, mottled now by bruise-colored blotches and dried to parchment by hot, husky-whispering summer winds, had no one to hear its rustling secrets.

Way back yonder, during the Hoover Depression, they raised chickens out there. Money was hard to come by; every jackrabbit had three families chasing it with the stewpot in mind. Back then, in rural Texas, people said things like "You can hear everthang in these woods but meat afryin' and coins aclankin'." No matter where a boy itched and no matter how high his fevers, it wasn't easy to come up with $3, even in exchange for a girl's sweetest gift. And so the girls began accepting poultry in trade. That's how the place got its name, and if you grew up most anywhere in Texas, you knew at an early age what the Chicken Ranch sold other than pullets.

You might have originally thought it a honeymoon cottage. Except that as you came closer on the winding dirt road that skittered into the woods off the Austin to Houston highway on the southeastern outskirts of La Grange, near the BAD CURVE sign, you would have noticed that it was too sprawling and too jerry-built: running off on odd tangents, owning more sides and nooks and crannies than the Pentagon. It had been built piecemeal, a room added here and there as needed, as with a sod farmer watching his family grow. Then there were all those casement-window air conditioners—fifteen to twenty of 'em, Miss Edna wanting her girls to work in comfort.

Since the 1890s, at least, the Chicken Ranch had been one of the better pleasure palaces in all Texas. You didn't have to worry about clap, as when free-lancing on Postoffice Street in Galveston, or risk your hide in machismo-crazed whore bars on Fort Worth's Jacksboro Highway, where mean-eyed, juiced-up, brilliantined, honky-tonk cowboys presumed themselves a nightly quota of asses to whip. Miss Edna, like Miss Jessie before her, didn't cotton to hard-drinking rowdies. Should you come in bawling profanities or grabbing tits, Miss Edna would employ the telephone. And before you could say double-dip-blankety-blank obscenity, old Sheriff T. J. Flournoy—"Mr. Jim"— would materialize to suggest a choice between overnight lodgings in Fayette County's crossbar hotel and your rapid cooperative leave-taking. The wise or the prudent didn't pause to inquire whether the latter opportunity included a road map. You just did a quick Hank Snow. Yes, neighbors, it was as cozy and comfortable as a family reunion, though many times more profitable. Then, one sad day last summer, the professional meddlers and candy-assed politicians closed 'er down.

God and Moses, what a shock to the 3,092 residents of La Grange, Texas, to say nothing of Chicken Ranch alumni around the world! Imagine corned beef without cabbage, Newcastle without coal, Nixon without crises. The Chicken Ranch was an old and revered Texas institution, second only to the Alamo and maybe Darrell Royal. History lurked there. Some claimed that La Grange had offered love for sale since 1844, back when Texas was a republic, which would put the lie to the Dallas *Morning News'* claim of being Texas's "oldest business institution." For sure, the Chicken Ranch traced, by document, back about sixty years. In a more primitive time, when there were fewer squirming concerns with goddamned imagery, the winning squad of the Texas-Texas A&M football game got invited by joyous alumni to the Chicken Ranch on Thanksgiving night. Think how fiercely a team might fight to win the Pussy Bowl! Yeeeeaaaah, *team!*

247

Anyhow, businessmen and state legislators were comforted during their carnal wanderings; the wise telephoned ahead for reservations. Indigenous hill-country Teutonics, Slavics, and rednecks of many faiths brought their sons in celebration of maturities that an older culture more gently signified by bar mitzvahs.

Man, listen: The Chicken Ranch was gooder than grass and better than rain. Registered with the county clerk as Edna's Ranch Boarding House, it paid double its weight in taxes and led the community in charitable gifts; you could go into the lobby of the gleaming new community hospital and see Miss Edna Milton's name winking at you from the engraved brass plaque honoring donors, the same as the name of the banker's or the preacher's lady. The Chicken Ranch plowed a goodly percentage of its earnings back into local shops to the glee of hairdressers, car dealers, and notions-counter attendants. It was a good citizen, protected and appreciated, its indiscretions winked at.

They say that some years ago a young district attorney, who had made his own sporting calls to the Chicken Ranch, sheepishly appeared at the front door as the reluctant head of a raiding party mobilized by crusading churchwomen. On spotting the young DA, Miss Edna is supposed to have sung out, "Not *now*, George, the law has me surrounded!" And during Prohibition, an old sheriff called on Miss Jessie to say sternly, "I don't like to say nothin', but this *drankin'*, now, has just plain got to stop!" When Miss Jessie died, her obituary identified her as "a local businesswoman." Yeah, they had 'em a real bird's nest on the ground out there. Then along came Marvin Zindler.

Marvin Zindler was a deputy sheriff in Houston, enforcing consumer-protection laws, until they fired him. Not for inefficiency or malfeasance—Lord, no! Marvin wore more guns, handcuffs, buckles, and badges than a troop of Texas Rangers; he brought more folks to court than did bankruptcy proceedings. Some folks said Marvin would jug you for jaywalking; it's of record that he once nabbed a drugstore merchant for failure to stock the kind and size of candy bar at the price the merchant had advertised.

Marvin got fired for being "controversial"—which meant that he couldn't, or wouldn't, make those fine distinctions required of successful politicians. After all, Marvin's boss was dependent on public favor.

No, sir, the law was *the law* to Marvin. Soon Houston merchants were screaming of how they received fewer considerations than did common pickpockets or footpads. They howled when Marvin tipped off television stations where he would next put the collar on a Chamber of Commerce member accused of selling fewer soap flakes in a container than its label claimed, and they were outraged when—a time or two—Marvin lurked around the magazine rack while television cameras were established and *then* made his bust.

A lot of good people, long goosed and flummoxed by many avid practitioners of free enterprise, dearly loved and cheered Marvin. But fellow deputies judged him insufficiently bashful when it came to personal publicity, and his superiors soon got a gutful of bitching merchants. Perhaps, too, the more sensitive wearied of daily contact with Marvin's ego, which may be approximately two full sizes larger than Howard Cosell's. Marvin keeps scrapbooks. He dresses like a certified dandy in his 200 tailored suits and has bought himself two nose bobs; he does not permit his own family to view him unless he's wearing one of his many silver hairpieces. Anyhow, they fired Marvin. Who landed on his feet as a television newsman for Houston's Channel 13.

Marvin approached news gathering with the same zeal he'd brought to badge toting. Not for him Watergate values: *The law was the law.* So Marvin began telling the folks out in TVland how a whorehouse was running wide open down the road at La Grange, which was news to Yankee tourists and to all Texans taking their suppers in high chairs. Even though a lot of people yawned, Marvin stayed on the case; you might have thought murder was involved. Soon he repeatedly hinted at "organized crime" influences at the Chicken Ranch.

One day in late July, Marvin Zindler drove to La Grange and accosted Sheriff Flournoy with cameras, microphones, and embarrassing questions. The old sheriff made it perfectly clear he was not real proud to see Marvin. Later the sheriff—a very lean and mean seventy-year-old, indeed—would say he hadn't realized the microphone was live when he chewed on Marvin for meddling in Fayette County affairs; perhaps that explains why the old man peppered his lecture with so many hells and goddamns and shits. Marvin Zindler drove home and displayed the cussing sheriff on television.

Then Marvin called on State Attorney General John Hill and Governor Dolph Briscoe: "How come yawl have failed to close the La Grange sin shop down?" Those good politicians harrumphed and declared their official astonishment that Texas had a whorehouse in it. Marvin told them they'd have to do better than that. Governor Briscoe issued a solemn statement saying that organized crime was a terrible thing, against the American grain, and since it might possibly be sprouting out at the Chicken Ranch, he would call on local authorities to shutter that sinful place. If they didn't comply, the governor said severely, then he personally would employ the might and majesty of the state to close it. *Me, too,* said Attorney General Hill. Veteran legislators, many of whom could have driven to the Chicken Ranch without headlights even in a midnight rainstorm, expressed concern that Texans might be openly permitted loveless fucks outside the home.

Old Sheriff Flournoy was incensed: "If the governor wants Miss Edna closed, all he's gotta do is make one phone call, and I'll do it." The sheriff may be old and country, but his shit detector tells him when grander men are pissing on his feet and telling him it's a rainstorm. The governor didn't have to bother with the telephone charade. Soon after the story hit the national news wires, Johnny Carson was cracking simpering jokes about it and every idle journalist with a pen was en route to La Grange. They found the Chicken Ranch locked and shuttered, a big CLOSED sign advertising a new purity. Miss Edna and her girls had fled to parts unknown, leaving behind a town full of riled people.

Sheriff Flournoy was extracting his long legs from the patrol car, with maybe nothing more on his mind than a plate of Cottonwood Inn barbecue, when this fat bearded journalist shoved a hand in his face and began singing his credentials. The old lawman recoiled as if he'd spotted a pink snake; for a moment it seemed he might tuck his legs back in and drive away.

But after a slight hesitation he came out, unwinding in full coil to about six feet five inches. Given the tall-crowned cowboy hat, he appeared to register nearer to seven feet three and some-odd. Flournoy is a former Texas Ranger who looks as if he might have posed for that bronze and granite Ranger statue guarding the old Dallas airport lobby. You sense that he knows how to use that big thumb-busting revolver thumping against his right leg as expertly as legend insists. The fat bearded journalist also sensed that the old sheriff may have done plumb et his fill of outsiders asking picky questions; he suddenly remembered that the third wave is the most dangerous one when beaches are assaulted, the first two waves having stirred things up and put the locals on notice. So he was real polite and friendly, grinning until his jawbone ached, and careful to let all the old native nasal notes ring, in saying he sure would admire to talk a little bit about the Chicken Ranch situation, please, sir, and would the old sheriff kindly give him a few minutes?

The old sheriff's face reddened alarmingly. He stared across the hot, shimmery Texas landscape, as if searching for menaces on the horizon, and he rapidly puffed a cigarette; the hand holding it trembled as if palsied. Then he said, *"Naw!* I'm tard a-talkin' to you sonsabitches!"

Well. Uh. Ah. Yes. Well, the journalist had come a fer piece; he had a job to accomplish; he'd hoped the sheriff might—

"You hard a-hearin', boy?"

The journalist cupped one ear and said, "Beg your pardon?" He didn't want to leave any doubt.

The old sheriff spat. He said, "My town's gettin' a black eye. All the TVs and newspapers—hell, *all* the mediums—they've flat lied. Been misquotin' our local people. Makin' 'em look bad."

Had the sheriff himself been misquoted?

"You goddamned right!"

To what extent?

"About half of it was goddamn lies."

Well, Sheriff, which half?

The sheriff put a hard eye on the visitor. Puffing the trembling cigarette, he offered a long look at his face. The sight was no comfort. You had time to concentrate on his mountainous great beak, deciding: *If he ever gets in a wide-nose contest with Nixon, he'll fair threaten the blue ribbon.* More terribly, however, the visiting journalist recognized bedrock character and righteous anger, knowing, instinctively, that T. J. Flournoy was the type of man described years ago by his father: *"Son, you got to learn that some folks won't do to fart with."*

Then the sheriff said, "It's pure horseshit what they say about that

251

being a multimillion-dollar operation out yonder. Hell. Goddamn. *Shit!* Them people was just scratchin' out a living like everybody else. The mediums, now, you goddamn people reported Edna running sixteen girls. And in all my years, I never knew more than nine. And it was all lies about organized crime."

Had the sheriff . . . uh, you know . . . received any er—ah—*gratuities* for services to Miss Edna?

The sheriff put his hand on his gun butt—*oh, Jesus!*—and fired twin bursts of pure ol' mad out of his cold blue eyes. "Listen, boy, that place has been open since before I was borned and never hurt a soul. Them girls are clean, they got regular inspections, and we didn't allow no rough stuff. Now, after all this notoriety, this little town's gettin' a bad name it don't deserve. The mediums, the shitasses, they been printing all kinds of crap."

Had the sheriff talked to Governor Briscoe or to the attorney general?

"Naw. No reason to. The place is closed."

Would it stay closed?

"It's closed *now*, ain't it?"

Yes, Right. And, uh, what was the prevailing community sentiment about the future of the Chicken Ranch?

"I ain't answering no more questions," the old sheriff said, stomping his cigarette butt with a booted heel. Two or three hot August Texas centuries limped by, while the visiting journalist vainly sought a graceful exit line.

The sheriff said, "Just you remember we got other thangs than Miss Edna's place. This is as clean a little ol' town as you'll find. Hardworkin' people. *Good* people. That fuckin' Marvin Zindler, if he'd start cleaning up Houston today, why, in about two hunnert years he might have him a town half as clean as La Grange. I'm a-gonna go eat my supper now."

The old man wheeled, lunging away, stiff-gaited and jerky. At the door to the restaurant, he turned and paused to stare his tormentor out of sight.

The fat bearded journalist opted to permit La Grange twenty-four hours of cooling time. In truth, the salty old sheriff had unnerved him. For years the crazed back part of the journalist's brain had whispered that he might one day be riddled by rural lawmen, as had happened to Bonnie and Clyde: a penalty his mind paid, perhaps, for growing up in rural Texas during the violent outlaw days of the thirties. There had been lynchings in his home county and backwoods feuds and tempers shorter than a deadbeat's memory; his paternal grandfather, in 1900, had died of an old indiscretion complicated by a shotgun blast.

They tell a story in La Grange of how, years ago, a bad nigger rejected a deputy who came to arrest him by throwing down on the deputy with a shotgun. When the cowed deputy reported failure, old Sheriff Flournoy first fired him and then drove out to face the same shotgun: "Flipped up his pistol, by God, it still in the holster, now, and drilled that mean nigger smack 'tween the eyes!" Well, who knows? There were no eye-witnesses; maybe it was just another case of Texas brags. The journalist was in no position to judge the yarn's veracity; one of his ambitions was never to be able to. Besides, the journalist had an unfortunate habit of trick driving late in the day; obviously, if he were even slightly demented behind the wheel, it would profit him little to encounter an aroused Sheriff Flournoy on the sheriff's back-roads domain.

So, safe in Austin's familiar comforting precincts, he rang up an old associate to enjoy what proved to be a fourteen-hour group lunch. There was Brett Haggard, the freewheeling lawyer, who had visited jail for purposes other than counseling of clients. And Egbert Shrum, successful novelist and screenwriter, who semiheavily dopes. Willowy Kasha, who had no visible means of support unless you counted the guys who always seemed willing to pick up the check. Babs, the visiting schoolmarm from New Orleans, with the great bone structure and the $99 smile, who, curse it, appeared content in the company of a scraggly-bearded advertising man named Bubba Pool. As events progressed, we would be joined by Egbert Shrum's tasty young wife, Darling, along with assorted actresses, musicians, free-lance writers, and dopers, a retired prostitute, and other social marginals. Originally, however, when they gave us a humorless ejection from the Driskill Hotel bar—something about breakage and noise levels—there were but six of us. We were at that stage where we felt momentarily uncon-

253

querable, to say nothing of how much we knew: Is there anything better or more beguiling than the whiskey smarts?

We repaired, hooting, to a dark motel lounge on the banks of the Colorado River. Egbert Shrum, crazed by oven temperatures, many young scotches, and periodic deep sniffs of his Methedrine inhaler, flopped out his dingus in requesting that Kasha give him head. As the cocktail waitress was then approaching, Egbert had much help in storing his dingus. When it came his turn to order, Egbert said, "Would you mind very much if I smoked a joint in here?" Well, *Jesus,* you haven't heard such general shushings since John Dean told 'em at the White House he had the truth on the tip of his tongue!

The cool young cocktail maiden said, "It's fine with me. But somebody else might come in."

Egbert said, with unimpeachable logic, "They might not, too. You ever think of that?" Then he fired three joints of the killer weed; everybody puffed mightily in hopes of reducing them to harmless ashes before the crazy bastard got us arrested. Texas courts take even *light* doping real seriously; better to steal a cow.

Somebody suggested an orgy. Sweet Babs and Bubba offered their two-bed motel room upstairs. Lawyer Brett Haggard said excuse him, please, but being more thirsty than horny, he preferred to drink; he wouldn't mind watching, however, should we guarantee bartender service. Darling Shrum dashed cold water on the idea, leaving Egbert room for a speech on the folly of marrying narrow-minded women who'll cost you too much strange. In the end, it amounted to no more than drunken gropings under the table, a few wet kisses and ear-blowings, and discombobulated dope babble. Lawyer Haggard laid his head on the tabletop and gently snored. Bubba Pool traded the cocktail waitress a joint for her phone number and a free pinch of ass, though she instructed him not to call until her boyfriend had left Thursday to go back to Baton Rouge.

Many hours past dark, the luncheon party moved to the Soap Creek Saloon, in Austin's rural hills. A folk-rock band crashed and banged, turning conversations into face-to-face shouting matches; the average customer appeared little older than a prep schooler: hairy young hippies and their braless ladies. Egbert Shrum passed around his Methedrine sniffer. On spotting a young mother breast-nursing her child, he was reminded of how one Christmastide he'd made hisself eggnog from a visiting mother's milk. Egbert claimed that her product shamed Carnation. Hours, dope, and whiskey passed.

Around midnight a dozen hot, crazed, half-deaf children of darkness milled about an unpaved parking lot, chased there by smoke and noise and hopes of new adventures. Egbert Shrum, having cornered a trio of edgy youngsters, railed at them that he was Governor Dolph Briscoe, by God, demanding they support his closing of godless whorehouses where red-blooded daughters of Texas, some of whose great-granddaddies had martyred themselves at the Alamo, were being held in white slavery by agents of the Kremlin and Marlon Brando. "The Godfather's in this up to his Eye-talian ass," he railed. In the background, while Babs assisted his gadget, Bubba took a big splashy piss into scrub-oak trees. Salli Ann, the ex-prostitute, professed how much more fun it was to give it away than to sell it; the difference had driven her into retirement.

The Byrds slammed out a high-decibel version of how they liked "The Christian Life" while the luncheon party moved by stereophonic Ford camper to a private home. A half dozen revelers gasped and pawed at one another from a mattress laid in the rear, nothing much satisfactory happening, though a lot of wine got spilled. Arriving, the party found lawyer Brett Haggard slumbering under a fine old tree and guarded by a mean-tempered, spitting, and humping cat. "Brett brought his own pussy," somebody laughed in the moonlight.

Inside, the air soon knew more Mexican boo-smoke pollution; pipes and home-rolled objects passed around the circle, along with Methedrine inhalers, amyl nitrite caps, and doses the fat bearded journalist was not yet chemist enough to identify. Prone on the soft, furry white rug, he discovered himself experiencing serious time lags. In the midst of Willie Nelson's singing from twin speakers about Los Angeles smog, it would become apparent that Kinky Friedman and the Texas Jewboys had somehow thrummed halfway through "Sold American." Or his brain would stubbornly fight to grasp that which Egbert Shrum was shouting into his face, and then he would blink and open his eyes to find that he was alone or talking to any number of other people about a like number of things. The room reeled; his brain crackled and burned; he was aware, dimly, of distant desperate merrymaking shouts.

At an unknown hour he was aroused from a nap he had not been aware of taking: Shrum had popped an amyl nitrite cap under his nose, causing him to greet consciousness with his earlobes on fire, his head expanding as if with a winter cold, and his throat full of senseless, humorless, drugged giggles; his heart pounded fit to burst through skin. Candles had burned down. Three or four indistinct inert figures lay like grain sacks in the gloom.

"They're having a small orgy in the back bedroom," Egbert Shrum said; he was on his hands and knees, crawling. Well, was it any good? "I don't remember if I joined in," the fractured novelist said. "I *meant* to, I assure you. But I think I forgot. No, wait: I ran into Darling; yeah, that's it. And she spoke evil of my participation." He rolled over from all fours, snuggled into the furry rug, and quickly went night-night.

The journalist stepped over him and muttered, "Sleep on, faithful husband. . . ."

Finding the kitchen, the fat bearded journalist gasped and wheezed in sousing his head under the water spigot. Everything in him hurt, sizzled, or jangled. He wished much to throw at a Nixon dart board on the wall but knew the motions would cost excessive pain. "You getting too old for this shit, podner," he told himself, and spat lightly on the dart board. He thought about Hemingway's final solution, wondering enough about whether ol' Hem had had the right answer that he was glad no firearms offered themselves. Kasha, sleepy and moody and tousled, materialized to drive him to his motel. She did ugly to him for a bit, he permitting her to do the main work, while he drifted toward sleep, at once begging her pardon and muttering thanks. . . .

La Grange, in the morning sun, appeared as pure as rainwater; the aching journalist closed out its splendors with dark glasses. You'd be surprised how painful light blues and greens can be, the sun striking sparks on trees and grass and turning the high sky into one giant reflecting mirror.

At noon, Buddy Zapalac, ordering another beer, recalled the Chicken Ranch of his youth. He is a gleeful fiftyish, of iron gray hair, a stubby heavyweight's torso, and a blue-ribbon grin. You see him and you like him.

256

"In the thirties," Buddy said, "they had a big parlor with a jukebox, see, that they used to break the ice. You could ask a girl to dance, or she'd ask you. And pretty soon, why, you could git a little business on. Three dollars' worth." He laughed in memory of those old days when Roosevelt nookie had been cheaper than Carter coffee is now.

"You couldn't get any exotic extras. Miss Jessie—she ran the ranch back then—she didn't believe in perversions. They had wall mirrors in the parlor, see, where the girls could sit in chairs and flash their wares. But if Miss Jessie caught 'em flashing a little more than she thought was ladylike, she'd raise nine kinds of hell.

"Miss Edna, who was thirty or forty years younger, was a little more modern. I've heard you could get anything you could pay for: ten bucks for straight; fifteen for half-and-half; twenty-five, I believe, for pure French. The girls wore smart sports clothes for day trade and cocktail dresses at night. They tell me each customer was urged to buy a Coke for himself and one for the girl, see, at fifty cents each. Miss Edna, counting the bottles, knew how much trade each girl had done. Or so I heard. I understand each girl kept half of her earnings and donated the rest to the house. And the house paid room and board."

Buddy Zapalac owns the biweekly La Grange *Journal.* When the Chicken Ranch got busted, he was widely quoted as saying he intended to lend editorial support to Miss Edna and her girls. Over Cottonwood Inn beer he admits: "I didn't do it. Lost too many of my supporters. Businessmen, even a couple of preachers, told me in private they'd back me up. But people in a little town can't stand much heat. As the publicity built up, see, people started calling up or slipping around to say they'd decided against going on record. I didn't even run a news story."

There had been media reports of outraged La Grange housewives taking to the streets with petitions, howling that the governor should— or should not—close the Chicken Ranch. Some said the infighting between the pros and the antis had been fierce.

"Ain't we in a nutty business?" Zapalac chuckled. "Exaggerated. Nothing much to it. Oh, yeah, some people circulated a petition. At one time, I heard, they had over four hundred names to keep the place open. Then people had second thoughts and took their

257

names off. They ended up with about a hundred and twenty-five names, tops, so they junked the petition. Too much heat, see."

From what sources?

The editor spread his hands, shrugged. "Everywhere. Nowhere. Anywhere. People tend to believe, see, what they read or hear or see on TV. Or, at least, to be influenced. So they ran. Yeah, sure, I'm for the Chicken Ranch. I grew up with it, and I never once felt corrupted. When we were kids—big ol' bunch of rough Czechs and Germans, natural rockheads—we had a lot of fistfights. But never at the Chicken Ranch. It was traditional to be on your good behavior out there. You honored unspoken rules. See, if a local man got sweet on one of the girls, they'd ship that girl out in a New York minute. *Boom!* Gone. They *never* hired a local girl. Most of 'em came from Austin, Houston. Everbody always took care to keep the townsfolk and the girls from mingling off the job.

"Those gals put a hundred thousand dollars or more into this little town's economy. Every year. Outside money, mainly. And I read in a Chamber of Commerce bulletin that each tourist dollar is really worth *seven* dollars, the way it circulates locally. By that formula, Marvin Zindler ran off about seven hundred thousand dollars' worth of business. Not many of us here feel like thanking him.

"People treated those girls good. Went out of their way to be friendly. Let 'em come to the beauty shop or any store, and they got the red carpet. Having 'em marry and mingle was one thing; being plain courteous was another."

Deep in his craw, would Buddy Zapalac personally miss the Chicken Ranch?

He laughed. "Hell, I haven't been out there in years. Except, you know, to take some visitor who had his curiosity up. But, yeah, I guess so. I guess I'll miss it. It's been there since my memory has; it's a landmark. Some people, you know, they're talking about getting the Texas Historical Society to put up a marker out there. And, yes, I'd be for that."

It was unspeakably hot and stuffy in the La Grange telephone booth; all the journalist accomplished was breaking into a rare honest sweat. No, said a testy minister, he had ab-*so*-lutely nothing to say about the Chicken Ranch and, if quoted, would surely sue. Samey-same, more or less, when one reached businessmen, the community's semiofficial historian, and a suspicious old justice of the peace. Well, screw research; fall back on perceptions. Besides, beer halls are more fun than telephone booths anyway. . . .

In the cool dark Longhorn Lounge, where Tom T. Hall warbled from the jukebox of old dogs and children and watermelon wine, the journalist discovered four beer-drinking middle-aged men in sports jackets and business suits and an older citizen in khakis.

"Hail," one said, "La Grange has lots to offer besides the Chicken Ranch. There's Monument Hill State Park, as purty a place as you'll see. You can see the river from there. Go up there! Accentuate the positive!"

The old nester in khakis belched and said, "That shitass from the Houston TV, he didn't say a goddamn thang about our boys winnin' the state baseball championship."

Winking, one of the locals said, "That place has been shut down before. Back in the sixties, when Will Wilson was attorney general and got it in his craw to be governor, he closed 'er down." Winks. Sips beer. Winks again. "Yeah, for about two weeks."

Over the laughter he said, "They put up a big ol' CLOSED sign out front. Newspaper people came and snapped pictures. But if a regular customer went out there, he knew what back road to park on, and the girls slipped him in the back door."

Yeah? Anybody slipping in the back door now?

"Naw, sir. No way. Been too much publicity. Edna and the girls, soon as the story got reported on national TV, they shucked on out."

Where were they?

"Well"—one grinned—"I doubt you'd locate 'em in a nunnery. Likely they went on the regular red-light circuit. Big towns. Houston. Dallas. San Antone."

The old nester said, "*Gal*-veston, too. Yeah, and Corpus. That Dallas, it's got more thugs and prostatoots than New Orleans. You recollect Jack Ruby?"

What of Miss Edna?

"Rumor is she's got an old man over in East Texas. Owns a farm. Some say she's hiding there till this blows over. Don't anybody know, for sure, unless maybe our sheriff does. But ol' T. J., that stubborn cuss, he wouldn't tell if you helt his feet to the fahr.''

Well, come on, fellers, whose official palm did Miss Edna grease for the pleasure of operating?

Shouted disclaimers clued the journalist that he'd overplayed his hand. In some heat a silver-haired man in a natty sports coat, who may have sold for Farmer's Life and Casualty, said, "That wasn't necessary, understand? That place paid good taxes, friend. It was clean. The girls had good manners. The prices didn't hold you up. Friend, they never so much as gave a *hot check* out there! I had a buddy, he was overseas during the Hitler war, and one of the girls out there, she mailed him cookies. Regular.''

"Only people around here ever tried to close Edna down," the old nester said, "I guess you could call 'em religious fanatics, *they* quit after people stopped talking to 'em and they woke up to find garbage and such like dumped on their lawn.''

Well, now, what about *that*? Didn't it show some long-range, perhaps less-than-gentle influence of the Chicken Ranch on the community and its standards?

"No comment," the khaki-clad one snapped, as if he'd waited a lifetime for the opportunity; his companions nodded agreement and turned to give full attention to their beers, showing the meddling outlander eight shoulders suddenly gone very cold.

Lloyd Kolbe. Lean. Well barbered. On the rise. Mid-to-late thirties. Quick to smile even when his eyes retain calculations in judging the moment's worth or risk. The quintessential Young Businessman: no bullshit, now, what with children to educate and two cars to feed and status to climb.

The owner of radio station KVLG in La Grange, Kolbe is large in civic clubs; he rarely misses the weekly Lions Club fellowship luncheon, where, should you fail to call a fellow member Lion Smith or Lion Jones in addressing him, the club Tail Twister will fine you two bits while everyone whoops and hee-haws. On Kolbe's desk, yes, is a picture of about thirty men in drag: startling, until he explains that it depicts local civic leaders in the Rotary Club's Womanless Wedding, staged, like the annual Lions Club broom sale, purely for purposes of charity. Close, Lloyd. You boys better watch it.

"I'm a native," Kolbe said, drumming fingers on a polished desk top. "I grew up knowing the Chicken Ranch was out there—no, I don't remember how early, it seems I just *always* knew. As kids we joked about it, though it didn't preoccupy us; didn't mark us, didn't make any grand impression. You noticed as you grew up that adults didn't joke about it. Local people, you actually didn't hear them mention it until the big bust."

Like—and no offense, Lloyd—but like, maybe, those good burghers who didn't know what went on at camps outside their hometowns of Auschwitz and Dachau? Knowing it was a grossly unfair comparison, though nagged by the worry that somehow it might be *relevant*, the journalist couldn't translate the thought to words.

Kolbe was saying, "Some people think the Chicken Ranch discouraged industry from moving here. I don't think it did. And *if* it did, was that truly bad? We're progressive, and all that, but why should we ruin our pure air and clean streams and pretty farms? Industrial rot and blight . . . do we want to trade for a paycheck? People all over America are looking for La Granges to raise their families in.

"My own two children, I've watched and listened to see what effect the Chicken Ranch might have on them. And I can't see that it's had any. They accept it, as I did—it's just *there;* it has nothing to do with them or their lives. We talked about it one night right after the bust.

"On the other hand, I can't believe the town's lost significant revenue. I doubt if those girls spent anything like a hundred thousand dollars a year here. And, hell, even if they did, that's no money. You take three or four little ol' mom-and-pop stores, they'll equal that. The economic factor has been greatly exaggerated. Probably not over six or eight merchants benefited from the Chicken Ranch. The thing I hate is that La Grange is now known nationwide as a whore town. And we're better people than that."

Soon after the bust, with the town in an uproar, Lloyd Kolbe had proposed that three each pro and anti Chicken Ranchers debate on his radio station. "But it fell flat. People who privately favored the Chicken Ranch simply refused to go public. We settled for two programs where people called in. They could identify themselves or not. Most didn't. And those who did, well, yeah, I've erased their names from the tapes. I don't want to take advantage of people."

261

He flipped a switch. The tape brought forth the quavery voice of an old woman: "I was borned and raised in La Grange, and I've always been proud. But when we traveled to other states, people would say, 'Oh, that's where that Chicken Ranch is at.' And it was embarrassing. You didn't have any answer. Yes, I pray the thing is shut and *stays* shut."

A high school girl: "It's been here for about a hundred years! And I doubt the Mafia's been in La Grange any hundred years, don't you? After Marvin Zindler cleans up Houston . . ."

A housewife: "I'm definitely for the Chicken Ranch. Those girls got regular examinations. You knew, if your husband went out there, why, at least he'd likely come home clean."

A dissenting housewife: "Talk about regular inspections, it was no more than weekly. How many times you think they might've been exposed to syphilis and gonorrhea *between* inspections?"

Another housewife: "It's been a disgrace. Our kids, when they went off to college, were ashamed to name their hometown."

The Englishman: "I'm relatively new, from England, and I've observed the hazards of street prostitution. It's bad. Young girls—sixteen, eighteen, twenty—live the most sordid lives. I think the Chicken Ranch was the best thing that ever happened, a true community asset. You've had no rapes, no murders, no dope. . . ."

Old woman: "I'm from over here in Schulenburg. We don't have rapes and murders over here, and we don't even have a Chicken Ranch. So I don't think you need it." (Lloyd Kolbe, chuckling, broke in: "You mean, ma'am, that nobody drives the whole fifteen miles from Schulenburg to visit the Chicken Ranch?")

Local businessman and civic honcho: "I think Edna ran a real nice clean place. . . . I've traveled more than anybody in La Grange. In places like Chattanooga or Georgia or Illinois, I was proud when people knew about the Chicken Ranch. They spoke well of it. In my business place here, a fine-looking lady walked in one day with her son to ask directions out there. Her son had been sent by a specialist doctor to the Chicken Ranch for his health—'cause that's what he needed! I say bless the place. It should receive a medallion as one of the best-known historical spots and recreational facilities in the United States."

Old nester with prime Texas twang: "I'm from [a neighboring town], and I never heard nobody was hurt by the Chicken Ranch. If I didn't have no more faith in my sheriff's department than some of you people, why, I'd just move on down to Houston with the gay fellers. . . ."

Many invoked the Bible. Others awarded brimstone to Marvin Zindler and Governor Briscoe. The majority cited the town's prosperity and cleanliness in objecting to publicity "recognizing us for just one thing." The topper was a salty-sounding young woman: "I'm one hundred percent for the Chicken Ranch. And I think we ought to have a studhouse for the women."

Lloyd Kolbe shut off the tape, laughing. "Boy, we sure nuff had some phone calls requesting *that* lady's name. . . ."

Journalists are predators and vultures; they will rut around in anything, including trash and garbage, seeking firmer understandings or, perhaps, nothing more than cheap titillations or a lucky spin of the wheel.

When the Chicken Ranch closed, to judge by its trash bin, Miss Edna and her girls shredded their personal papers in the manner of diplomats under siege in a disadvantaged embassy. One surviving letter—stained and ink-smeared—addressed to April and signed by Gene, spoke first of the weather, laundry chores, onion planting, and other mundane matters before addressing the human condition:

> I had been toying with the idea of skipping our August get-together and planning a longer one for September. But, when I heard from you, I couldn't see not coming to see you next weekend.
>
> April, please let me know if there is any chance of your coming to New York with me for a weekend on my vacation. If it is just wishful thinking on my part, please let me know so that I can make plans. Please don't leave it hanging in the air, like seeing you at the beach, until the time is past. . . .
>
> I don't expect you to write every day. I realize you have problems in that respect. You asked me to be patient with you, and I sure will try. But I hope that you can be patient with me also.

After all, remember when I gave up a weekend of girl watching in Wichita Falls to be with you? I will be happy to wait for you, but you have to let me know from time to time that you want me to wait.

There has always been the possibility that your interest in me was purely professional. I haven't really felt that was the case, and if I ever do, I will probably become conspicuous by my absence. . . . You are a very wonderful person, and I am glad that I met you, April, and I hope to keep that feeling for a long, long time. . . .

There was a little row of purple *X*s, representing kisses, in the traditional code of lovers, directly below a carefully drawn solitary heart and a single flower.

Yeah, I know. Corny. You wouldn't dare put it in a screenplay. But it happened, and real people were involved, and I couldn't get it off my mind. One line kept humming in my head: *There has always been the possibility that your interest in me was purely professional.* . . .

Credits

Contributors

LEE K. ABBOTT, JR., grew up in the southwest and took his M.F.A from the University of Arkansas. His first book, *The Heart Never Fits Its Wanting*, won the St. Lawrence Award for Fiction for 1981. He has been a fellow of the National Endowment for the Arts and has recently won an O. Henry Award. Abbott teaches English at Case Western Reserve University in Cleveland.

LISA ALTHER was born in Tennessee and grew up there. She contributes articles to a variety of magazines and is the author of *Kinflicks* and *Original Sins*. She lives in Vermont.

FRANKLIN ASHLEY is a regular contributor to such magazines as *Harper's*, *The New Republic*, *New Times*, *People*, *Paris Review*, *T.V. Guide*, and *Sport*. He teaches English at the College of Applied Professional Sciences at the University of South Carolina in Columbia.

ROY BLOUNT, JR., a contributing editor for *The Atlantic*, is from Decatur, Georgia. He is the author of *About Three Bricks Shy of a Load, Crackers, One Fell Soup,* and *What Men Don't Tell Women.* He lives in Mill River, Massachusetts, and claims to be working on a "strange piece of fiction" and to be available for a "genius grant or a free T-shirt."

HARRY CREWS grew up on a Georgia tenant farm, an experience he describes in *A Childhood: The Biography of a Place.* He is the author of ten books, probably the best known being *A Feast of Snakes,* and has been a regular columnist for *Esquire.* He teaches writing at his alma mater, the University of Florida in Gainesville.

WILLIAM PRICE FOX is a native of Columbia and is currently Writer-in-Residence at the University of South Carolina. His numerous articles have appeared in publications as diverse as *T.V. Guide,*

269

Sports Illustrated, and *Harper's.* His books are *Dr. Golf; Ruby Red; Moonshine Light, Moonshine Bright; Dixiana Moon;* and *Chitlin Strut & Other Madrigals.* He is perhaps best known for his classic collection of tales, *Southern Fried Plus Six.*

LEWIS GRIZZARD is a nationally syndicated newspaper columnist based with *The Atlanta Journal* and *The Atlanta Constitution.* His books include *Kathy Sue Loudermilk, I Love You; Won't You Come Home, Billy Bob Bailey; Don't Sit Under the Grits Tree With Anyone Else But Me; They Tore Out My Heart and Stomped That Sucker Flat;* and *If Love Were Oil, I'd Be About a Quart Low.* He won the National Headliner Award in 1983.

BARRY HANNAH was born in Clinton, Mississippi, and teaches writing at the University of Mississippi. *Geronimo Rex,* his first novel, won the William Faulkner Prize and was nominated for a National Book Award. His other books include *Nightwatchmen, Airships, Ray,* and *The Tennis Handsome.*

FLORENCE KING grew up in Virginia and attended American University in Washington, D.C. She worked for two years as a reporter for the women's page of the *Raleigh News and Observer* before turning to writing confession stories and adult fiction. After some thirty-seven paperback novels, she began working for such magazines as *Harper's, Cosmopolitan,* and *Viva.* She lives in Seattle.

LARRY KING is a native of Texas who has written for the *Washington Star, Harper's, The Texas Observer, Texas Monthly,* and *New Times,* among many others. His *Confessions of a White Racist* was nominated for a National Book Award in 1971. He is the coauthor of the hit Broadway musical, *The Best Little Whorehouse in Texas.*

GEORGE WILLIAM KOON, a native of Columbia, South Carolina, writes for a variety of magazines and is Head of the English Department at Clemson University. His biography of Hank Williams came out in 1983.